Further Afield

Journeys from a Protestant Past

Marilyn Hyndman

First published in 1996
by
Beyond the Pale Publications
PO Box 337
Belfast BT9 7BT
Tel: +44 (0)1232 431170
Fax: +44 (0)1232 301299

British Library Cataloguing-in-Publication Data.
A catalogue record for this book is available from the British Library.

ISBN 1 900960 01 X

Printed by
Colour Books Ltd, Dublin

Cover design: detail from NOTHING IS LOST by Tom Bevan

CONTENTS

Acknowledgements

Iowe a great many debts to people who have helped me produce this book. First and foremost, my thanks to all the people I interviewed. They participated in this project with considerable enthusiasm, often suggesting other people for me to interview. Sadly, Sadie Menzies and one other interviewee died before the book was published. Bill Rolston was a tremendous source of encouragement and practical help throughout my endeavours. I am very grateful for his friendship and the sensitivity with which he offered suggestions too various to detail. My thanks also to Tom Bevan for allowing me to use one of my favourite pieces of his work to illustrate the cover, Carol Coulter for writing the preface, Northern Visions Media Centre for their material support, and Ann Hope, Anna Eggert, Kevin McCorry and Colin Devine for their kind suggestions of people to interview. For her unflagging support of all my endeavours, my thanks to Marie Therese McGivern, and for their inspiration and emotional support, my deepest thanks to my partner and children.

In memory of my friend
Madge Davison
tireless campaigner for civil rights and
a woman's right to choose, whose
story also belongs here.

Glossary

Alliance Party – Political party in Northern Ireland, founded in 970 in an attempt to provide middle ground between Catholics and Protestants.

An Phoblacht – Newspaper of Sinn Féin.

Anglo-Irish Agreement – Agreement signed in 1985 between London and Dublin governments to work in closer co-operation towards a political solution in Northern Ireland.

Battle of the Boyne – King William III's victory at the Boyne river in 1690.

King Billy – King William III.

Bloody Sunday – The shooting dead by British paratroopers of 13 civilians during a civil rights demonstration in Derry on January 30, 1972.

Bonfires – Eleventh night (July 11th) bonfires in commemoration of the Battle of the Boyne.

Boys' Brigade – Akin to Boy Scouts, with more emphasis on religious pursuits.

Burntollet – People's Democracy march from Belfast to Derry in 1969, modelled on that led by Martin Luther King in 1965 between Selma and Montgomery.

Connolly, James – Socialist and trade union organiser, executed after 1916 Rising.

Craig, Bill – Ulster Unionist politician who formed the Vanguard Unionist Party in 1972.

Cruithin (or Cruithne) – A people thought to have lived in Counties Down and Antrim in ancient times. Contemporary relevance in the construction of an 'Ulster' loyalist identity.

CSE – Certificate of Secondary Education.

Cuchulain – Ancient champion of Ulster who single-handedly triumphed over the men of Connaught. Contemporary relevance in the construction of an 'Ulster' loyalist identity.

DUP – Democratic Unionist Party, loyalist party founded by Reverend Ian Paisley in 1971 in opposition to Ulster Unionist Party.

Fair Employment Agency (FEA) – Later Fair Employment Commission, British government organisation to combat discrimination.

Faulkner, Brian – Ulster Unionist leader, Prime Minister of Northern Ireland, 1971-2.

Fianna Fáil – Political party in Republic of Ireland founded by Eamon De Valera in 1926.

Field, The – Destination of Orange marches on Twelfth of July for church service, political speeches, food and drink.

Fine Gael – Political party in Republic of Ireland founded in 1933. Main opposition to Fianna Fáil.

Girls' Brigade – Akin to Girl Guides, with more emphasis on religious pursuits.

Hunger strikes – Main hunger strike took place in 1981 when republican prisoners refused food in demand for prisoner of war status. Ten prisoners died. It followed on previous hunger strike at end of 1980.

Inst – Royal Belfast Academical Institution, public school for boys in Belfast city centre.

Lemass, Séan – Fianna Fáil politician and Taoiseach, 1959-66.

Lundy – Key figure in loyalist history, traitor who opened the gates of Derry for the forces of King James in 1689. But gates were closed by apprentices loyal to King William and Seige of Derry began.

Mackies – Engineering factory in West Belfast with traditionally Protestant workforce.

Murrays – Noel and Marie Murray, anarchists who shot dead a police officer in Dublin in 1970s, and were sentenced to death. Sentence was later commuted to life imprisonment.

New Ulster Movement – Precursor to Alliance Party.

NILP – Northern Ireland Labour Party, founded in 1923.

NICRA – Northern Ireland Civil Rights Association, founded in Belfast in February 1967.

O'Neill, Terence – Ulster Unionist, Prime Minister of Northern Ireland 1963-69. Widely regarded at the time as a modernising unionist and as such opposed by loyalists, led by Reverend Ian Paisley.

Officials – Official IRA. Espoused political rather than military methods to a establish a United Socialist Republic.

Orange Order – Formed in 1975, a secret society pledged to defend the British crown for as long as it supported the Protestant ascendancy. Three principal aims: protection of Protestants from Catholics, support for the Protestant religion, and maintenance of the monarchy and British constitution.

Paisley, Ian – Free Presbyterian who founded the Democratic Unionist Party, and strong supporter of Ulster Workers' Strike.

INLA – Irish National Liberation Army, military grouping with connections to the Irish Republican Socialist Party.

IRSP – Irish Republican Socialist Party.

People's Democracy – Socialist movement founded in Queen's University, Belfast in 1968 which sought equality of civil rights throughout Northern Ireland.

Provies – Term to denote members and supporters of Provisional IRA.

Provisional IRA – Republican paramilitary organisation.

PUP – Progressive Unionist Party, loyalist party with links to UVF.

PTA – Prevention of Terrorism Act.

RACs – Relatives' Action Committees, formed to support republican prisoners struggling for political status in mid to late 1970s.

RAF – Royal Air Force.

Red Hand Commandos – Loyalist paramilitary group.

Revolutionary Workers' Groups – Marxist groups founded in Belfast and Dublin in late 1920s, precursors of Communist Party of Ireland.

RUC – Royal Ulster Constabulary, the police.

Sandy Row – Loyalist area in inner city Belfast.

Shorts – Short Brothers in East Belfast, major manufacturer of military hardware.

Sinn Féin – Irish republican political party aligned to Provisional IRA.

Stormont – The parliament of Northern Ireland, built in the grounds of Stormont Castle in East Belfast.

Thompson, Sam – Belfast shipyard worker and playwright.

Tone, Theobald Wolfe – Founder of United Irishmen

Trinity – Trinity College, Dublin, founded in 1592 and modelled on Oxford and Cambridge. Originally the centre of education for the Protestant ascendancy.

Twelfth – July 12th, public holiday in Northern Ireland commemorating King William III's victory at the Boyne in 1690 and main day in the marching calendar of the Orange Order.

UDA – Ulster Defence Association, loyalist paramilitary organisation.

UDP – Ulster Democratic Party, loyalist party with links to UDA.

UDR – Ulster Defence Regiment, regiment of British army raised solely in Northern Ireland.

Ulster Workers' Strike – Strike called by loyalist Ulster Workers' Council in 1974 to oppose Sunningdale Agreement and power-sharing with nationalists.

United Irishmen – Formed in 1791 to seek 'a cordial union among all the people of Ireland' and an Irish parliament which included 'Irishmen of every religious persuasion.'

Unionist Party – Ulster Unionist Party which ruled Northern Ireland from 1921 and which remains the dominant unionist party.

UVF – Ulster Volunteer Force, loyalists paramilitary organisation.

Vanguard – Ulster Unionist organisation founded in 1972 by Bill Craig as a reaction to introduction of political reforms.

Preface

It has been commonplace for politicians and commentators in the South of Ireland to state that they 'understand' the fears of Northern Protestants concerning nationalism, citing the IRA campaign on the one hand and the many imperfections of Southern Irish society on the other. There was a widespread willingness to accept the argument that the Protestant 'culture' and identity might be threatened within a united Ireland, though no one examined very closely what that culture and identity might consist of.

This understanding was shattered by Drumcree. What kind of culture and identity demanded the 'right' to stage offensive marches in areas where they were patently not welcome? What kind of religious conviction was expressed by turning a church yard into an armed camp? What were constitutional politicians doing helping to blockade roads to force an unwelcome march through nationalist areas?

This incomprehension was perhaps all the more keenly felt among Protestants in the South, especially members of the Church of Ireland, the majority Protestant church in the South and the denomination of the church in Drumcree. Day after day appalled church members watched on their televisions as Orangemen grouped in the church yard and bands gathered among the grave stones, all with the vocal support of the local rector. There was not even a word of protest when a digger was moved in, or when known members of loyalist paramilitary organisations joined the demonstrators. This dismay has now begun to surface as synods of the Church of Ireland meet around the country.

This has prompted the beginning of a debate on what Protestantism is in Ireland, and a questioning of the relationship between Protestantism and Orangeism among Protestants in the South. It is a debate that has not yet taken place in the north, and one which was never posed by the Catholic majority in the South, who accepted unquestioningly the contention that Protestantism and Orangeism were two wings of the same entity. There has been no serious attempt in the South to closely examine their fears and, where they are without foundation, to challenge them; or any effort to look at the great diversity within Protestantism in the north, the nuances of political attitude to be found there. Instead the existence of 'two communities' and 'two traditions' has been taken as self evident.

This is not just true in the South. In the north a whole industry has grown up aimed at introducing the 'two traditions' to each other, and explaining their 'cultures'. The effect of this has been to reinforce stereotypes, and to encourage only those who fit into this mould. There has also been a widespread reluctance to challenge the relationship between Protestantism and Orangeism, and to critically examine the ideology of Orangeism. There have even been attempts to link it with the progressive heritage of Protestant Enlightenment. In fact, Orangeism has nothing to do with the heritage of the Enlightenment and is profoundly conservative in every way. It is opposed to all change, to modernisation, to the exercise of the individual conscience outside the narrow prescriptions of Biblical literalism, to pluralism and dissent. There is no room in this kind of Protestantism for any kind of dissent, for creativity, for bohemianism, for personal, cultural or sexual self expression, let alone toleration of nationalism or Catholicism. It is significant that there is no place for women in the activities of the Orange Order, except in a supporting role, and this finds its way into the unionist parties, where women with few exceptions still occupy a tea making role.

In one way or another, all those interviewed for this book have experienced this narrowness and have rejected it in their different ways. They come from different perspectives and reach different places after their journeys. In so doing many felt themselves to be 'outsiders': some, because their families were more interested in radical politics or trade unionism than in political unionism, or because one parent came from England or the South. Others felt themselves to be outsiders because of their sexuality. Yet others came in contact with like minded young people from Catholic, Southern or English backgrounds through political radicalisation or cultural interests, and then found themselves rejecting the assumptions and preoccupations they had grown up with.

One of the most poignant things about this book is the loneliness of some of the journeys undertaken. Some have crossed a literal Rubicon and can never go home again. This is especially true of those who have politically embraced republicanism. They are happy in their choice but they have paid dearly for it.

These stories also contain valuable insights into the religious life of many Protestants in Northern Ireland, one which, in its level of observance and its all pervasive nature, will be unfamiliar to most people living in the South, Protestant and Catholic. It will also be unfamiliar to most people who live in Britain and it goes some way to explain why so many of those who write here had to leave that environment to express themselves culturally, personally and politically.

But more than anything this book is an indictment of all those involved in dealing with the North who have excluded the real voices of dissenting Protestantism from their consideration. What encouragement have such people ever had? Who has listened to them? Yet it shows that there is an estimable number of people from Protestant backgrounds in the North who struggle with these questions. They are a living contradiction of the notion that there are 'two traditions', 'two cultures', 'two nations' in Ireland or in Northern Ireland. Instead there is something much richer, much more interesting, a people with a multifaceted culture, varying, not only according to religious background, but also according to geography, class, gender and, above all, the choices made by thinking individuals.

Carol Coulter

Introduction

The idea for this book arose from a conversation with friends after the republican and loyalist ceasefires had been declared at the end of the summer of 1994. As the conversation switched from lively anecdotes about the previous twenty five years to a more reflective mood, I found the experiences of those friends who had been brought up to be Protestant and loyalist compulsive listening.

Some had experiences which involved feelings of guilt and shame at being a Protestant (a false guilt, it seemed to me), while others observed that for the last twenty-five years they had 'passed for a Catholic'. These memories served to highlight the myriad of convolutions that masquerades as normality in Northern Ireland. For those who had become Irish republican socialists, the knowledge that they were now seen as Lundies or traitors to their own people had been accompanied by sadness that, as far as former friends and often family were concerned, they were completely beyond the Pale. They could no longer express their political views openly and in some cases could not physically return on visits to what had once been their home territory. Everyone puzzled over why they had questioned everything they had been brought up to believe in. Why them? Why had former school friends and siblings not felt the same need? It was this puzzle which drove me to find others who had had similar experiences.

Some of the experiences recounted by my friends were already well known to me, especially those of emigration and of being Irish in Britain. But I had given little thought to the paradox of being seen as British in Ireland and Irish in Britain, and the effect that might have on the politics of those who had been brought up to be loyal to God and the crown. My parents had emigrated to England when I was young, but although my father, a Protestant, told stories of being poor and barefoot in Fermanagh, I had no sense that he was any different from the many Irish Catholics who were his friends and workmates. Everyone was defined as Irish and, beyond jokes to his more devout Catholic friends to say a prayer for him too, religion had no relevance in our lives. By then anyway my father was an atheist and had come to believe that Ireland should be reunified. That was what the majority of Irish people wanted and, so he thought, would bring the greatest happiness to the greatest number of people.

We came home to Fermanagh most summers on holiday. I do remember inexplicable incidents and remarks made by aunts and cousins which I now realise stemmed from the belief that one should 'keep to one's own kind'. Not that that had much influence on me or my behaviour. More than anything summers in Fermanagh reaffirmed the economic reasons why my parents had left Ireland. My extended family lived in what had originally been the workhouse in the last century and where my great grandmother had worked as a cleaner all her life. It was also where I was born – a huge, draughty grey stone building on the top of a hill which had been sectioned off to provide 'living' accommodation for several families and space for a clothing factory. There were few amenities and as a child, it felt like stepping back into the past. When part of it was pulled down in the 1970s, my family discovered that beneath their wooden floor were not foundations, as they had thought, but a sheer twelve foot drop leading to the original escape bolt from Lord Balfour's castle. No doubt this was an essential architectural feature in troubled times when his relationship with the natives deteriorated.

When I began interviewing people my first thoughts were to make a film on the subject, but it soon became apparent that that was not going to be possible. It is notoriously difficult to convince British broadcasters and financiers that any film about Northern Ireland will hold the attention of the 'national' audience and the preoccupation of the regional media centred around the decommissioning of weapons. Interest in any in-depth analysis of the peace process was non-existent, never mind the experiences of Protestants who did not fit neatly into the stereotypical norm.

I had other doubts. Film can be a crude medium and I wondered how adequate it would be at representing the complexity of experience in so many people's lives. Even in written form I was conscious that I could only impart fragments from the lives of the people interviewed, distil the essence of their words and trust that all of the interviews, when taken together, would shed some light on the totality of experience. I am not an academic; I had no interest in writing a political essay on Protestantism and editing quotations from interviews to fit the text. To me that was the story of a familiar cast in familiar costume. It would have told us nothing of the individual and I wanted to restore the individual to the centre of the narrative.

One question I was asked should not have surprised me as much as it did. Was I also interviewing Catholics who had become unionists? Actually, the thought had never dawned on me and I failed to see its relevance. I think we have all become inured to accept the media's absurd notion of balance – that there must always be two sides to every discussion, Protestant and Catholic, unionist and nationalist, and that objectivity, an elusive concept at the best of times, lies somewhere in the middle ground. I don't believe in cultural and political straitjackets. It seems to me that anyone who has questioned and challenged their own culture and background is less likely to allow themselves to be bound over again. It did not occur to me to interview Protestants who might conform to simple categories. This was borne out when the publisher asked me to arrange the interviews in sections for the benefit of readers. I was only too aware that everyone I interviewed had overlapping identities, all of which were important to them, and that it was an arbitrary decision on my part which placed people in the categories I had invented for them. The running order is at the suggestion of the publisher.

The interviews in this collection are united by common themes. Given the importance that others have attached to the assembly line of new mythologies – the Cruithin, Cuchulain, the Ulster-Scots language – I was relieved that so many spoke of the influence of popular culture and contemporary music on their lives rather than the pull of simulated folklore. Several people made reference to the divide between secular Protestantism and religious fundamentalism as opposed to the divide between Protestant and Catholic, and I began to see how central this division is and how little importance is attached to it. I find it difficult to imagine a childhood spent struggling restlessly within the rules of Protestant fundamentalism and the experiences documented here made me realise how rare is my contact with a swathe of people whose lives revolve solely around the church.

From the accounts of many of those interviewed it is clear that division is endemic across generation, class and gender and that contact with Catholics is often minimal until adulthood. Even then, there tended to be specific turning points: an interest in folk music, the sixties' revolution, the punk movement, rather than friendships created through work or university. One account which stayed with me for a long time was of first socialising in a meaningful way with Irish Catholics on a visit to Russia in the 1950s!

As to loyalism, my feeling is that it is more at ease with celebration of itself than revelation of itself, and so I was not surprised when people looked further afield to international political movements for a vision of an alternative social order. Many left Northern Ireland altogether in the belief that history has not passed and the future does not exist here. Their experiences in other countries brought them to a greater understanding of the society that they had left behind. Only then did history regain its importance, or more accurately, the thread of dissenting Protestant views in Irish history and the discovery of integrity and generosity within the colonizing community.

Still others discovered that free and open discussion within their own community was impossible and the cost of their silence, with its accompanying loneliness, was too high a price to pay. Ethnic cleansing is not just about burning and shooting people from their homes. It is also about the purging of dissenting voices.

This is not an 'objective' book. I am quite sure that others will be quick to pass judgement on the extent to which these interviews represent the Protestant experience in Northern Ireland. I was struck by the sincerity and frankness of everyone I interviewed. I hope that I have done justice to their experiences in so far as that is possible within the restrictions of the printed page. Some interviews inhabit an anonymous space. I wanted the scope of the book to encompass experiences, particularly around religious fundamentalism, republicanism and sexuality, where I knew it would be difficult for people to speak out without the cover of anonymity. In the event, issues around sexuality have been freely expressed and acknowledged, a sign of the confidence that the gay and lesbian community has achieved over the last ten years. To those who wished to remain anonymous, I offer my deepest thanks for their contributions and hope that we will all live to see the day when everyone will feel comfortable to express their opinions openly.

Marilyn Hyndman
November 1996

Diversity

I came to understand that there can be a celebration of diversity. There can be lots of differences but we can still all try to move forward together, each having their own power and respect.

1

Georgie McCormack

Counsellor. Born 1951.

There were two streets at the bottom of the Newtownards Road in East Belfast, Harland Street and Wolff Street, which directly faced Seaforde Street where the Catholics lived. We lived in Harland Street, about the length of a large house. My mother was born there and so were all her children. There was a difference between whether you lived at the bottom of the street or the top of the street. We lived at the bottom. The biggest dare when we were children was to run up Seaforde Street and I just never managed to do that! However, I did learn to respect boundaries and territory.

It was a rough area; a lot of fighting went on between streets and there was abuse both within families and within the street environment. I don't have those happy colourful memories that other people seem to have of community life. I was glad to see the houses being knocked down in the 1960s. They knocked them down with ladders. They have preserved some of them at the Ulster Folk Museum. I went once to see them; I was surrounded by people saying how lovely it all used to be. It was the pits; in our house the bedroom walls were all painted with this disgusting chewing gum pink distemper which was designed to kill anything that might be alive. There was a place called O'Kane's Lane just beside us; I think it was a Catholic street. I don't know how the people who lived there survived. Big houses, rooms full of people, and the toilets were down the middle of the lane. All the customers coming out of the local pubs would have used them. It was a nightmare of a place. I was glad when they moved us out to tin town in Sydenham. Those houses have been pulled down now too, to make way for a red-brick estate. My mother loved living there. It was like the little house on the prairie towards the end. Her house was one of the last left standing.

I'm sure that I must have internalised the Protestant culture that existed in the area, how far I don't know. For me there is a huge difference between religious Protestantism and Protestantism as a culture and whilst I'm sure I would have absorbed Protestantism as a culture, I never absorbed Protestantism as a religion. I went to Sunday school. After my father died when I was three we were classed as orphans and the Orange Widows' Society gave my mother money every quarter, as long as she attended church and we went to Sunday school. She didn't like going to church. She was scathing of authority in whatever guise – ministers, priests, doctors, policemen – so we had great permission to rebel. We couldn't rebel against her but we certainly had permission to take the system on.

Whenever I brought loyalist or orange ideas into the home they were always challenged and I was told that, regardless of religion, everybody I knew and could see was working class and that was where my loyalty lay. Loyalist ideology was always there in the outside world. Slogans like 'We shall not surrender the blue skies of Ulster for the grey mists of an Irish Republic' were painted on kids' school bags and along walls, but there were other things which had a more powerful impact on me. I remember my mother couldn't sign for things like hire purchase because she was a woman, and because my father was dead, her name couldn't go on the rent book. I remember walking down the street with her, her body rigid because she had to go and ask a man on the street to sign for her. I will never forget the tension in her.

With half the road being Catholic and half being Protestant there was an underlying violence during the Twelfth of July. Fights were part of the general course of events and occasionally the chapel railings got painted red, white and blue. I was frightened of the men who carried the swords and terrified about not crossing the line, not cutting across the bands that were marching in the Twelfth parades. That would still be something that stays with me. As a child I was convinced they would definitely use those swords! Actually the only time I went to the Field I was beaten up!

Although I didn't realise it at the time my upbringing was unusual. My mother was more or less a recluse and absent in a worldly way. Her father had been in the UVF, one of those who had signed the 1912 Covenant in blood, but her mother had been totally the opposite. She had led a spiritually based life, not necessarily a religious one, more like one with all the hocus pocus of religion but without the God bit. I think she was close to being a witch – a white one, but a witch none the less. My mother was very like her; she saw herself as Irish and, if a name had to be put to her politics, it would have been socialist. My brother who was 13 years older than me was a huge influence in my life. He was an ardent socialist, trade unionist and atheist.

There was always a big split between my home life and the reality of the outside world and I'm still making the transition. When I was young, I didn't do it very successfully. What also made it difficult for me to fit in was that I looked oriental. The first time I was asked if I was Chinese was when I was four years old. When I said I didn't know, I was beaten up. There were two of us in the family who looked very different and were always bantered and hassled because of it. When you are young it's awful to feel that you don't fit in but as I got older I started wearing my difference like a badge.

I never had any career ambitions. I have a form of dyslexia which meant school was difficult. I learnt survival skills; I learnt to go in at a certain level where it gets you a minimum amount of attention, good or bad. It didn't always work. There was one year I got so much physical abuse with canes that on one occasion my legs were caned until they bled. My mother had to go to the school; that made it mega bad. My mother going to the school was big stuff. It was also a bit of a failure to not have a father. I remember one day in school we had to write about what our fathers did, what his job was, and then stand up in class and tell everyone. There was me and another girl in the class; her father was a bin man, and we shared a common shame. I remember just standing there not speaking, with the teacher blasting me. It was all part of the system abuse that was so prevalent and probably still is. I have another friend who came from a family of 17. They lived in a two-bedroom house and she used to fall asleep all the time. Her school desk was probably the biggest bit of space she got to herself. She got awful stick. They called her the Dormouse and I was called the March Hare because most of the time I hadn't a clue what was going on.

The happiest time of my childhood and adolescence in the outside world was between the ages of 12 and 16 when I joined the Young Socialists. Nothing seemed to make sense to me until then. They were good years for me, very creative and without boundaries. When I look back, my mother must have found me unbearable. I was always on at her about why she wasn't doing something about the starving millions, why she didn't get politically active. We used to have our meetings in the Pigeon Hall in Dee Street but then we got rooms in Great Victoria Street beneath the Young Unionists' rooms. They didn't get as much hassle from the police as we did! The regular meetings were on a Sunday afternoon so I went to them straight after Sunday school.

It was totally idealistic, a small group of people with very dedicated hearts. I was determined to change the world and I spent a lot of my time selling *Keep Left* and being thrown out of places like the Crown Bar. This was long before it was renovated; it was still a 'man's' pub. We drew up various plans. We had a plan to get the Labour government elected so we could show them up for not being socialist. We had a plan to infiltrate the Young Women's Orange Order. That wasn't very successful because I could never remember the password to get in from one week 'til the next! We read and debated political essays, argued over the trade union movement and I remember sitting on top of Glengall Street bus shelter writing notes on Paisley's speeches as he exhorted young men to become more active.

I feel some of our people, especially our young people, have been pushed past the emotional pain barrier to a place beyond comprehension. Some of the happenings over the years have been defended or explained as necessary political acts – maybe they were – but the impact at a personal level on people's lives, that's something different.

I mellowed out in my late teens and became a bit of a liberal, started to go out to dances and enjoy a different social life. I have one daughter and I met her father during that time. He was from Beechmount on the Falls Road which I thought was quite cool because they had wee front gardens and it was more upmarket than tin town. Seeing it decimated after a riot came as a big shock. During those years in the early seventies I worked for the Blood Transfusion Service. We had to work all hours and I remember the incredible sadness there was in Belfast of a people struggling to find their way.

As I have got older I've come to see the Protestant community as an abandoned community with a culture built around a people who were displaced and created, sent here by Britain, their mother country, to occupy and defend but with the promise of a reward for that stance. Whatever that promise held I don't know; perhaps it was a promise of further occupation in Ireland. Whatever it was, it didn't happen and I think Protestantism has been struggling with it not happening. A people can hold and protect for a limited amount of time only. It can't be done forever or else their culture stagnates. For so many years Protestants have been looking questioningly towards Britain which has long since negated the original contract. I think Protestants need to accept that in fact they did achieve what they were asked to do; they did occupy and they did defend but that's it; whatever was promised in the original contract is never going to happen.

I lived in London for two years, which certainly gave me a dislike of the English. I found work as a copy typist with a large firm. I was sat down at this desk and once they realised I was Irish, that was it. I worked there for four weeks and nobody spoke to me, not one single solitary word. They didn't tell me where the toilet was, when the tea breaks were, lunch time, nothing. It didn't matter what part of Ireland I came from, what my politics were, just total blank. They used to have conversations about spitty Irish; that was what they called us. Then the radio and television networks began warning landlords and landladies that if they had any Irish tenants they had to watch them. Our mail began to be opened and read. When we challenged the landlady, who was German, she said she was just terrified having us living in the house; every time she looked at my face she said it made her physically ill. I lost about two stone during those years. I stopped speaking in public. We would be sitting in a pub and somebody would come over and start telling us Irish jokes or they would start into us about their sons being in the army and what had happened to them.

I lived and socialised with people from Northern Ireland, Protestants and Catholics, people who were in England because they just weren't fitting in here anymore; some had experienced people trying to trail them into cars or had lost somebody in the 'troubles'. Of course their humour was so god-awful black. It got us into terrible trouble no matter where we went, but I'd still have preferred to be at home.

I came back in 1976 and since then I never lived in a Protestant area again. I deliberately chose to live in a mixed area, one that has as much diversity as the North of Ireland has to offer. I became a mother, which was a huge learning experience for me; I think anyone who survives parenthood is amazing. And I began working voluntarily in counselling; now it's an established part of my work.

I've worked with all types of women in this culture. One lovely incident I remember was in Crossmaglen. I went to a family planning meeting attended by women who had travelled miles to be there. One of those workers that women always seem to have, also attended. Nobody spoke. I kept rambling on like someone demented and then I just asked the worker if she would mind going out of the room; I would feel more comfortable. Then all these women started. They were all using contraception and travelled miles to get it so that nobody else would know. They all had concerns and worries and were dedicated to looking after themselves and making sure that they had some control over their own lives. After that session I went in next door to Social Services who refused to believe that any of the women were using contraception. I think that in our culture women are very good at looking after egos and living their own lives at the same time; that is where they put a lot of their energies.

Sexuality or sexualities? Labels like homosexual, heterosexual or bisexual aren't sufficient to describe how people experience their own sexuality. I'm not talking about people who live somewhere else; I'm talking about men and women from the North of Ireland. Those labels identify, they don't describe human experience. I don't want to be placed anywhere.

I love diversity and I think it's a nonsense to say that the whole human race can be boxed into three sexual identities. Within those three groups there are cultures of people and lots of differences. People trip up and down a hidden continuum. There is a shame attached to that which is a burden people shouldn't have to carry, but nevertheless it's all here in the North of Ireland. Men and women who have deep desires and longings to be a different gender or live as a different gender without changing their body or to have sex with somebody of the same sex or be able to have it with who they want or not have it at all. The sexual self influences so much. It is a central part of people. It has to be because sex is the gateway from not being to being. I think that in any culture there is very little which allows for a deep exploration of sexuality but what is totally denied in our culture is the experience of sensuality. It is one of our great taboos, well and truly censored. I don't think that's just about religion. I think as a people we have internalised a level of brutality. Our country now has a generation of parents who have had to learn to live with political and civil conflict. It's bound to affect the development of the sensual and sexual self.

As I said, I became more liberal in my late teens and then about ten years ago I decided that socialism made more sense to me after all. I feel a bit like a dinosaur but I am holding on to it and I'm going to look forward to being a red or dead targe in my old age. I can see socialism encompassing feminism but I don't see feminism encompassing socialism. Nationalism scares me when I see it acted out in other countries. I think of English nationalism and I don't like it. It has no commitment to diversity. I think socialism has. As to the North of Ireland, I think we have two cultures, one based in defence and one based in struggle, and I would like to see us owning all of that in all its vastness and using it to reach our full potential. We have been along a road that has had a lot of learning in it; it has challenged so much in people and I know through my work that people who have had to travel a challenging road in life find new dimensions to survive and live. Some cultures have not had to do that and have no understanding of it; we have. I look forward to a future where curiosity, equality and diversity are valued and encouraged. I feel lucky to have had some of that in my life.

I spent most of my younger life wondering what the questions were, never mind the answers. I'm 45 now; I relish getting older. I revel in the internal freedom age is bringing to me.

2

Peter Quigley

Actor and Theatre Director. Born 1950.

It's strange how people assume what you are or are not. I was in the corner shop when news of Gerry Adams' electoral victory came in and the girl behind the counter said to me: 'You'll be pleased about that.' I asked her why that was and she said: 'You know, all you lot.' I looked at her for a moment and then said: 'Did you not know that I'm a Protestant?'

Most people just presume that I'm a Catholic. Mainly I think that's because of my name, but it's also because I'm involved in the arts. Actually Quigley isn't my real name at all. I had to change my name when I joined Equity, the actor's union. They already had a Peter Turner on their books and in entertainment your name is your trademark. So I changed it to my mother's maiden name, Quigley. The irony is that all my Quigley relatives are Protestants! I think that if you are not partisan – you know, I would never talk about 'fenians' or 'that lot' – then people have to guess and make assumptions as to where your loyalties lie.

I was born and brought up in Duncairn Gardens. There were Catholics living in the area and my parents allowed me to play with them and to bring them into the house. I was aware that they were Catholics and that we were not, but certainly I wasn't encouraged to hate them. My family was Methodist; my uncle was once the President of the Methodist church. My mum sang in the choir but my father had very little time for organised church activities. As a young child I was sent to Sunday school, but then my parents bought a television set and I discovered that every Sunday afternoon they were broadcasting Hollywood musicals. Well, Sunday school wasn't as exciting as the musicals and I stopped going. It wasn't as if there was a great deal of pressure from my parents to make me go.

I remember at school how we were all asked what we wanted to do for a career. I said I wanted to work in the theatre and it was greeted with howls of laughter. I always felt that people saw the theatre as a sign of decadence, of non-utilitarianism. Certainly, my parents were very keen for me to go into teaching which was considered a respectable profession and so after I finished school, I went to study at Stranmillis College. It wasn't until I was 27 that I finally went into acting.

The 'troubles' started whilst I was at college. By that time I had moved into a house in Sandy Row. My lecturer equated this decision of mine as akin to Van Gogh going to live with the miners but actually the house was cheap and I wanted to do a visual record of the redevelopment which was happening in the area at the time. When I look back I can see that there were two influences on me at that time. The local news carried the 'troubles', but the British news was quite different; it reported on the hippy movement and it was the hippy movement which was really sweeping me along. There was an urgency about Belfast at that time; the city was in shock and people reacted in different ways. I look back on it now and see incidents which were incredibly bizarre. On the Twelfth my friends would come over to see me, so inside the house people would be smoking dope whilst outside they would be hosing down the house because the bonfire was just outside the door. I experienced a lot of bombs going off because we lived behind the Europa Hotel and it was being blown up all the time. The woman next door to me always seemed to get a bit of a car through her window and one day she said to me that her shed was like the Imperial War Museum and would I like to see it? She brought me in and I discovered that she had labelled all the pieces of scrap. Here was the Cortina that was blown up in 1971, and so on; she had bits of all the cars.

I came out at this time too. I had always felt different when I was younger, had been attracted to other boys at school but I didn't have a concept for what I was feeling. I couldn't put a name to it until I became aware that there was this group of people that were known of as gay. One good thing about the gay scene is that the separatism between Protestants and Catholics only surfaces now and again. It does surface though. It's a myth to think that being gay modifies one's politics. With me, I do think that when I accepted my sexuality it meant that I questioned what other people in our society deemed to be right and wrong. When you question society on a sexual level then most people also question on a political level and every other level, but that doesn't always happen. I have met gay Paisleyites and gay republicans. I met a young man recently at a party who gave the assembled company this great lecture on republicanism and how Ireland was a slave to England. Yet this same young man told us that he couldn't tell his father that he was gay because he feared his father's approbation. As someone in the company pointed out, he would be much better going and trying to liberate himself first before he tried to liberate a country! It's the same with the gay Paisleyites. I would say that they should claim loyalty to themselves before they claim loyalty to any crown.

There simply isn't enough questioning in our society. So many people are obsessed with wanting to be identified, wanting to be classified, which I can't understand. I see this in the theatre. The themes in modern Irish plays have this search for identity and a preoccupation with the past. It's introspective. I would prefer to think of what we can do now, how we can make it easier for the next generation, more tolerance, more respect for the rights of other people. It disappoints me that we concentrate on Brian Friel type plays in the theatre and Marie Jones for the community drama scene. Where are productions of Genet, Pinero, Pirandello, Lorca, the German Expressionist playwrights? We are European and we should be broadening our horizons. I'm always being told that you wouldn't get the audiences, which I think is patronising and underestimates people. The great playwrights explore and bring out the darker side of human nature and that negativity can be a source of connection between you and someone else. Even if you think someone is despicable, I believe that if you take the time to look closely enough you will find a connection with them.

Certainly whenever I was employed by the Belfast City Council to go around Belfast and recruit young people for theatre projects I had a better response from the Catholic community. I think that outwardly the Catholic religion is a more dramatic religion. It's more theatrical, with the candles and the confession boxes and the stations of the cross which are like mini tableaux, and their buildings which are ornate when you compare them to the spartan pine pews of Protestantism. In the old

Hollywood films you never saw James Cagney dying on the steps of a Protestant church!

I was in Ulick O'Connor's play *Execution* at the first West Belfast Festival. I was the only Protestant for miles. Similarly, during the three-day passion play at St. Peter's cathedral, I was the only Protestant in the cast, and they cast me as Judas! I was up dancing with the rest of them and afterwards sat at a table drinking and making a few camp comments. A prominent republican leaned over and said: 'We all know you are gay, but do you have to be so public about it?' To which I replied: 'That's rich coming from you. I could say to you: "We all know you are a republican, but do you have to hand out leaflets? Do you have to form a party? Why don't you keep it a wee secret. After all, we are both in a minority."' I was surrounded by people wanting to build the new society whilst women ran round wiping ash trays and making tea. So provincial and so Irish!

I remember once when I was going down to Dublin one year over the Twelfth and there were two Americans on the train and they were saying how disappointed they were to miss the Mardi Gras. That made me smile! A Mardi Gras the Twelfth is not! I once said, rather campily, that I could never attend a parade which restricted me to three colours. The Twelfth is not a glamorous, abandoned, wonderful occasion where the whole city joins in. Belfast is dead during the Twelfth. No one is at home; well, you might find a few poor unemployed Catholics, but everyone who can gets out of the city. I'm all for more festivals but I think that they should be imaginative and I think that festivals like the Twelfth which celebrate separatism or bigotry or prejudice, whatever you want to call it, can be harmful. The problem is that whenever you criticise events like the Twelfth people start accusing you of wanting to do away with their tradition. I think it is more a case of breathing life into it! Traditions are only useful when you add or subtract to them. If you look at the history of any other cultural development, take the visual arts, what you find is a history of movements – how one movement in art developed into another, how someone introduced an idea and it developed into another and another. Within that context I suspect that Protestantism has given us very little over the twentieth century. The culture is dead, fossilised. In fact it's not a culture anymore; it's a habit.

There are too many silent people in Northern Ireland. We need to encourage people to put forward ideas even if in the end those ideas are deemed impractical. People should have the right to fail. Politicians are the last people I would ask for ideas; they have probably spent them all anyway. Unlike acting, where you feel that your vocation is one of questioning and of learning all the time, politicians here seem to have learnt it all years ago and are adhering to the same position whatever happens. By their performing nature they have to be so certain all the time, whereas it would be refreshing to hear a politician who turned around and said, 'I don't know everything' or 'I'm not so certain about this', 'I'm not so secure about this'; but then would they be leaders; would people follow them? I very much agree with what John Hume said about the accommodation of people with differences. We have a Protestant community, we have a Catholic community, we have a Chinese community, we have an Asian community, we have a gay community. All the multifarious groups of people here should be capable of living on the same island with each other and besides, it can be refreshing to mix with people who are different from you.

The Protestant work ethic is probably still with me. I feel that I don't exist if I'm not working, which is very hard on an actor, but if you were to ask me about Protestantism in the strictly academic sense, ask me about people like John Wesley and Luther, I couldn't answer. I don't know enough about the tenets of the religion; I just know that I don't like the smell of it. I don't like how it affects my life, its practical application from day to day. I'm not reacting from any deep theological thinking; it's the political aspects. The denial of people's human rights, that's what I reject. If I had to define what being a Protestant means in Northern Ireland then I would say that it means that the taigs are our enemies and vice versa, being brought up a Catholic means that you are one of the underprivileged people.

I don't feel passionately about a united Ireland or a British Northern Ireland. The problem with swearing allegiance to any ideology is all the sub-clauses and I've never felt that I fitted in with any category. But I am fervent about self-liberation and I'm fervent about political liberation in terms of equal opportunities and equal rights and basic civil rights to everyone. People being fulfilled in life and having the potential for growth in our society, that's what I think is important.

3

Jean McMinn

Counsellor. Born 1962.

The classic statement, my best friend was Catholic, was very true in my case. I was aware of the difference in economics between my own family and my friend's family because they had more children and I was aware that they were Catholic within the predominantly Protestant Knock area where we were brought up, but I wouldn't have thought about that within sectarian terms. My father died when I was a few weeks old and my mother struggled to support my sisters and I. She was from the South of Ireland and her experience of being Protestant within a very nationalist environment had made her genuinely inclusive and non-sectarian. That was a big influence for me. She isn't a nationalist but I think she has a greater appreciation of the dilution of cultures, whereas my father's side of the family were unionist and from Belfast and more rigid in their approach.

In many ways I feel I had a sheltered upbringing until the late seventies when my own political awareness began to form. Two instances from my childhood come to mind which made me aware of difference. One was the Ulster Workers' Strike. That was when I realised that there was some force which was protecting the tradition I was supposed to be brought up in. There were barricades at the bottom of the road and huge rallies at Stormont which was just around the corner from where we lived. My mother had taken over the running of the family shop after my father died and she had to close during the strike. She was informed that I would be kidnapped if she opened the shop; not that she told it to me in that way until some years later, just said that if any strange men spoke to me, I was to let her know. So as a young teenager I became aware of violence and threat. The other instance was when a policeman who lived in our neighbourhood was shot. Again I knew that this had happened because he was a Catholic but I didn't know why.

Up until I was 18 I was very much the dutiful daughter and quite a child. I do feel I stayed in innocence for quite a long time. The girls' school that I attended was academically abysmal, unsupportive of its students and devoid of critical thought. I finished my education at the College of Business Studies in Belfast city centre and that was a basic changing point. I was treated like an adult, given responsibilities around study and genuinely began discussing ideas in Politics and History, the two subjects I was studying for 'A' level. The feminist debate interested me greatly; my elder sister was politically active within the Women's Movement and she was a strong role model for me, but I don't remember having much consciousness of the political situation in Northern Ireland. There wasn't the dialogue at that level and I still think we don't talk enough about it. I met women from the group Women against Imperialism but their politics seemed quite distant from me and it wasn't until I spent a year at university in England that I became much more aware of the Troops Out movement, or even that Britain was imperialistically governing our country. My year away was quite a catalyst for thought and change. I came home that first Christmas and for the first time I actually became aware of tanks on the streets and soldiers with guns and of feeling very scared. I really hadn't encountered them in East Belfast.

The year that I came back was the year of the hunger strike and it just broke my heart. I lived in the Holy Land and I could feel the anger and tension in the city. Even though the nationalist struggle was not part of my consciousness, I couldn't believe the inhumanity of Margaret Thatcher in letting the ten men die. I started reading a lot more about Sinn Féin and voted for them at that point. Republicanism still held personal conflict for me, particularly as a feminist. My role models in the feminist movement were women who were trying to provide services and opportunities for *all* women and they weren't involved in the nationalist struggle; indeed whenever the question was discussed it caused divisions within the women's movement. I still would have put feminism before nationalism but listening and trying to understand the views of women in the anti-imperialist movement really did broaden my perspective on nationalism.

Another huge learning exercise for me was the debate around lesbianism. Before I went to England I had no awareness at all of lesbianism and there I met a strong movement which was confronting heterosexual women around their homophobia. At this time the AIDS virus was impacting and I thought it could be a positive force for social change and strong debate on sexuality. Our society would have to look at sexual relationships within the heterosexual world; women and men could maybe negotiate more; women's sexuality and pleasure could be explored more fully. I felt very much out on a limb with these thoughts but excited by the possibilities and became more involved in sex education, AIDS and HIV awareness.

Back in Belfast I started going out with a woman. I was totally in love with her and didn't feel any big trauma or guilt about it, but there was some fear. I really wanted to tell my sister but something held me back. On a personal level I didn't feel I could be out about my sexuality and my own inner sense didn't feel a need to be out. Even today, being involved with a woman, I find one exists in a bubble within our culture. There are significant threats when one chooses to be out in this society, emotional threats of humiliation, shame and judgement, threats of physical harm and losing one's job. Back then in 1982 I didn't feel that need to be out. Part of that, I'm sure, was due to some fear. Now it is strongly attached to the belief that my sexuality is private and, whether I am involved with a man or a woman, I do not feel the need to flout it or to make a political statement.

I worked within the women's movement for ten years, working with the student women's movement, women's groups, family planning, counselling and AIDS awareness. In the late eighties I felt very depressed about the political situation here. I really got a sense that there was no hope of change and we were in an endless spiral of violence. I've never identified with unionism but I really couldn't sympathise with the IRA and the armed struggle. I knew that the British government were manipulating power. Although I still had a mild sympathy with Sinn Féin during this period, I didn't know what the solution was. I wanted talks and dialogue but they seemed impossibly far away. I also felt there was some shame around being a Protestant here and that I had to take some responsibility for that. It's a false guilt but something I held on to until quite recently.

At that time I was working with young people between 13 and 17 years of age and coming head on with sectarianism. The young people were mostly Protestant but the residentials were cross-community ventures and I didn't experience nationalist young people as any less sectarian. If people say that is true then I think it could be purely intellectual. Our society does not have models of dialogue, communication and respect and our children, whether unionist or nationalist, are not brought up in a way where they are given respect and power to dialogue and where they are listened to. We all live our lives in Northern Ireland with a degree of violence. We are not allowed to speak what we feel without the threat of physical violence being upon us; we are not allowed to feel what we feel. I think our capacity to listen in this society is minimal. The impact of that has to be immense. It is particularly acute where there is economic struggle, where young people are living in a disadvantaged, poverty-ridden community, their parents are struggling, there is no comfort, everyone is under pressure at an economic level. I don't see how children who experience this raw, violent impoverishment can have the capacity to tolerate another when they are not tolerated themselves.

I left for the States for what I thought would be a few months but in effect turned into six years. America was so different. I adored the anonymity; no one placed me; no one made demands ot me; it was just glorious! When I left here I was very troubled inside and America gave me an environment to relax in. There is a huge personal growth movement in the States which, given the political struggle in Northern Ireland, can appear to be selfish, luxurious and very individualistic but for me at that time it was a total godsend. Living here I felt I always needed to be politically active whereas in the States, because I wasn't part of that society, I didn't feel the same need. That gave me the space to explore more creative aspects of myself which would have felt like an indulgence here. I developed self-esteem and confidence on a much deeper level which ultimately allowed me to question what my political responsibilities were, how involved I wanted to be, rethink my spiritual beliefs, my emotional beliefs and my desires as a sexual person.

Within Northern Ireland I had found that lesbians had great difficulty if I did not identify as lesbian. It was difficult for them; they wanted me to take on a label of being lesbian, gay or straight and I always felt this was disrespectful of others' experiences. I can understand that lesbians need to be precious of their achievements and the safety that has been created, but I have difficulty belonging to any group which from my perception has narrow criteria of 'membership'. My experience in this country would lend itself to this perception. When a group of people are exclusive, then I feel this can alienate people or leave them on the fringes. I have a fear of being ghettoised and I would wish to have a broader criterion for belonging and to acknowledge and celebrate diversity. I do not wish to take on a sexual label. I do not find it empowering for me and would rather identify as a sexual person, a person who is sexual, full stop.

Really what America taught me was that it was okay to be different. That sounds very simplistic but what I mean is that it allowed me to give myself permission to be different. Just because I felt different from others didn't mean that I was bad or sinful or was leaving the tribe. Here I was always challenged on my experiences whereas in the States if I said something, it was left to be; it was accepted without the challenge. There was a place for me to be bisexual, a legitimate place that was articulated and respected. In the later years in the States I came to understand that there can be a celebration of diversity. There can be lots of differences but we can still all try to move forward together each having their own power and respect.

Ultimately though I missed here, I missed the familiarity, I missed the culture. I started spending nights in a local Irish bar, tragically hanging out with people I really had little in common with. I was excited and delighted by the peace process and that encouraged me to come home. It angers me that the British government has not utilised the opportunity for peace but has created numerous barriers to its progression. I don't understand their short sightedness in excluding Sinn Féin and I'm rageful at the way they are still imposing their will and supporting the unionists to impose their will on this society.

I think a lot of people from the community where I was brought up don't have the political awareness or understanding of the inequalities in our society. They don't understand, for example, the impact on the nationalist community of the RUC being almost totally Protestant and the bigotry, sectarianism and abuse of power that accompanies that. Given the leaders they are choosing to elect at present like Paisley, Trimble and Robinson I don't see how there can be more explanation and understanding. I suppose what I want to see is the British government standing up to the leaders of unionism, really confronting them around their behaviour, introducing penalties which force them to be inclusive of the minority loyalist parties and the nationalist parties. I do get angry with unionists; I want them to learn their lesson, but it has to be given in a way that they really get it. Ultimately that has to be in a way which accepts them and listens to their story too and I'm aware that sometimes in my anger, my own humanism doesn't always embrace that.

What I miss most about the States is their ability to hold and celebrate difference. American society is fraught with difficulties; it is also very violent and yet they manage to dialogue between themselves much more effectively than we do. I think people flourish best in an environment of acceptance, non-judgementalism and lack of shame, an environment where there is support and encouragement and where people can truly express themselves even if that expression is bigotry and sectarianism and homophobia. Expression isn't enough of course. We still need to listen and accept that another's experience is as valid as our own and to realise that in doing so we don't have to compromise our own experience, we just need to make room for others. I think then we can actually move on to building bridges through dialogue and begin to celebrate diversity as opposed to being threatened by it.

4

David Grant

Theatre Director. Born 1959.

I knew from an early stage which side my bread was buttered on. I've memories of living in Malone Heights as a small child of about seven and looking out from my bedroom window to the Black Mountain and being very glad that I came from a comfortable family. I knew there were people who weren't comfortable because I went to Taughmonagh Primary School and there were children there who had an awful lot of brothers and sisters. In my family there was just me and my brother; that always seemed to be a good thing. I was also very glad to be male, but only because I had picked up by this stage that having babies was very painful, and of course, as I grew up I would have added that I was pleased to be a Protestant – not from any conventional bigotry towards taigs and the Pope, more that being a Protestant was comfortable, that these three states combined – middle class, male and Protestant – were much more comfortable.

Talking about one's origins does bring out the difficult definitions of Protestantism. My grandfather was the Northern Bank manager for Newry. Although Church of Ireland, I remember him as a typical dour Presbyterian, still with a heavy sort of Scottish feel to him and largely concerned with money. I remember when we were children, the telephone was still a fairly new acquisition, and my granny would phone twice and hang up. That way we knew we had to phone her back because woe betide her if the bill showed any outgoing calls. Because my grandfather worked in the bank he moved around a lot and by the time my father was of university age the family had moved to Dublin.

21

My mother met my father at a hop in Rathfarnham. She was a Dublin Protestant which is a very different Protestantism altogether. To begin with, in the 1950s, Dublin Protestants had been assimilated much more into society in the South of Ireland than Catholics had been in the North. There was the tail end of the ascendancy which certainly relatively lower middle class Protestant families like my mother's would have aspired to. There is also a terrible snobbishness which exists in Dublin and which I don't think exists here to the same extent. It was fantasy really. It was important to my maternal grandmother to be the granddaughter of the disinherited granddaughter of Sir Roland Blennerhasset who once owned half of County Kerry!

My mother never really understood Northern Protestantism. When she moved with my father to Portadown she began teaching in Catholic schools. She had always taught in Catholic schools in Dublin where all schools were Catholic apart from the ones that she had been too. It made trying to get a house in Portadown quite difficult. I wasn't aware of the underlying politics at the time but looking back, it was quite obvious that our neighbours saw my father as this man with impeccable Protestant credentials, employed by one of the local Protestant building firms and a Territorial Army Major, but who had this wife who went across town every day to the other side of the tracks. It raised a few spectres and took a couple of houses before my parents found somewhere without that sub-text running through.

Most of my friends at school would have been the sons of academics at Queen's. I still have a slight Englishness to my accent which is nothing to do with having studied in England but the fact that my school in Belfast, Inchmarlo, was like an English prep school: lots of well spoken little boys all mixing together in their yellow quartered caps. I went on to Inst during the height of the 'troubles' in the 1970s and looking back, I can see that I led a truncated life. My first day there coincided with the first daylight bombs in Belfast city centre, but it became so normalised and internalised that I just got used to it. It's hard now to realise that there really was nowhere to go out. Those days came back to me a few years ago when I was working for the Opera House and we had tickets to distribute to schoolchildren for a show. Two of us sat down and contacted Inst, Methody and Victoria, I think we even went to Belfast Royal Academy, until the wife of somebody in the Arts Council who worked in St Dominic's got wind of what we had done and phoned us up saying: 'Don't you realise what a sectarian selection this looks like?' Myself and the other organiser – he was an old Campbellian – looked at each other with incomprehension until she told us that we hadn't included any Catholic schools on the list! Neither of us actually knew how close St Malachy's and St Dominic's were. It brought home to me that right through the whole time that I was growing up in Belfast, my Belfast was very closely defined. That's a reality for more people than would admit to it, particularly of my age.

I would have met Catholics in Dublin. My mother retained a lot of friends in Dublin but I don't know that I was very conscious of Catholic institutions. Even to this day it would be very rare for me to go to a Catholic Mass or attend any explicit Catholic occasion apart from maybe the odd wedding, and even then it's always a big deal. I remember going to Rome to meet the Pope with my mother's school when I was 16. It was a lot of fun because my teenage contemporaries on the trip approached the whole religiosity of the experience with varying degrees of cynicism. I remember being taken with great glee by one lad to some monastery in the darker regions of Rome to get a holy medal for his mother. We banged on a door, a grille slid across and the medal was handed out for a few lira. He explained to me that it contained strips of cloth which were put on a roller and rolled under a carpet that Pope Paul had walked on. He had promised his mother not to come home from Rome without one. I discovered that aspect of Catholic culture through Catholics themselves. In general, though, I had no real sense of living in a divided culture at all. With hindsight, it surprises me that I could go through 18 years and not be aware of those differences. That does seem to be at the root of life in Northern Ireland, that it's not avoidance but circumstances that create the difference.

Ours was not a very religious household. My mother was a Territorial Army widow on Sundays with my father away playing soldiers. We would have gone dutifully to church as small children and to Sunday school. Church on a Sunday morning was quite therapeutic. I went through the motions of confirmation as a teenager but there was something about the evangelical stance of even the Church of Ireland that was alienating in the extreme. I was cynical about the whole confirmation process, but I think that was more to do with an intellectual arrogance than any sense of being uncomfortable with my roots. I did go on these inter-school camps which were run by evangelicals. They were intended as a summer-long boost to teenage spirituality. My main achievement the year that I went was helping market the tuck shop. I remember at the end of the camp there was a scathing reference in the closing reports in respect of Camp C's tuck shop sales which had exceeded all expectations. This was in a paragraph which was talking about the number of religious conversions in Camp B! I'm afraid that aspect of fundamental Protestant life never really got into my psyche at all. At school I was very curious about boys who were exclusive brethren and who weren't allowed to join in certain activities. I think that children whose religion imposes lifestyle restrictions have a terrible time in terms of being subjects for bullying. There was a boy at primary school who wouldn't go to religion classes and if there was ever an outing he wouldn't go either. Even his food was different and he would sit apart for meals.

There was a conveyor belt at Inst. If you were good enough, you just kept doing the exams until eventually there were no more to do and then you went on and did more exams at university. In those days there was seventh term teaching so I had an extra term with a teacher-pupil ratio of three to one, and I was the pupil. It was a pampered, intensive existence far better than university from the point of view of the quality of teaching and learning. I applied to do Law at Cambridge, which is what people in my stream did if they didn't do pure sciences.

Cambridge was an extraordinary experience of privilege. The wonderful thing about the college system in Cambridge is that most colleges have 300 to 600 students in them. In a normal university everybody is competing; for example, if you want to be in the Drama club, then there are 3,000 people who might want to be in it, or sports facilities or whatever. In Cambridge each college had its own drama society and rugby team. On a higher level the university facilities are also very good and the opportunity to specialise is very available; so I immediately got into things like the Cambridge Mummers, what we used to call the 'white plimsoll' theatre. It is interesting looking around at who is in the theatre now at the highest level. A lot of the people who are artistic directors and significant figures in British theatre, including the starry names like Stephen Fry, Emma Thompson and Tony Slattery, went through this system.

There was also something wonderful about being Irish which of course you suddenly became once you went across the water. I remember there was an obnoxious boy from Belfast Royal Academy who used to run the local Unionist club and I was invited to an Ulster evening at which I suddenly realised how many awful people there were in Cambridge from Northern Ireland that year! Equally there were highly politicised people from the other side. I wasn't interested in the Ulster Club. It was very obvious that it was the unfashionable part of being Irish. Not that I aspired to being nationalist at that stage at all. I rather liked John Hewitt's dictum where he says: 'I'm Northern Irish first, Irish second, British third and European fourth'. When my friends and I did talk about identity it was very much in the way one analyses and distances oneself from the issues which seemed to bother other people. My friends in Belfast were much more concerned with punk rock and the music culture. If people talked about politics at all, it was an embarrassment. We certainly wouldn't have had the degree of political sophistication of some of the kids one sees nowadays on television from Hazlewood Integrated College, talking about their role within the modern world.

During the hunger strikes of 1981 I was doing the Edinburgh Festival and I remember we were all rehearsing away and I have to say, in spite of ourselves, we gathered around the television for the Royal wedding preparations. It was just the news report; we didn't watch the whole thing, I hasten to add! The three items on the news were two from Northern Ireland and one from London. The first item had people out on the Falls banging bin lids because a hunger striker had died, the second item had the Orange marches and the third item had the Dean of St Paul's out polishing the steps in preparation for the Royal wedding. I remember thinking that, however absurd you may feel the whole Northern Irish thing is, at least there is some kind of cultural vibrancy in both cultures. There was noise if nothing else compared to the blandness of the Royal Wedding fever.

I didn't feel comfortable with the hostility of the Thatcher regime towards the hunger strike, but still, a residual sense of Protestantism came through. I always think of that David Rudkin play, *Saxon Shore*, where he characterises Protestants in Northern Ireland as werewolves who are perfectly normal when you meet them but when there are certain conditions, like a full moon, they go north. He represents Protestants as

Saxon planters from the Roman Empire. When the Romans withdraw the Saxons are nice most of the time but every so often they suddenly go north and kill Picts. Then they come back the next morning and they don't remember it! For me there is almost a psychosis whereby you are not quite in control of how you feel. I've felt that a few times in my life and one was during the hunger strikes when I really couldn't bring myself to believe that this wasn't all some kind of propaganda plot. I also felt it when I was working in the Dublin Theatre Festival. There was a huge vogue at the time in marches for the Guildford Four and the Birmingham Six. All my friends were artistically involved, playing drums and making models for the Parade of Innocence. It used to anger me because I felt they were safe from the firing line; they were not actually in Belfast; they didn't really know what Belfast was like and it was just a trendy cause to them. It is difficult in retrospect actually trying to come to terms with the resistance you feel when the truth and justice of the situation is so palpably documented. It goes deep and it is one of the hardest things I think about this whole process that we are engaged in at the moment. It is one thing hearing rational arguments, it's another absorbing them, accepting them and actually seeing that it is in your interest to move on. I felt very similar at the start of the ceasefires.

I had always been interested in drama, which made me a bit of an oddity at Inst because it was tolerated at best. At Cambridge I began organising various programmes. I remember we organised a programme of Irish writing in which we performed extracts of *Waiting for Godot* and *The Importance of Being Earnest*. It was a gimmick really. In one scene two men squabble over muffins and in another over the last carrot which, to us, was an intellectual conceit. Because of what was happening in Ireland at the time, one of the critics said that it was a searing indictment of bourgeois comfort in the face of political deprivation. Beckett summed up the aspirations of the Irish people and it was a powerful comment on the hunger strikes. Nothing could have been further from the truth as far as we were concerned. It was really quite dilettantish. During this time I began playing at being a real live theatre person, going to Edinburgh, putting on the more arty stuff, leading on to the footlights and more and more contacts with other people in the world of theatre. I remember once after we had performed our poetry programme, a very earnest Home Counties girl came up to me and said how fascinated she had been to discover so much about Northern Ireland. There was one thing that puzzled her. She just wanted to know exactly what part of Belfast Ulster was in. I really knew we had made a breakthrough there!

After university I came back to Belfast to work for the Queen's Festival. The Festival is an establishment institution – there are no two ways about that – and I came to know the great and the good of Ulster society. My life from 1982 to 1986 was concerned with getting further up the tree in the Festival so that I had a secure post. Then a number of things happened. My parents moved away in 1983, leaving me with a flat and a car and a very comfortable lifestyle which could have gone on indefinitely. There were two problems with that. One that I really was not in any sense content with myself and my sexuality. University should have been when I came out and everything would have been cool but it wasn't for me. My friends there used to say it was because I was Irish, though I never quite knew how it could be blamed on being Irish. It became harder and harder to sustain the older I got. Ten years ago a gay person did not advertise their sexuality. Unfortunately I didn't rationalise at the age of seven that, along with male, Protestant and middle class one had to presume straight. The second problem was a sense that I was going to be in the Festival job forever.

I went to see a piece in what has become the Old Museum Building and thought that the space was wonderful, that we should really do something with it. I don't know what snapped but just that cycle ride home really did change my life and that's when the mould broke because, instead of accepting the comfortable salary and the circumstances, it just seemed sensible to say 'no', invest in something a bit reckless, which is what I did. I signed on, helped to establish the Old Museum Building and picked up work where I could.

I began to work on Friday mornings in Scala, the Youth Training Programme on the Springfield Road. Nothing could have prepared me for the total contrast between the world that they lived in and the world that I lived in. I used to be so terrified I didn't sleep on Thursday nights. On the first day I brought all these bits of newspaper and string with me as a workshop aid. They used it to truss me up with and set fire to. I realised rather quickly that I would have to use slightly different techniques! We were working in a dire building. The girls used to come into work at 8 o'clock in the morning and stay in this windowless building until they left at 6.00 pm without ever seeing daylight. Eventually I got the classes moved to the Old Museum Building but they stopped abruptly when the class was accused of shoplifting during the breaks. I had strips torn off me; I think they thought I was running Fagin's Den.

At about the same time I was asked to be Assistant Director for the Passion Play at St Peter's. It was the church's strategy to regain the initiative from the IRA in terms of creating social confidence building. It was an extraordinary experience, not least the day we were rehearsing and a bomb was thrown from the flats on to a jeep. A priest had to go out and pick the bodies up. I had never been as close as that to the actual firing line. Suddenly having tinkered with notions of community drama and its relevance to people, I began to realise that here was a play about God, a concept which had never made any great inroads on my life, but was the most important thing in some of these people's lives – even to the extent that two ladies got up and tried to help Christ carry the cross up the aisle until a quick thinking centurion threw them back into their pew. That was a salutary lesson. I realised that the kind of art that would make a connection with people's real lives wasn't necessarily the kind of art that interested me and that all the time one had to make compromises and define one's work in terms of what people were actually interested in.

I also assisted in directing a youth theatre production piece. Both the Director and Musical Director were openly and unashamedly gay and didn't see their sexuality as an issue. That was a shock to me because I found just thinking of what I was afraid of, quite terrifying. It was a bizarre time being surrounded by teenagers all oozing hormones whilst trying to come to terms with my sexual self and complicated by the fact that, however I behaved with my peers, it was something that I wanted to keep from my parents. When I came out to my mother she was quite hysterical. Thankfully all that is behind me now but it got to the stage where I wanted to make a statement and so I devised, wrote and directed a play called *Tangles*, one of my achievements I'm proudest of, for a young people's theatre company in Dublin. That was a public statement which included coming out in the *Irish Times,* mainly because I was quoted as saying, being gay myself, I thought it an issue from which so many people suffered needlessly and that it should be addressed among teenagers. I still do feel very strongly about the routine violence that people go through because they don't conform and don't have the opportunity and the freedom that I had.

In Northern Ireland I think there's no question that there are deeply entrenched suspicions in certain quarters about the other side but I also feel that there is too great an emphasis on defining cultural differences. The kind of work that I undertake has a lot to do with finding a culture which isn't aligned. For instance, the theatre that I want to do must have a world context and it worries me that so much of policy thinking and arts funding, particularly in audience development, has, as its main justification, Protestants and Catholics 'being got together'. It is a real issue. We can be as rarefied as we like about it, we can say it isn't the priority, but it is. When I get the chance I speak out about defining the arts in sectarian terms and the need to find other hooks rather than just the Protestant tradition or the nationalist tradition. We also have a youth tradition, a gay tradition, a black tradition as far as it exists here, a Chinese tradition. I'd like to see us move on to a pluralist society. Pluralism, I think, has been the defining change in the South in the post-Mary Robinson Ireland.

One sad aspect about Northern Ireland is that I don't think one can attain any recognition here until one has gone away. I wouldn't have been considered for my present job if I hadn't had my three years in Dublin. It's entirely to do with the attitudes of those people who make the appointment decisions, their obsession with outsiders; they want to be seen to be appointing someone who doesn't come from here. The great absurdity with all the reports on religious discrimination emanating from the University at Queen's is that no one points out how so many of the appointments actually made are to English people. What does religion really mean when you are English?

The biggest frustration I had working in Dublin was the blindness to what was happening in the North. The North is a direction not a place; it's up there somewhere. Northern Ireland is a pimple on the top of the island which stops the southern Irish from being real Europeans. If there is ever to be a United Ireland, I think that will be a big struggle. The people who would need most education would be Dubliners and particularly the lesser informed Dubliners who still think very much in black and white terms of imperialism and the IRA as a counter to that. What does encourage me by contrast in Dublin is that, during youth theatre workshops, kids from the worst imaginable housing conditions in Dublin always have a spark and a life about them that their counterparts in the North of Ireland lack.

I think that at the moment Northern Ireland is clearly a world which has been a Protestant world, which has been a male world, and has now to cope with the Protestant culture being under threat. To an extent the male culture is under threat as well. I don't feel great allegiance to either culture. I suppose what a Protestant culture means for me is that the majority of people that I see on television or meet in the institutions of power are people who have come from a similar background to myself. That doesn't necessarily mean that you are at an advantage, but you do notice when suddenly you meet a civil servant called Seán or Eugene. I stress that I don't have any problem with that, but obviously there are many Protestants who do. We live in a changing culture and I suppose the fear comes from not knowing what is going to take the place of a Protestant world.

I don't feel the Protestants I meet who need that kind of political reassurance have anything to gain by staying in the United Kingdom. They have the conviction that there is a conspiracy, that the world out there is completely stacked against them. I don't agree. I think it will be possible for Protestants to influence the new establishment, whatever form it takes, in a future United Ireland which I would wish to see. The division of Ireland seems to me to be a cultural, economic and political absurdity. I face practical absurdities all the time working in the arts. Ireland is a small island, the potential audience is right across it and yet funding structures, buildings, all the things which make the arts what they are, exist on two tracks. There are institutions with similar briefs North and South, associations in the South which don't exist in the North but should exist. It's not so bad when you're in Belfast or Dublin which have their own catchment areas, but it's particularly acute in places like Enniskillen and Sligo where the natural confluence is across the border. I want to see cooperation grow. I want to see change, but the problem is finding a way of letting that happen without pandering to the insecurities that Protestant people, in particular, here feel.

Out of the Sixties

There was so much happening in the world as I was growing up – Czechoslovakia, Paris in 1968, the American civil rights movement, the feminist movement and of course, all that was happening on the streets of Northern Ireland.

5

Desmond Bell

Academic and Film Maker, Born 1949.

Looking back on it, I think that the period I grew up in, in Derry, was a curious 'make believe' period. Indeed it was a 'make believe' period elsewhere in Western Europe, a post war era of social democratic optimism. There were tremendous social advances taking place, a welfare state was in place for the first time and there were new opportunities in education. There was rock and roll on the juke boxes. Certainly by the time I was in my teens there was a feeling that a new world was being ushered in in Northern Ireland, a world which seemed at last to transcend the narrowness and the bitterness of the past. I was a teenager during the period of the O'Neill administration, a time when people believed – rather erroneously, it turned out – that Northern Ireland was going to evolve into a normal democratic society, rid of the forms of sectarianism and discrimination which had been such a feature of the six counties from the foundation of the state. It was as if that past was giving way under the impact of dramatic changes occurring elsewhere in the world, as social democracy seemed to triumph in Western Europe.

But the dream couldn't last. I remember watching the rioting in Derry at the very beginning of the 'troubles' in 1968 and for the first time in my life, my father began to tell me about the fighting in Derry in the 1920s which had involved murderous shooting in Bridge Street between republicans and loyalists. As the conflict deepened, with the loyalist backlash to the Civil Rights Movement leading to violence on the streets, more people started to talk about similar past experiences. It was almost as if, from 1939 to 1969, people had forgotten history or chose to put it aside. But now the repressed had returned and with a vengeance.

I had a relatively quiet childhood in Derry on the city side. At that time the North Ward had substantial areas that were religiously mixed. There wasn't the same ghettoisation as today in Derry which sadly is now divided into areas predominantly Catholic or Protestant. Actually, my father had grown up in the Bogside at a time when it was still a mixed neighbourhood. We would find his attitudes to religion and politics rather peculiar today. He was a 'Southern Unionist' which doesn't mean anything in Northern Ireland today. That is to say, he was someone who preferred Ireland to remain united but within some structure of the British Empire. He had been born and brought up before partition and disliked the fact that Derry had been cut off from its wider hinterland and culture. As a family, we were like many Protestants, cut off from our larger extended kinship network in Donegal. He certainly was never a Northern Unionist. As a junior clerk to the County Court in Derry, he saw sectarianism and unionist bigotry at close quarters and intensely disliked both. One of his jobs was to go round and check electoral registers and he had many amusing anecdotes about the political brokerage that took place at election time – bar room deals between nationalist and unionist election agents about how many dead men from each side would be permitted to exercise their suffrage! Nor was he happy about the reconfiguration within Presbyterianism which had occurred with Home Rule with the annexation of dissenters into what later became the Unionist and Orange bloc. This political development had coincided with an increase in Protestant fundamentalism which he intensely disliked. Presbyterianism was always wracked by doctrinal schisms and theological disputes and through him I was made aware of the debates which took place between 'New Light' (the sceptical rational tradition of dissent) and 'evangelicalism'. Evangelicalism of the 'born again' variety always scared me as it did my father.

During my childhood and adolescence Derry was still the major market town serving the Donegal hinterland and the north west right down to Sligo. As a family we looked west rather than east and I grew up knowing relatively little about Northern Ireland. Most of my holidays and spare time were spent in Donegal where my father seemed much happier and relaxed than he appeared to be anywhere in Northern Ireland. My school was an all Protestant one but there would have been a lot of children from Donegal in my class. Outside school I played and fought in gangs with Catholics and Protestants. The gang structures which existed in Derry then were not organised on religious grounds but by street. A hell of a lot of stone throwing and fighting went on but we fought the next street! Obviously there were divisions in that we went to separate schools but street life was unified. Sectarianism existed however. I used to come across this when I was sent to organisations like the Boy Scouts, not sectarian organisations in themselves but ones which recruited on an exclusively Protestant basis. I was beaten up several times as a child when wearing my boy scout uniform in the street by gangs of marauding, less privileged kids from the Bogside. I had my scout scarf ripped to shreds with a knife on one occasion so one had a certain amount of fear and tremulation when travelling through certain areas. Class divisions seemed to be as important as religious ones.

I was also aware of another world, that of industrial working class Lancashire where my mother had been born and which I visited each year. This was a completely different world to the one I lived in either in Derry or in Donegal. Some of it was highly attractive: cinemas, rugby league, street markets, pop culture, considerably less prohibition on what you could or could not do and less concern with Protestant propriety. It was a vibrant industrial culture and I liked that very much. I felt a real sense of difference of course when I went to visit my relatives in Rochdale. Indeed I was told I was different. I was 'Irish'. I was treated as if I was Irish by people who drew no distinction between Protestant or Catholic Irish. The south Lancashire community my mother was born into had historically been anti-Irish and anti-Catholic in the context of mass Irish emigration into Lancashire after the Famine. Sectarianism is not an exclusively Irish phenomenon!

The Protestant grammar school I attended laid claim, rightly or wrongly, to being a liberal establishment and I was encouraged to study Irish history. Indeed, I even tried to study the Irish language although I didn't succeed terribly well. I was trying to impress my Catholic girlfriend at the time so it was perhaps more a case of teenage lust rather than disinterested love of the language. But I was very interested in history and spent a lot of time coping with the intricacies of Irish history and the complex role of the Protestant community within this. I shouldn't however give the impression that I spent all my time reading scholarly work! I also had an intense interest in rock music, in blues, in girls and a thousand other distractions. But, from the age of 15 onwards, I would have been reasonably familiar with the history of Ireland, with the character of English colonialism, with the complexities of Protestant political identity and aware of the historic injustices that Catholics had suffered.

I was actually 'on' the first civil rights march in William Street. That provided a rapid political education! I can't claim that I was there because, as a fun loving teenager, I was fundamentally committed to civil rights activity in the first instance. I had been practising with my rock band over on the Waterside of Derry and, as I was coming home, I ran into the march and joined in as one does, partly out of curiosity, partly as something I felt I should be seen to be involved in. All I can remember is seeing Eddie McAteer, then nationalist leader, jostling with the police at the head of the march, the roar of the crowd and the next thing, having to jump over a wall and almost breaking my leg as the RUC charged into the crowd, wielding batons and sending people fleeing in all directions. That night after the march I went on the walls of Derry and looked down on the Bogside as the crowds gathered in angry mood below. To be honest I was still nervous about entering the Bogside. It struck me that this was the start of some momentous event; it wasn't just a passing street disturbance as my father was telling me; it was actually a major political event, a turning point. In school I had been reading about the French Revolution and the storming of the Bastille; now I was actually witnessing a real, live popular revolt. This was scary but exhilarating.

At that time most of my school friends would have sympathised with the civil rights cause and some of us were involved in the sit-downs at the Guildhall, called as part of a strategy of non-violent resistance to a Stormont regime seen as politically bankrupt. I can't think of anyone I knew well who was actively involved in Orangeism. Green nationalism and Orangeism struck us as equally absurd. You can't imagine in what derision the Unionist oligarchy and nationalist hacks like Eddie McAteer were held by young people, whether Protestant or Catholic. We were into American youth culture, the Beatles, the Rolling Stones. We were mods and rockers rather than Unionists or Nationalists. Derry at this time had an American base and we were able to hear the sort of music that wasn't as widely available elsewhere in Northern Ireland. Black servicemen brought Stax, Tamla Motown and blues music in. It was a cultural strand which was very important, particularly for musicians. By its nature, that music was cosmopolitan and concerned with youthful experience – not with religious background. It seemed to us that this modernising wave was sweeping away the accumulated heritage of sectarian shite that we had all had to deal with. I think we were rather naive but then that was a period of innocence.

There were more opportunities for young people in Northern Ireland than there are at the moment. Unemployment was lower than it had been for many years. Higher education was now free. I was the first member in my family either to go on to grammar school or to have gone to university. The world seemed to me and my generation to be a big stage available for us to operate on, certainly bigger and more complex than the world my parents had experienced (or were prepared to talk about).

After school, most of my friends, Catholics and Protestants, got out of Northern Ireland. This was a generation on the move. I left school without sufficiently good exam results to go to university, a performance which caused problems between my parents and myself. They thought that I had misapplied myself by spending too much time playing in rock bands. I left and went off to Edinburgh and worked as a labourer for nine months in a cold storage depot. I came back to Derry briefly after this. By then the 'troubles' had worsened and life was becoming more polarised so I decided that I didn't want to stay. I went to England, first to train as a music teacher, then I opted to study philosophy at university. For the next seven years I really didn't have much interest in Irish affairs and I was glad to be out of the place as the violence spiralled out of control. Even during vacations, when I came home I spent most of my time in Donegal. I may as well have been in Canada for all the connection that Donegal had in my mind with the North. Still caught up in the dream of an alternative cultural space to sectarianism, it became for me a sort of Tír na nOg. Quite a lot of my Protestant friends actually went to live in Donegal in search of an alternative life style. We felt we couldn't be part of the Protestant side in the struggle but we weren't completely convinced of the merits of the republican and nationalist position either, particularly after the onset of the Provisional IRA's bombing campaign. There wasn't really any option but to leave.

The hopelessness that affects people in Ireland when it comes to political life seemed to be in complete contrast to what was happening in the labour movement and in student politics in England. The campaigns against the Vietnam War, the Paris students, direct industrial action, community politics, squats, sit-ins and the political ferment on the Marxist left that I was to become involved in, all seemed preferable to what was happening in Ireland. There, constitutional parties were still bickering away and any direct mass action to achieve social justice had been eclipsed by the barbarity and severity of the paramilitary campaign and by the British repressive response to this. At this time I couldn't make a link in my mind between the forms of political radicalism that attracted me in England and the mired nature of Irish politics. I don't think that I was alone in that. I think there is a generation of people, particularly Protestants, who were radicalised in England and found it very hard to make the additional leap involved in taking those politics back to Ireland either organisationally or in their heads. It's a problem which I think still exists to this day and is not helped of course by the traditional cowardice of sections of the British Left in facing up to the Irish Question.

It really wasn't until the trauma of Bloody Sunday that the penny dropped and I was forced by events to bring the Marxist politics that I held in England into a relationship with political activity in Ireland. I was being asked to speak on Irish issues in student debates and I was having for the first time to make commitments which would finally sever my relationship with my Protestant community of origin. I still disliked nationalism intensely. I disliked the militaristic strategies and tactics that were being used which substituted physical force for mass political mobilisation and deferred socialist objectives to those of a nationalist popular front. It seemed to me that republican politics were divisive and unable to address the working class interests that made sense to me as a socialist. There was, it seemed to me, something short-sighted about Sinn Féin's increasingly cynical, if not explicitly sectarian, strategies and tactics. There were fundamental questions like the Protestant working class and their relationship to a socialist agenda in Ireland, questions of women's rights and a variety of other radical issues that I regarded as highly important and which were not being addressed within the Republican agenda. There were other more practical problems. My family's next door neighbour in Derry was shot dead by the Provos in a string of attacks on local businessmen which made it impossible to discuss politics with my parents. They had been quite liberal but like many Protestants they had moved to a more authoritarian position as the war continued. Even to this day I cannot talk politics in my parents' household. It is too explosive. I had kept the Northern Ireland conflict and my socialist politics apart in my mind. Usually what happens to most Protestants is that the war forces them into a right wing 'law and order' political mentality. Those of a more radical disposition tend, in the first instance, to separate their personal politics out from the conflict and then only at a later stage can they reintegrate them.

After university I moved to Liverpool. I got a job in a Catholic teacher training college run by the then Archbishop Heenan of Liverpool, a very powerful figure in the English Catholic hierarchy. (Whether this career choice was accidental or chosen I don't know). The college was meant to be the jewel in the crown of Catholic teacher training education. Perhaps I was given the job because I applied from Donegal and they assumed I was a Catholic. They had a shock however when they discovered that first of all I was from a Protestant background and furthermore an apostate, an atheist and a marxist socialist! It was an interesting time. Most of the students were first and second generation Irish kids, many were from families involved in the labour movement. Struggles took place inside the college around issues like contraception, abortion and authoritarianism within the church. I feel privileged to have had these insights into a form of questioning Catholicism which was very different from that which I had seen in Ireland.

I returned to Derry in 1976 to a teaching post at Magee University College lecturing to social and community workers. I'd involved myself in community politics in Liverpool and back in Derry there were hopes that a radical community work agenda could bring working class Catholics and Protestants together to work on housing and social issues. After six to nine months I became intellectually and politically convinced that this wasn't going to be possible. The nature of the British state in Northern Ireland and the apparent inability of community activists to bring Protestants and Catholics together in any meaningful political way until the national question is resolved meant that the political debate around community action was always going to be marginal.

I led a bifurcated life. During the Hunger Strike I became loosely involved in the protests against the treatment of the prisoners and for my pains had the house raided a couple of times by the police. This was absolutely normal for vast swathes of the nationalist community in Derry but it wasn't quite so normal for Protestant university academics. My young children were looked after by a lady in the Creggan and I remember pushing them up there everyday through the barricades of smouldering tyres and burnt out cars. The place did look like Armageddon. I still moved socially within the Protestant community but the condition for doing that was that I didn't talk politics.

I became a member of the Socialist Labour Party. It was a loose collection of people, republicans and socialists, some who had been in various Trotskyist groups. We gathered together to seek to play an active role in national politics around a radical agenda. The experiment only lasted for about a year, but it seemed to me to be a better forum for debate and platform for action than anything else which was on offer. A number of us would go along to meetings with Sinn Féin republicans in Derry. Maybe in Belfast it is different but certainly in Derry there were republicans who tried to make me feel guilty because I was a Protestant. I think it's all part of a general inability in Ireland to see beyond the ethnic in politics. But, more importantly, the SLP contingent would be the only people who would actually contest the republican line at the meetings! Most other people accepted slavishly that the republican movement had some sort of moral right to command the debate. I never accepted that. If I thought they were wrong I said so. It didn't make one terribly popular, particularly if you were a Derry Protestant! You were always subject to the accusation that the reason you held the views that you did was because you were not a card carrying member of the nationalist majority.

I'd find that no sooner did I arrive somewhere and then I'd have this urge to get out of the place again, to be somewhere else. I left Derry and went to teach at Ruskin College which is the Labour college in Oxford. I stayed there for two years. Perhaps I was in search of a purer socialist dream than was likely to be available in the intractable world of Irish politics. The ethos of Ruskin was changing with black students, women students and Irish students with republican politics coming into the college and the hierarchy of English Labour by and large hated it. They were incapable of addressing the pressing issues of racism and sexism as they were events in Ireland. Then the Malvinas war broke out and I discovered to my horror that a lot of Labour people were quite unable to see why there could be no support from socialists for the British Government's position. The Labour Party justifications for such bipartisan support – made in terms of the Falklands campaign being a struggle against the Argentinian Junta in the name of democracy – were spurious. It seemed time to leave England.

1983 and I moved on again, this time to Dublin. Here it didn't seem to matter at all whether I was a Protestant or a Catholic. I was to them primarily a Northerner and anyway Dubliners didn't seem to me to be the slightest bit interested in the North and its problems. There was at this time a discussion group called the 'Three Green Fields', whose political arguments seemed to summarise the partitionist attitudes I found in Dublin at the time. Their argument seemed to be that if the North, the 'Fourth Green Field', was torn off the cursed map of Ireland and sunk somewhere in the Atlantic – or at least if the national question was to be put aside, and the 1921 Settlement accepted as final – then the 26 counties could deal with its clericalism and disabling authoritarianism, and develop a liberal European agenda of social democratic politics. It was and remains a widely held view amongst the intelligentsia in Dublin that the politics of the Northern struggle has no connection at all to the advancement of a liberal politics in the south. And of course the inability of Sinn Féin as a political organisation to develop a programme addressing the interests of working people in the 26 counties has not helped to repair this rent in the liberal conscience.

As restless as ever and anxious to maintain my links with Derry, I began to spend more time in the North again, becoming professionally involved in research work around youth culture and in particular that of the Protestant working class. It was a world which still both fascinated and horrified me – one which hadn't been part of my immediate childhood and yet one which because of my background, I understood. I was able to return to Derry and slowly piece together a network of contacts that was to offer me ready access to plebeian unionism, including important echelons within the loyalist organisations.

What I found in Derry was this endangered Protestant species that seemed to have reversed itself into a historical cul-de-sac and couldn't find a way to get out of this. I was fascinated to discover that my teenage peer group, those that had grown up in the sixties and stayed in Derry, had not become involved in politics. Whatever the mode of recruitment into loyalist organisations was, it had seemingly skipped a generation. Loyalism however was appealing to a younger working class generation. The great mystery to me was how this group of young people in their leather jackets, many of whom listened to punk music or heavy metal, could have anything in common with their bowler hatted sectarian elders. The dynamic at work it seemed had little to do with traditional unionism but more with changes that had occurred within the Protestant working class. Protestants, as a result of losing their privileged economic situation and with the rise of unemployment after the onset of Thatcherism, were experiencing hardship at a level normally only experienced by Catholics in Northern Ireland. What I was seeing were the tensions within the Protestant working class being played out in various forms including around the youth agenda. It was all about marginalisation and immiseration. The identity of young Protestant people was in a sense up for grabs with old certitudes gone and the young trying to fashion a new sense of themselves as Protestants, as the Union weakened.

It struck me that there was no point bleating on about the failures of the Protestant working class unless there was some real attempt on the part of republicans and socialists to understand the transformations which had taken place in this culture. The left had a political analysis of loyalism – not a terribly sophisticated one – but it didn't have an informed sociological one which could understand the Protestant mind set. I saw myself as filling in some of those missing links. The difficulty was that my sociological and film work was taken up in ways which rather appalled me. I was invited by people all over Ireland to go and talk about the Protestant working class and loyalism as if I was a 'card carrying' representative of this tradition – which of course I wasn't. My politics are, I hope, very different! My argument that one ought to understand the phenomenon of loyalism became confused with the secondary argument that because one understands loyalism that one has to sympathise with it!

The documentary films I made dealing with loyalism and Protestant identity were popular in the south of Ireland. People would say 'Oh we never knew that' and 'you made us understand loyalism much better' and I would say well, yes, that's fine but I am not saying that as non-partisan nationalists you have to side with the unionists which of course was exactly what certain sections of the liberal intelligentsia seemed to want to do! For the 'Dublin 4' luminaries the Protestants and the loyalists in Northern Ireland suddenly became the oppressed minority! I have never ever made such an absurd claim and indeed the statistical evidence is absolutely incontrovertible. Catholics still suffer inequalities in Northern Ireland and are on the receiving end of British state repressive activity. However, it became fashionable to redefine the whole Northern Ireland problem as if it was a problem predominantly about Provo violence and about the plight of the poor 'alienated' Protestants. I've had to stand up several times recently and say that I may possibly have added to this confusion by making the films which I did. I was in fact trying – in my films 'We'll Fight and No Surrender' and 'Redeeming History' – to show the nullity of the loyalist political position and indicate the heavy price paid by unionists in terms of dignity and self image for their loyalty to a Britain which ultimately does not want them. This doesn't make me a 'Provo fellow traveller', an accusation some academic apologists for unionism have levelled at me recently.

I used to show my documentary films to loyalists and I was very pleased when they liked them. The films sought to provide a forum around which to debate issues. I think that one of the problems with loyalist culture is its lack of intellectual and political confidence. Despite all their bravado and sabre rattling loyalists usually find it hard to string four sentences of a political argument together. I don't think that this difficulty is something which should be relished by nationalists. I see it as a real problem affecting all of us in Ireland for without a growth in that confidence within the loyalist community the opportunities for progressive change will not exist. It's not as if loyalism has to be any more regressive on a variety of social issues than Catholic nationalism. In fact the irony is that in its own self image in the past, unionism has seen itself as more progressive! The absence of political debate within Protestantism has meant that a rigid mind-numbing fundamentalism has filled the vacuum. It's dangerous and nasty, and a lot of Protestants are very unhappy with it but they seem to have no political resources to contest this. For me the cultural realm seemed to offer such a resource. Film making provides an imaginative space, a forum where ideas can be debated, just as they often are by young people within youth cultural formations.

I often find my ethnographic work concerned with mapping Protestant mentalities difficult. The price that I had to pay for the co-operation of the young loyalists in my research, or indeed older loyalists that I worked with, was one of having to remain politically silent. That's not to say that, had I ever been asked, I would have denied my politics, but there had to be a certain amount of pragmatism if the films were to be made and the research programme accomplished. Would loyalist militants have talked to me if I had more fully revealed my own views and more explicitly challenged theirs? I don't know but sometimes I felt not so much like the scarlet Pimpernel but like the traitor Lundy. Like all 'double agents' on occasions I suffered crises of identity. But I had to be realistic. Sadly, within the Protestant community in Northern Ireland there is at present no room for dissenting voices, and for those who would question the prevailing unionist hegemony.

Within loyalism there are contradictions and divisions of class, age and sentiment. Today these are expressed in plebeian loyalism with the formation of parties like the Ulster Democratic Party and the Progressive Unionist Party, groups with intimate experience of paramilitary and prison realities. These parties, I think, are a symptom of the cul de sac unionism is caught in and not a solution to the problem of loyalism. They don't command widespread parliamentary electoral support and hence fall prey to the charge that they are unrepresentative. They don't put forward arguments which in any way differ from the canonical arguments put forward by more traditional unionist politicians. Despite their habitual reference to working class interests they have failed to develop a coherent social programme. Nor does plebeian loyalism represent any serious critique of unionism's sectarianism and its reactionary alliances. It would have to develop a different and more radical social agenda and indeed a different national agenda if it were to become truly 'progressive'.

I think that in the end we just have to accept that there isn't a rational answer as to why loyalists are loyalists (not that it's wonderfully clear as to why Irish nationalists adhere to the myths that they do). Loyalism is a position which seems sadly lacking in intellectual merit and political idealism. Worse still, in its supremacist and exclusivist mode it seems to be lacking the political generosity of nationalism and threatens to degenerate into ethnic savagery. It has no connection to any other significant political current or international association. It is important at the end of the day to understand historically and sociologically how Ulster Protestants have reversed themselves into this cul de sac in history. However the question which engages me certainly is how they can be got out of it as soon as possible.

For me the 'Northern Ireland problem' is in essence an unresolved colonial question in a post-imperialist age. The British have to decide to end this disgraceful political impasse by gracefully withdrawing. Their *raison d'être* for being in Ireland has long disappeared. The question of course is not 'if' they are going to go but 'when' they are going to withdraw and under what circumstances. If loyalists don't believe me then they should study the post war history of Britain's divestment of its empire. The core issue for me is how to convince Protestants that in the long term their future lies in a democratic, secular and unified Ireland and that a British withdrawal is to be welcomed. The struggle to create such an Ireland, within which Protestant voices and virtues will have their place, seems a much more interesting and worthwhile one than to join in the long, bitter whinge of unionism. We must break with the mean and miserable path of the bigot if we are to recover our dignity and speak once more to the world.

Times are changing. The Republic of Ireland twenty five years ago wasn't a particularly attractive society to be a part of. Although it still has many social problems, it is evolving rapidly in a pluralistic direction as Europeanisation advances. Conversely Britain and particularly England has become a nastier, more closed society. Fifteen to twenty years of Thatcherism has made the UK a more grasping, chauvinistic and inward looking society. The final Tory melt down has now started and the King Canute like folly of Thatcher and Major's attempts to arrest the long tern decline of Britain as an economic and political power is apparent to all.

I think that it is within this post-colonial context that a new debate in Northern Ireland is necessary. The trouble is that the generation of people who have the ability and the insight to lead such a debate have absented themselves from the political arena. Many of them have left, not just for economic reasons but also because they didn't feel part of Northern Ireland society and didn't feel there was anything they could contribute. It's a damning indictment of a society when huge swathes of its most talented people feel that. Even the ones that didn't go away seem to have taken a vow of silence. They appear to have held with that vow of silence for the last twenty-five years. We have all paid a high price for that. I don't anticipate however that the debate I seek will happen until there is an announcement of intention regarding a British withdrawal. This is the log jam which must be broken to free new voices within the Protestant community. Quite frankly there is really not much point talking to loyalists until that happens. As long as there is the slightest possibility that they can cling on by their finger nails to the miserable securities of the Union and to their veto over political transformation then they have no motive to negotiate with others who seek a fairer, more stable settlement.

I would like to see a democratic, pluralist secular Ireland capable of keeping its young people in the country and providing employment, social opportunity and cultural enrichment for its citizens. In the long term I feel that would deliver, 'the greatest happiness to the greatest number'. That's what I would like. But you ask what I think will actually happen? A difficulty always arises when sections of a national community for all sorts of historical reasons and due to perverse cultural and political alliances still feel more in common with the colonisers than the colonised. To the question of how that section of the population that I come from can be persuaded to abandon the politics of resentment and break the historic alliance with the most reactionary and regressive elements of the English polity is a difficult one. What will it take to bring the majority of the Protestant population to the realisation where their best interests lie? I don't know. The responsibility of dissenting Protestants clearly is to offer their co-religionists a new political imagination, one within which an emancipatory politics rather than a politics of despair has a privileged place.

I don't have immediate answers. I'm not a politician. But I think if people could realise that as Protestant and Catholic we share a common history and culture, and a common plot of land – if we spent some time reflecting on how we might best live on this narrow ground together and speak from it to each other, and to the world – then that might be useful. Britain, the British state, is the missing part of the Northern Ireland jigsaw puzzle, one to which much more attention should be paid. The British government has the historical obligation to play the leading role in attempting to convince the loyalists that their future lies in an historic accommodation with other ideologies and sentiments in Ireland.

6

Aid Worker for
the Developing World

Born 1957.

There was so much happening in the world as I was growing up: Czechoslovakia, Paris in 1968, the American civil rights movement, the feminist movement and of course, all that was happening on the streets of Northern Ireland. I was the bookworm in our family and I just read all the books and magazines I could find. Although my parents didn't read a wide range of books themselves – my dad read the occasional thriller and my mum read her Bible – they always found the money to buy the books I wanted. I remember the first place I ever was thrown out of was the Lisburn Road Adult Library. I was ten; I'd read all the books that I wanted to in the children's library and they wouldn't allow me to read the adult books.

I had a traditional Protestant upbringing which centred around the church. We lived in a two-up, two-down terraced house off the Lisburn Road in South Belfast. My mother was a shop assistant and my father worked in a weaving factory, checking the cloth and repairing looms. My father was a member of the Orange Lodge and in some years would have been the Master, but I didn't think of this in any other way than other children whose fathers would have had interests like pigeon fancying. Both my parents had a strong class perspective. There was always the realisation in our house that those in power look after those with money and the working class do the best they can with their lot in life. I found that confusing because, when you are brought up to be a loyalist, you are expected to be loyal to those in power.

Our family were Church of Ireland, which some Protestants consider little better than Roman Catholicism. I think my mum hedged our bets because we were also encouraged to go to an evangelical Sunday school and to an evangelical Friday night Christian club. The Christian club was an experience in literalism. They taught me that there was a boxing ring inside my stomach and in the boxing ring there was a little white boxer, who was Jesus, and a little black boxer, who was the devil – I had no concept of racism in those days – and whenever I yielded to temptation, the little black boxer won and Jesus got thumped by the little black boxer. I remember one winter night going to bed with my hot water bottle and waking up really hot and panicky, thinking, 'Oh no, I've burnt Jesus; I've melted him!'

By the time I was 14 I'd become disillusioned with religion. I'd stood and renounced the pomp and vanities of the wicked world and all the sinful lusts of the flesh and I'd never even had a lust of the flesh! I knew my Bible inside out. It was God's word and the word is the law and as a Protestant I was privileged to have direct access to that word. This alone gives Protestants a feeling of superiority over Catholics whose relationship with God is mediated through a priest. Of course it is all a sham. Our Bible is a politically constructed book, a mixture of translations from Greek and Hebrew, many of which are missing since the Council of Trent decided that all those books classified as the Gnostic Gospels were not to be included. Protestantism holds out the illusion of freedom of thought, whereby the relationship between the individual and God is one of their own making, without having the understanding that the word of God has already been sanitised and censored.

I know I was an exception within my circle of friends and family. I don't know why or where the questioning came from, but I do remember being the lone voice in arguments. At home my parents' view would have been that if there had never been a Bernadette Devlin there would never have been any 'troubles'. When I look back to my days at school, I remember having quite ridiculous arguments to which there were standard responses. If a united Ireland was mentioned, my peers would reply that we had never had anything to do with the people in the South and it would be ridiculous if the countries were unified now. They didn't believe me when I told them the country was partitioned in the 1920s; it just wasn't part of their understanding. There was always much more of a link with King Billy. King Billy came over to Ireland and fought at the Boyne and won. That is why we are here, why it's our country. It has always been like that and we have to fight to maintain it. There was an incredible level of ignorance. I can remember being taught in P4 how Belfast got its name. Belfast got its name, just in case you didn't know, when King Billy arrived at Carrickfergus on his way to the Boyne. He was on his favourite white horse called Bell and he had just got near this town when news was brought to him of the impending battle that was about to take place and how urgent it was that he come at once. He cried out, 'Bell, fast, Bell, fast, and so the town was named. That is what I was taught at school!

Apart from King Billy and the Battle of the Boyne, the only other individual who emerges is Lundy, the traitor during the Siege of Derry. He is a very important figure. There is this belief generally among Protestants that Catholics are not to be trusted, that they will stab you in the back as quick as look you in the face. They do that because they are Catholics; that's understandable. What is completely beyond the pale is being a lundy, a traitor to your own people. This was rubbed home to me in a very horrific way. One of my childhood friends married a Catholic and they began life together in a loyalist area after the wedding. A fortnight later she was murdered. Loyalists broke into the house and shot her whilst she was sleeping in bed. They didn't shoot her husband. That was the point. She was the lundy, the traitor; she had dared to do this. There is no concept within Protestantism of forgiveness for lundys.

I was lucky to have a brilliant History teacher. He came into the class one day and just spoke in German for five minutes and then said, 'Zeig heil'. Everybody laughed at him. By the end of the class he had everyone on their feet shouting, 'Zeig heil'. When the bell went he told us: 'That's how it happened; the Germans were people like you and me. Don't laugh when you see it happening again.' I began to read more and more about British history, about their colonialism and imperialism around the world. I became curious about Ireland and read about the missed opportunities, the gerrymandering, people's ignorance of how the state was controlled and perpetrated. I remember being terribly shocked when I read how the Northern Ireland unionists had tried to block the extension of the British welfare state to Northern Ireland, not because Catholics were lazy but because working class people were lazy and state benefits would only encourage them to continue being lazy.

Of course when I was young I didn't have words like feminism or socialism to express myself. I just felt very strongly that there was a lot of injustice in the world. One book that was published in Northern Ireland had a profound effect on me. It was Bernadette Devlin's *The Price of my Soul*. I was just so impressed by this woman who had been elected to parliament at the age of 21. The demands she was calling for, like one man one vote, appeared utterly reasonable to me. I know that it is people rather than individuals who change society; for example, it wasn't the Pankhursts who won the vote for women; it was those hundreds of thousands of women who struggled together and who will remain nameless to history. But nevertheless, I still feel that there are exceptional individuals like Bernadette Devlin who stand up for what they believe to be just and they give hope to people like me.

You never know how events happen by accident or design, but one event which had a profound effect on me was the Ulster Workers' Strike, the loyalist strike. It sounds crazy now but I remember quite vividly that I was reading *Bury my Heart at Wounded Knee* at the time. In the beginning no one wanted the strike; no one within my family circle, not one of the neighbours thought it was a good idea. What happened was a political education for me. The UDA was very well organised in our area; they made sure that old people living on their own didn't suffer; they engendered a strong sense of community feeling. I remember my mum saying that it was bit like during the Second World War. Some enterprising neighbour would rig up what we would call a barbecue these days and people would cook meals; others would make sure that the old woman down the street got her loaf of bread. Within a short period of time people had forgotten that they had originally been against the strike.

There were a few Catholic families who lived in the block of streets where I lived. They were identifiable because their children wore different uniforms and went to different schools from us. They kept to themselves and I wasn't particularly friendly with them. As the bombs went off and people were being killed, the neighbours who traditionally stood talking outside their houses would turn their attention to their Catholic neighbours, asking themselves whether it was safe to have them in the street. Some Catholic families became afraid and moved out and Protestant families were welcomed into the area to live in the houses they had vacated. I welcomed these families too but with time I began to realise that this wasn't an elaborate game. Everyone has a choice about how they behave and that included me.

I remember distinctly the last time I spoke freely about politics with my friends. I was 17 and I argued that it made sense for Ireland to be united. One of the guys pulled me aside and asked me if I realised that his dad was the commander of the UDA in our area. He told me in no uncertain terms what would happen if I was heard saying that sort of thing again.

After school I went on to university. I began to read books about the Spanish Civil War and in Philosophy I read George Woodcock's book on anarchism. One day, one of the lecturers began to tell us about these anarchists that he knew in Belfast. I buttonholed him and said: 'You mean there are anarchists in Belfast; is that what you are saying? I want to meet them.' I ended up chucking in my degree course, getting involved in campaigns and opening Just Books in Belfast with them. It was hard to chuck in the degree course. I was the only girl in my family to get to university and I thought that my parents would be terribly hurt and upset because, no matter how short money had been, I only had to say 'if only I could read such and such a book' and the money was found. My mum actually said: 'Well, you have been talking about changing the world for long enough, it's about time you started to do something about it.'

Since then I have spent some time in England working in co-operatives and for a trade union. The experience of being a paddy in England wasn't a positive one for me. As the war went on and on here I got the feeling that people in England were uncomfortable asking questions. There were times when you would throw a story into the conversation about such and such a night when you were caught up in a riot or a bomb and people just didn't want to know. In the end my friends tended to be Irish although I never intended it to be that way. I was living in the east end of London where there were horrible racist attacks and stabbings and murders. It felt like it was another Northern Ireland waiting to happen in that there were communities completely alienated from the state and the police. There were gross miscarriages of justice after the most appalling attacks had happened.

One evening I went to hear Linton Kwesi Johnson speak, a very powerful exponent of black rights and defender against racism. I got up my courage to ask one question about the similarities between the black struggle and the nationalist struggle in Ireland. His answer was: 'We subscribe to their journal and they subscribe to ours.' I thought it was a pathetic answer but perhaps it's unfair of me to point that out. I could have said: 'You want to talk about SUS laws? Have you heard of the PTA, other laws like the Payment of Debt Act, which were never enacted in England?' It confirmed to me that people in England were not only very ignorant of Northern Ireland; they really didn't want to know.

I was very homesick for Belfast; it's a beautiful city with the hills all around. London was claustrophobic by comparison. I've only been back a few months but most of the people I have become friends with are Catholics. I find my assumptions about the news and political events are not ones that Protestants can take. I feel no sense of unease when I am in Catholic areas, but the first time I had to cross the peace line into a loyalist area in connection with my work I was terrified. I know some of my friends find that hard to understand. I'm a Protestant; why should I feel so uneasy? Well, because people usually get into difficulties during a conversation and I was afraid that I would not pass muster as a good Protestant. The problems of Northern Ireland are political; they are not to do with where you were brought up or what religion you are.

Since coming back I have noticed there is a lot of soul searching going on into the Protestant identity and what it means. It is a search which verges between the bizarre and the desperate. I see only the trappings of how to cling to power, how to justify why Protestants are in Ireland. There is 1690, King Billy and the Battle of the Boyne, the sash my father wore, and a penchant for celebrating disasters like the Battle of the Somme and the sinking of the Titanic. I saw an horrendous exhibition on how bowler hats and balaclavas symbolised Protestant cultural traditions. I've read the attempts by Protestants to reclaim the ancient Irish hero Cuchulain as their own lost son of Ulster. I went to a play about the men who went to the Somme where they lamented going into battle without having had an Ulster Fry. Soda bread suddenly became part of our cultural heritage! There is a desperation in all this, almost like we let these nationalists steal a march on us. There isn't an equivalent Protestant alternative to Irish culture and for me that's okay; Protestants are part of Irish culture; we've been here for hundreds of years, we can be here for thousands more. This is where we belong and where our future lies.

7

Richard Doak

Lecturer. Born 1952.

I was brought up in the Bishop Street area of Derry on the edge of what became known as the Bogside in the period of the 'troubles'. It became a completely nationalist area after 1971 as Protestants moved across the river, but I remember it when it was a mixed area of working class terraced streets. The big difference, I think, between myself and my Catholic friends was that we didn't go to school together. Contact was at the informal level of street games and although we didn't have a 'gang', as such, we certainly identified with the streets where we lived. It was also a very male street culture. All the boys played soccer and shared the same soccer heroes. Many of these would have been English, but we were also enthusiastic supporters of Derry City Football Club which was very successful in the sixties at winning competitions and, in fact, the club got into Europe before going out of the League altogether with the advent of the 'troubles'. Sectarianism was institutionalised in education and obvious celebrations like the Twelfth of July and the Derry Apprentice Boys parade in August, but I think the fact that Protestants and Catholics lived so close to each other meant that it didn't have the same impact on my childhood as it would have done if, like today, we lived in our separate communities. To take one example, Protestant kids like myself would enjoy going to the Catholic bonfires on the 15th of August, the nationalist equivalent of the '11th night'.

When the Civil Rights campaign began in the autumn of 1968, I went to watch. I regarded the marches as a great piece of urban theatre to liven up a Saturday afternoon, but I was also aware of experiencing a period of political excitement and change. I was just 15 at the time and was very naïve, just beginning to think politically. I did identify with the demands of Civil Rights and I think that the reason for this was the effect the global media culture was having on me. Civil Rights for me was more about music and style and protest than about nationalism or hard politics. Looking back, my political consciousness was probably informed by a vague leftish liberalism emanating from the American hippies and from rock stars like Dylan and Lennon.

Not that there had ever been a powerful loyalist or Orange influence in my family. My father was a bricklayer and secretary of the trade union. Both my parents were Methodists, liberal in their politics though not in their theology. By the time Civil Rights came along I had stopped going to church and religion meant very little to me, but it was the Civil Rights campaign which made me realise for the first time that unionism too was not for me. I couldn't identify with those hard-nosed guys that I was seeing; to me they were reminiscent of South Africa and how could anyone possibly identify with the police batonning people who were protesting for civil rights? The irony, though, was that I still identified with Britain. During the early 'troubles' I thought Britain were the good guys; after all, what did I know about Irish history? To me there was a Labour government in power and a straightforward debate which said people should be given civil rights and integrated into the United Kingdom as first class citizens.

In 1972 I went to university. I had come to regard Northern Ireland as the epitome of narrow mindedness and backwardness. Unlike most of my peers who went to Queen's or the New University at Coleraine, or unlike my brother and sister who had done the conventional Protestant thing of going to teacher training college in Belfast, I set my sights on going as far away as possible, which for me at that time was studying Sociology at Kent. I had no social science background at all, I'd studied Greek and Latin at 'A' level, but this was the moment of Sociology and I thought it was the radical thing to do. Of course it wasn't as radical as I thought; the vast majority of students in Kent were from the home counties and very bourgeois.

That was a culture shock for me and, for the first time, I realised that I was Irish in the worst sense of racism. Like a lot of Irish people who go to England, I played the role, tongue in cheek, drinking more than other people, being the Paddy that they called me. However, I did feel safe in England. Back home the situation in the early 1970s was changing dramatically with gross acts of sectarian murder, particularly from the loyalists. I took the view that the sectarianism in the North was a lot worse than the polite racism of England; no one was going to slit my throat or shoot me in Canterbury!

I've often asked myself why I came back in 1974. The logical thing would have been to stay in England. Derry had become a dangerous city to live in and my mother had moved across the river to a Protestant suburb. Many of my school friends had become hardened in their unionism and there was no such thing any more as a liberal Protestant. The only reason why I did stay was that I was offered a full-time job in a Further Education college in Omagh, a mainly nationalist town where there was very little trouble. There I could have a fairly normal extended adolescence, socialising in bars and at dances. My job, teaching Sociology, was easy. It gave me a space. I was teaching British metropolitan Sociology; all of the syllabuses were British, so I could talk about radical issues and avoid Northern Irish politics. What happened was that gradually I found that most of my friends and contacts came from Catholic nationalist backgrounds, mainly because of the local demography; but even on the college staff, Protestant teachers didn't go out drinking; Catholic teachers were a bit more sociable.

Many of my Catholic friends still perceive me as a Protestant. I think it is very hard to get away from that. When it comes to the crunch there is a sense of it's them or us. I think, mixing in mainly Catholic circles, it was inevitable that I would marry a Catholic. My wife comes from a Catholic housing estate and I was well received into the family. It wasn't any tremendous leap for me. The housing estates in Omagh are segregated, but they are physically close to each other. There isn't that sense of moving from one geographical community to another that you find in Belfast or Derry. There is a sort of benign sectarianism, especially in the middle classes where people know each other very well.

My wife and I had a long debate about what school our children should go to. My wife didn't insist that the children be sent to Catholic schools. Like me she is an atheist; she'd had a bad experience of Catholic schools herself and was happy for the children to be educated in a more secular setting. It was problematic. We visited every primary school in the town, but eventually the problem we faced was solved by default. An integrated school was opened the very year my oldest child was about to go to school. I wouldn't say that I am tremendously pro-integrated education in the same very optimistic way in which liberal Alliance types are, but, in fairness, it does open up an important space and I'm glad we at least had the choice.

I have never been politically involved in the sense of going out and doing anything. I feel I'm half in, half out of the nationalist community. I suppose I do something that a lot of people do and it's not a very noble thing to do. I drop out of Northern Ireland emotionally and intellectually, that is until recently. Logically, as a Sociologist, I shouldn't have been in a small town like Omagh; I should have been doing something in Derry or Belfast where I could have reflected on or added to the political situation and I have a certain regret that I didn't do that, but when you have a job and just stay on in a place the years fly by and that's what happened to me.

The research that I am engaged with now has forced me to become more political, at least on paper, and I have found myself identifying with nationalism more. Looking back to my teenage years I can see that I supported Civil Rights because of the effects of a metropolitan liberal culture. I was anti-unionist in the sense that I couldn't identify with what I saw as semi-fascist politics. That's easy intellectually, but where do you move on to? Nationalism as an ideology has associations with political rightism in Europe generally and Germany in particular; it was a bad word. I've really only become comfortable about Irish nationalism through reading more about it. Although it has its excesses, I can see that Irish nationalism holds out the possibility of inclusiveness and pluralism. It is more akin to the nationalism of Third World resistance and anti-colonialism than to the nationalism of political rightism. It articulates oppression, life as an underdog; that's an easy leap for a Sociologist to understand intellectually, but my problem is that it is only intellectual. I have never experienced harassment, never had a brother who was lifted, never had an uncle who was shot, my father always had work. Whilst I can identify with nationalism intellectually it is more difficult to identify emotionally.

Could I give you what I think is a really good example of this? The whole Drumcree affair. When the news came through on the Thursday that the Orange guys were being allowed to walk through, I quickly became aware of the hurt and anger in the Catholic community, people crying, the mood being as bad as the period of the hunger strike. I knew the decision was completely unjust and I broadly agree with the residents' groups principle of consent, but there was no way I could be into that kind of communal grieving. My reaction was more of an academic researcher; a number of issues were whirling through my mind – the different reception of events in the nationalist community between Sinn Féin and the SDLP/clerical fractions, the various fractions and constituencies within unionism, the marching issue as the site of a bitter and unsubtle fight for hegemony, the shifting balance of power between the blocs, the paradox of unionism as representing both strength and weakness at the same time. But nobody that I spoke to in the nationalist community wanted to hear about such things as settler insecurity – it was frustrating for me and I just listened passively to what people were saying. One guy, a conservative SDLP-clerical type, who was completely incensed by Drumcree, said that if you are lying on the ground and someone is kicking the shite out of you, you don't worry about his motivation; you just worry about yourself. Another thing that came out of Drumcree was Sinn Féin reactivating the slogan, 'Disband the Orange State'. I can understand why people might want to use this type of slogan politically but to call the North an Orange State is in my opinion a serious misreading of the last 25 years – it doesn't see the dynamic nature of the sectarian relationship. Drumcree happened precisely because the North is not an Orange State. Don't get me wrong here – I'm aware, through my research, that there is a lot of inequality of power and advantage between blocs, but it's not a static thing. I would find it hard to actively support a political party; I suppose I'm a nationalist but in a very unaligned kind of way.

The research I am doing into the GAA has meant that I have had to think carefully about the whole issue of sectarianism. In one sense, what I would call the descriptive level, the nature of sectarianism is similar between the two blocs – school, neighbourhoods, work places, sport. But in another sense, at a more analytical level, Protestants and their institutions here have been historically closer to institutionalised power. In the context of this state, I would regard Protestant institutions as sectarian and Catholic institutions as having been sectarianised. I know that some people might think this is just playing about with words, but I think the sectarian/sectarianised distinction is important theoretically. In my research I have become interested in the everyday language of sectarianism, the way people pair off certain things like the Falls/Shankill, GAA/Orange Order. This type of thing rolls off the tongue easily, but it doesn't pick up the fact that Catholic institutions like the GAA have never been part of the state apparatus. In this sense there is a fundamental difference between the nature of Protestant sectarianism and Catholic sectarianism.

There is a deep opposition in loyalism to any change of jurisdiction. There are also those middle class professional Protestants living in places like North Down who are not out on the Twelfth or voting for the DUP, who see loyalism as a culture of embarrassment, but they still want to remain British in a secular, metropolitan way. So far they haven't wanted their voices to be heard. The problem remains, though, that this is a failed state; it doesn't have a future without radical reform. I can't see how it can be reformed within a six county set up and be workable. Ideally I would like to see an all-Ireland secular and pluralist state and I think that in such a political set up it would be possible to safeguard the rights of everyone and respect their diversity. Over the last number of years the South of Ireland has changed positively and has moved in the direction of genuine pluralism. They have relaxed the question of nationality because most of them believe that they already have their nation. Some leading political scientists regard it as a more liberal, democratic society than the U.K. state. There is an irony in this which is at the heart of the whole problem – no matter how liberal or pluralist the South becomes, unionists will never want to join that state. The conflict is about different aspirations. I think that many elements within the SDLP, Sinn Féin and the southern parties now realise that unionists are not suffering from some mass delusion or false consciousness, and recognise their Britishness. Given that there are two sides whose ultimate goals are incompatible, any settlement must involve a compromise, with each side settling for something well short of their original objective – like some kind of joint sovereignty arrangement. My gut feeling is that nationalists and republicans would settle on these terms, but not unionists; they seem very insecure and compromise isn't really part of their mindset. I'm not terribly optimistic about the whole situation to be honest.

8

Johnston Price

Community Education Worker. Born 1954.

Today Stranmillis is seen as a relatively posh area but when I was growing up it was quite different. Obviously it was never a traditional working class area; most of the people would have been employed as clerical workers, so it was an upper working class or lower middle class area, however you want to categorise it. My memories are of a tight network of streets where you knew everyone and played games on the street. We would also have been more conscious of the differences between us and the adjacent middle class Malone area. The Boys' Brigade, for example, which played a huge part in my childhood – I was in it until I was 18 – would have been seen as too proletarian, not fashionable or proper for children from the Malone Road to join.

I had a religious Presbyterian upbringing and I was quite conscious of being a Protestant, more so as the sixties progressed and the political situation became starker. My mother had a sense of the difference between Catholic and Protestant and although we mixed with the few Catholic families in the street, I still have memories of Catholics being different; they were better to do because, where we lived, they were on their way up the social scale and to some extent the Protestants were heading downwards. They holidayed in different places – the South of Ireland or Portaferry – whereas we went to Bangor and Donaghadee, and of course they went to different schools.

Looking back, I can see that I took immense pleasure out of being in the Boys' Brigade. It was make-believe really. We marched on church parades, we were the most atrocious marchers, and at the end of the year there was a parents' evening of marching display and prize giving. I took a perverse pleasure in gaining a Queen's badge and progressing up the ranks from Lance Corporal to Corporal to Sergeant, receiving certificates and prizes for religious knowledge along the way. I used to swot it all up and if the truth of the matter be told, I was a prat; other boys just wouldn't have bothered! It was always a smart-assed thing to come first and get a book token! As I got older I went on training exercises. One which I remember as a very harrowing experience was with the Paras. It was so physical and rough and aggressive and they were cold and frightening, although they changed character altogether when they showed us the guns in the evening. I guess it is a very different way to come at the Paras compared to the ways some other people have come at them from.

Despite all the religious knowledge I had accumulated, I was never able to summon up a religious belief in my bones and after attending confirmation classes, began to articulate this vigorously. The year I was to be confirmed into the church I refused, but enormous pressure was put on me the next year round. I can remember the ceremony more as a spectator than in any sense being a participant. I would still have an attachment to the atmosphere of Presbyterian churches in the evening when there are only a few people in attendance, when you really find someone different but as to religious faith, it is non-existent for me.

Even by normal standards I read a lot. I think the first serious book I read was *Black Like Me*, about a white guy who took some tablets and changed the pigmentation of his skin and then went into the Southern American states and experienced racial hatred. I began reading more books like this, became interested in Irish literature, read a short book by Lukacs on Lenin, got a subscription to *New Left Review* and one Christmas rather pretentiously asked for *Das Kapital* as a present. Politics interested me. When he wasn't being elected to Stormont, David Bleakley used to teach us Politics at Methody. I can remember him having us correct the *Guardian* and send it off, detailing all the misprints as some sort of complaint. For me it was an introduction to liberal, vaguely socialist politics. I knew that a lot of issues weren't being covered by the school curriculum. Irish History wasn't covered; it was British coal fields and the Peterloo Massacre, radical in themselves but you had to dig pretty deep to find it. Similarly in literature, we would read E. M. Forster, which is all about imperialism and colonialism, but that wasn't being picked up by the students and sure as hell the teachers weren't picking it up.

The world around me revolved around leaving school, getting a job and settling down. I didn't want to do that but nor did I fit in with friends at school who were dropping out and taking LSD. That was too trendy for me and I never made it to be a hippie. I was a very earnest young man who always looked as if my mother had dressed me; my clothes were always too big for me, the music I was into was retro before retro came round. When the 'troubles' broke out I was a spectator. I'd put my head out of the window and look over at Divis and listen to the gun battles. I watched the students walking down past Methody, read the Hunt Report which called for the disarming of the RUC. I did write in the school magazine that the RUC should be disbanded not disarmed, not because it was an issue with me but because I had seen the RUC batoning people on the television. Now I can see that civil rights here can be compared with what was happening in Paris or America but then that wasn't so apparent to me. But there were a lot of lefty ideas around and I was drawn to that way of thinking; I'd like to argue that it was a very central way to see the world, but I felt and still feel very much part of the Protestant community. Even though I have never had any attachment to unionism, I still feel that they are my people.

I think the world that I lived in was summed up for me during the celebrations in the Botanic Gardens for the 50th anniversary of Ulster in 1971. I had a gut feeling that there was something bizarre about tramping around a muddy field to a succession of marquees celebrating things Ulster as I avoided tartan gangs and RUC men with their Alsatians. It is very much my world, that muddy field, a bleak world I would like to move beyond.

I worked in a number of jobs after leaving school: a clothing factory in Liverpool, odd jobs in Belfast, including a roofing felt company, a smoky place full of bitumen and asbestos. There were two sides to the factory, one side made the paper and the other the vulcanite. The foreman, a Catholic from Scotland, was killed by two Protestants from the other side of the factory. I left there and started working as a road sweeper, graduating to bin man. There were only certain areas of the city you could work in, dependent on your religion. This was always worked through without being formalised and I remember quite shamefully playing that to my advantage. If you worked in one area you could go to the pub in the afternoon whereas if you worked in another you couldn't and I, by my saying that 'I am not going to work with those Catholics', ended up in the area where I could go to the pub in the afternoon. The foreman perfectly understood my sentiments. It was disgraceful really!

If there was a Road to Damascus for me it was the hunger strikes. That's when I began to feel guilty, in the sense that it wasn't enough to have a view on things; people needed support. By that time I had enrolled at the Poly where I came into contact with more and more Catholics and one couldn't help but be aware of the stress they were under, being pulled and torn by the political situation. I began to attend political meetings in the students' union and public meetings around the hunger strike and increasingly felt the need to belong to some political grouping. Therein lay a difficulty. I don't support the armed struggle but I appreciate that it is a complex issue. If I was to argue what impact armed struggle has had on forcing change, I might have to admit that it has had an impact and yet I could not join a political party which endorsed armed struggle. All of this, I'm afraid, is a long winded excuse for joining the Communist Party!

I was introduced and welcomed into the party in this gloomy room and heard the low mumble down the back saying 'another bloody student'. It's questionable what impact my activity had. I wrote for the party paper, sold the party paper, tried to start a branch in Derry which never got off the ground and generally went to meetings which were useful to me on a personal level. I think the Communist Party wanted to be a broad church for socialism and so didn't apply those parts of the agenda which members didn't subscribe to. The national question fell victim to this and I would have been considered a republican by claiming that Ireland should be united even though that was party policy. I felt that at the time there was very little else I could have joined. In the event I never really left the Communist Party, just walked away from it over a period of time. I went on to study in England and did try to join the Communist Party of Great Britain, but they refused. This was in the days when democratic centralism meant something; you couldn't be in two communist parties at once! So I involved myself in Troops Out meetings and different fringe meetings around the Labour Party, arguing for a united Ireland against the Campaign for Labour Representation which was prominent in the mid-1980s.

When I returned to Belfast I became involved in community education. I don't adhere to this community relations ideology whereby you can get people to understand each other and share some agenda. Community relations is the British government's agenda rather than a people's agenda; I think it has had a disjointed impact on the situation, creating sectarian blocs in terms of cultural expression, but I do think it is important for people to know where they are coming from and have the ability to exchange views and information. That was becoming more and more possible during the ceasefires when the price of speaking out was not seen as a threat to one's life. It was always possible to get Catholics to listen to a unionist platform, much more difficult to attract Protestants to hear a nationalist platform never mind a republican one; that seemed to be breaking down a bit and a space was being opened up. Since the ceasefire has broken people are much more cautious.

I don't think there is an Ulster culture in the same sense that there is an Irish one, but it is an area where it is very difficult to be prescriptive. You can't tell people what their identity or culture is. A number of organisations have sprung up post-1985 which construct an Ulster identity in a deliberate way, in the same way one could argue that Irish nationalism was culturally and politically constructed at the end of the 19th century. I don't think that this Ulster construction comes from within the Protestant people. I have a folk memory of the sense of power and energy of the Orange bands and I can remember cajoling my father to get the flag out, which was a tricky operation because we didn't have one of those holes in the wall of our house and so it had to be tied with rope to my bed; but I don't know if that amounts to a culture, although it can be a way of life for some people. Or take the invention of the Ulster Scots language. Is that not so much a cultural project as an attempt to create a challenge to the Irish language, a crude blocking device which copper fastens sectarianism in people's mind set?

My concept is that the society I live in and the 'troubles' I am surrounded by are Irish, but there are other contexts. I am surrounded by mid-Atlantic culture and a British way of life, I support Everton football team, my favourite food is Indian but above all this, I live in Ireland. I wouldn't be insulted if someone called me an Ulster Protestant but it is not how I think of myself, or only in so far as I have done a lot of fishing in Cavan and Monaghan and a lot of drinking in Donegal and been to the other six counties as well! I think life would be a lot more enriching for people from a Protestant background if they could embrace some notion of an Irish culture but that is a matter of choice; it can't be rammed down their throats.

I am one of those crude people who think that the national question needs to get sorted out before other relationships will improve. Britain should be encouraged to work towards a resolution, to move unionism on, to have the sense to realise that the Northern Ireland state is unworkable. Twenty five years of the armed struggle have cemented people into rigid positions yet even despite that, people have shifted some ground. The relationships are complex but I think the solution is a process of working towards a united Ireland. I think that is attainable. Certain sections of the Protestant middle class are not necessarily opposed to a united Ireland so long as their economic interests are copper fastened.

Five or ten years ago I wanted a united socialist Ireland. Although there are all sorts of difficulties with socialism I am still not dissuaded of it. I think what has changed in recent years is that people have begun to think pragmatically; they have begun to question whether too high a price was being paid for ideals, given the sectarian violence and the death squads. There was also a question mark over how different people's lives were going to be even if they did get a united Ireland. As to whether, nowadays, they are being too pragmatic only time will tell!

Civil Rights

*All of my life I had been brought up to believe that the working
class people of East Belfast, the shipyard workers, the
engineering workers, the women in the factories, were the
salt of the earth. To be rejected by them as a traitor hurt me
but I could not have changed how I felt. I don't see that any
section of the people in Ireland or Northern Ireland or Belfast
can be free if they are prepared to accept privileges over
another section of the community. You can't be free at
somebody else's expense.*

9

Edwina Stewart

Communist and Civil Rights activist. Born 1934.

My mother and father were members of the Revolutionary Workers' Groups which were founded in 1933 at the time of the Outdoor Relief struggles in Belfast. The same year they became foundation members of the Communist Party of Ireland. We lived in East Belfast where my parents had the goodwill on a small shop in Templemore Avenue, on the bus route for the workers who travelled to the harbour estate to work in the shipyard, Shorts and in the engineering works. Ours was a shipyard shop where the workers would stop off to buy cigarettes and papers on their way to and from work.

My parents were atheists, not that it mattered much in those days in Northern Ireland; one still had to be educated either in a Protestant or Catholic school. Throughout my childhood I really didn't meet or know any Catholics. The membership of the Communist Party was in general made up from the Protestant section of the working class, although of course there were a few Catholics who joined. My father was always sarcastic about religion, but he didn't withdraw me from religious education classes at school or stop me from attending Sunday school if I wished. I think he knew that it was hard enough for me to have a mother and father as leading communists standing at election time. I was aware that ours was not seen as a respectable family and I did have a time in my teens when I went to the Presbyterian church with some school friends. That was an effort on my part to try and understand, maybe to be seen conforming to the norm, because I knew respectable people went to church. It didn't last long however.

The Orange Order was the organisation to join if you were Protestant working class and wanted to get a job and become part of the unionist monolith that ruled Northern Ireland. When I was a child, my father would have taken me to the Twelfth of July parades for the spectacle, but other than that the traditions of orangeism played no part in my life. In fact, I can remember going to a birthday party and playing 'truth or dare', and my dare was to sing the *Lily O*. When I said I didn't know it, the other children were astounded; you know the song – 'There is not a flower in Ireland like the royal orange lily o'. Apart from the popular music of the day and a couple of Irish songs like the *Rose of Tralee*, the only songs that I knew were Russian, like *The Soviet land so dear to every toiler* or international working class songs, a lot of them Wobbly songs, like *The man that watered the workers' beer*.

My attempts at going to church and being respectable came to an end when I was about 14 and became involved in founding the Youth League in the Communist Party. Peace and more especially the campaign against nuclear weapons were the big issues after the Second World War ended. The Cold War began and with it the view that the Allies had been fighting the wrong people during the war, the real threat being the Soviet Union and communism. There would have been a view in society that the Soviet Union should be bombed before they strengthened their position in the world. With the Chinese Revolution came the threat of the Americans using atomic weapons in the Korean War.

International issues and struggles on bread and butter issues concerned us far more than the border. As communists we believed that Ireland should be re-united and although we didn't approve of the IRA's armed struggle during the 1950s, we did campaign against internment and made collections of cigarettes at Christmas for republican prisoners. Their families were turned down for state welfare benefits and one of our members, Betty Sinclair, fought and won the case for their reinstatement.

There was such a backlash against communism after the Second World War. I remember in 1948 my father and the East Belfast branch of the Communist Party marched on the 150th anniversary of the United Irishmen. The republicans wouldn't allow them to be attached to the march, as it were, because they were communists! They had to walk so far behind the rest of the march. I think there was also an element of 'the prods were coming'! I remember a member of the organising committee telling us how he had been very happy at organising the anniversary but had been driven to despair when a Catholic girl from the Markets declared she was giving up her Protestant boyfriend in honour of Wolfe Tone!

Of course ignorance was on both sides. Belfast was ghettoised then; people either lived in a Protestant or a Catholic area. It wasn't really until the sixties that the viciousness declined a little and Catholics began to move out of their ghettos. We had no Catholic neighbours. The first time I had real contact with Catholics was when I attended the World Youth Festival for Peace and Friendship in Moscow in 1957. Various cultural groups from the nationalist community attended the Festival, including the McPeake Family and Irish dancers from the Mulholland School. That was also my first introduction to what you would call Irish traditional music and culture. As the sixties progressed it became more and more acceptable for Protestants to travel over to the folk clubs on the Falls Road and it was there that I socialised with Catholics and began to make friends.

Communist and socialist literature was a great help to Protestants wishing to understand Ireland, so it wasn't that I was ignorant of Irish history. James Connolly's *Labour and Irish History* had been published and the English Marxist Tommy Jackson published *Ireland Her Own*, an excellent analysis apart from the chapters on the early Irish clan system. Though the Communist Party didn't agree with armed struggle or abstentionism, we always maintained contacts with the republican and nationalist movements. We recognised that they were anti-imperialist and that they were fighting for a United Ireland. We certainly subscribed to that. In 1962 we published our programme, *Ireland's Path to Socialism,* in which we argued for civil rights, for one man one vote, the end of gerrymandering, the end of undemocratic rule, improved relations with the Irish republic, as it had become, and an alliance of all anti-unionists to elect a progressive government which would use public money to develop industry.

I was elected onto the Northern Ireland Civil Rights Association executive committee in 1969. At the time I remember being asked to try and stop events happening too quickly, but you know, when there are attacks on the Falls Road, pogroms and burnings, it really isn't possible to stem the tide of events. No one was going to sit back and allow another attack like Burntollet or the police rampage into the Bogside in Derry.

NICRA itself was an alliance of groups with different agendas. People's Democracy wanted to use confrontation politics to further the revolution. The people who became the Provisional IRA didn't want any concessions from Britain. They thought they could win a United Ireland and a socialist republic militarily. I didn't think that this was possible without the involvement of the Irish Republic, which was not an option because the IRA really had only a minority support base within the Northern nationalist community. How could you win with that? In the Communist Party we thought that we had reached a time whereby the majority of the Protestant population would back O'Neill and his reforms. We thought it was time to consolidate. When those loyalists who were against O'Neill's reforms started using violence, sectarian feelings built up and the mood for change, so fragile anyway, evaporated.

The years that I was involved in the Civil Rights campaign were the hardest for me. I was teaching in Ashfield Girls' School and I had a high public profile as a speaker at meetings all over the country. I spoke out against internment at a meeting in Leeson Street on the Falls Road and a campaign began in the school to get me the sack. Some of the other staff members would not speak to me. They saw me as a traitor. I didn't let that annoy me and, you know, I was speaking at so many meetings and teaching all day that, come lunch time I just used to fall asleep in an armchair anyway.

After Bloody Sunday the campaign against me reached a crescendo. I was attacked in the *Sydenham Defender* – I think that was the name of the paper – which reported on 'the lying spokeswomen for the IRA, Máire Drumm, Bernadette Devlin and Edwina Stewart'. I had also been charged with organising an illegal march against internment, which carried a mandatory six month sentence. I was threatened on the bus, my parents were threatened, my sisters were harassed. My children suffered too. I remember going to my younger daughter's primary school one day after she had forgotten her raincoat and finding her in the classroom by herself when the other children were out playing. The school couldn't let her out to play with the other children for fear of what might happen. That was a terrible kick in the stomach for me, when I realised that my children were suffering for what I believed in. Without my husband's support I couldn't have carried on. During all this time he was a full-time official in the Communist Party. We discussed everything together and supported each other and he understood all that I was feeling. His family were unionist and Presbyterian; he had really kicked over the traces far more than me.

People in the Party told me that I would be killed if I stayed any longer at the school and so I left to work voluntarily for NICRA. It was distressing having to leave my job. All of my life I had been brought up to believe that the working class people of East Belfast, the shipyard workers, the engineering workers, the women in the factories, were the salt of the earth. To be rejected by them as a traitor hurt me deeply, but I could not have changed how I felt. I don't see that any section of the people in Ireland or Northern Ireland or Belfast can be free if they are prepared to accept privileges over another section of the community. You can't be free at somebody else's expense. I think there is a guilt among Protestants that makes them shout all the louder, a guilt that sometimes they got their jobs not on merit but because they knew somebody, or their mother's uncle's cousin knew somebody, who could get them a job. I think that guilt lends itself to a lack of self-confidence and a fear that the way they treated the nationalists in the past will be the way they will be treated in the future now that they no longer have much power. In fact many privileges could be more illusion than reality.

NICRA began to lose its mass support. There were splits and divisions in the movement. The IRA split into the Officials and the Provisionals. It began to be impossible to work and make real progress for all our people in NICRA. After the UWC Strike in 1974, the divisions in the movement became too great. It was difficult for the trade unions or the progressives in the Protestant section to be openly linked with the Provisional-led organisations in support of what were, in fact, perfectly legitimate demands. Constitutional nationalists didn't want to be linked with the Provisionals. There was no co-operation between the two IRAs on issues like internment. It was heartbreaking to see NICRA, the people's organisation, fail. Something which Bernadette Devlin McAliskey said recently reminded me of how I felt, that in the beginning there was a preparedness among the Protestant population to accept O'Neill's reform package. That of course was before there was any violence. After the IRA ceasefire Bernadette said that nationalists had accepted terms that were not as good as they were offered twenty years ago. She said the good guys lost. I would agree with that. If people had been prepared to accept the demands of the civil rights movement all those years ago, we could have been much further on now.

After NICRA I began to devote more of my time to the Party, involving myself in internal affairs, building a financial base and securing ownership of our own headquarters. The discovery of the terrible weaknesses, the lack of democracy and economic failure of the Soviet mode of socialism has not stopped me believing in communism, from believing that production for profit rather than need will never solve the problems of the future. I would hope that and I believe that a better change in social ownership will be found so that the people who do the work can own and receive the benefits of that work.

And Ireland? I suppose the old dream of the United Irishmen, that Catholic, Protestant and Dissenter would unite under the common name of Irishmen and Irishwomen; the dream of the civil rights movement that civil rights would be granted and there would be peaceful political progress; that the workers who produce the wealth would run the country and get the benefits from it; that there would no longer be a need for using the great folk memory of the Irish famine to raise money to send out to India or Somalia or Romania; that we would all live in a world where the wealth is developed for the benefit of all the people who live in the world.

I was Honorary Secretary of NICRA from 1969 until the late seventies, a member of the National Executive of the CPI and became Northern area and National Treasurer. I joined practically every world peace and solidarity organisation and I'm not finished yet.

10

Bobby Heatley

Economist/Lecturer. Born 1934.

I remember my father dragging me into darts clubs on the Woodstock Road in East Belfast where they were showing movies of Russian ballerinas. I was about four at the time and I subsequently learnt that these clubs were also political debating clubs, or at least places where a lot of political debates went on, and I remember my father saying how he had collected donations there in support of the Irish Brigade in the Spanish Civil War. My father belonged to an Irish Socialist Republican group in and around the Woodstock and Beersbridge Road. They were followers of James Connolly. It wasn't a big or important group, but it certainly existed and would have tied in with the socialist thinking of the time which existed in the area, and which I think was due to the slump, unemployment and poverty of the 1930s. I do remember there being considerable anti-fur coat sentiment in those days. Later in my childhood Brookeborough used to come round the streets on the back of a lorry dressed in a fur coat canvassing the people at election time. He threw little packets of sweets out to the children. That anti-fur coat sentiment continued for a few years. The Northern Ireland Labour Party became quite strong electorally and the Communist Party within the trade union movement gained momentum. 'Wullie' McCullough polled thousands of votes in an election against Lord Glentoran.

Both my mother and father's families, and my father too, had been in the British forces. Family lore states that my grandfather and my uncle both had military funerals at Dundonald. Their coffins, draped in the union jack, were transported up the Newtownards Road in a gun carriage.

Interestingly enough, there was a radical streak on my father's side of the family which came from generations back, but the most immediate connection was my grandfather who was an active member of the Irish Transport and General Workers' Union and well versed in the teachings of Connolly and Pearse. My father picked a lot of this up from him, but I think that it was his experiences of being posted to India with the British Army, and later Aden and Egypt, that radicalised his thoughts about the political situation in Ireland and made him more aware of this side of his family tradition.

I didn't have a lot of contact with Catholics during my childhood years except when we were evacuated during the War to Ballynoe. We did live on the New Lodge Road for a while during the period that Tom Williams (the republican) was executed. I actually went to a Protestant school there. I remember being surrounded by a crowd of Catholic youngsters who were going to beat me up, but as always happens, someone came forward to defend me and said that I couldn't help where I was from. There can be a greater tolerance in the nationalist community even at such traumatic times. Another memory I have of our time in the New Lodge was during an air raid. I remember it because it was very hard on my mother. My father was in the Home Guard and he was on the roof of the BBC as an anti-aircraft gunner, so my mother was on her own with two children. Everyone else was taken away from the street and we were left alone. I remember asking where everybody had gone and why we hadn't gone too, but my mother didn't answer. Looking back on it now I realise why we hadn't been included. It happened just after Tom Williams had been hanged and there was the most terrible atmosphere in the area.

My uncle had a huge influence on my early childhood and he was probably closer to me than my own father. At that time my father was very much an adult's person. My uncle was an enthusiastic Orangeman, I remember he put the Orange sash on me and dragged me down to Jerome's, the photographers in North Street, to have my photograph taken. I loved him dearly, but as I grew older I became more aware of how unionism had shaped his life. In ways he was a victim of it in that he never got anything personally out of it. He had suffered hard during the depression of the Thirties, did difficult and dangerous work in the shipyard where his job was insecure and he was never highly paid. When

I was older, he took me by the hand down to Queen's Island. He walked me through it, describing the shipyard and telling me what it was all about. He was as proud as punch, calling it 'our' ship yard, 'my' ship yard. It was so incongruous, this little man who didn't own one screw of the shipyard and yet he had so much pride in the place. I saw him shortly before he died and by this time he knew that I hadn't grown up to be a unionist or an Orangeman and that I wanted to see Ireland united. He told me he couldn't understand how I could be a traitor to my own country. That hurt me, but there was no way that I could make him comprehend. We didn't part as enemies, we were still friends, but there was a gulf between us. It's terribly sad when that happens but I couldn't allow such feelings to imprison me, not even for someone that I felt a deep love for.

When I was 16, I went to work as an apprentice joiner for the City Surveyor's Department in Belfast Corporation. At that time those jobs were definitely the preserve of Protestants and I think that was the reason why I got the job. The trades were very stratified in that, for instance, Catholics could be pavers or slaters and some Catholics were allowed to be painters, where the trade was more mixed. All the 'aristocratic' jobs, such as carpenters and joiners, were totally Protestant.

Not all of the people that I served my apprenticeship with would have been stereotypical unionists. There were some who had a lot of inner conflict and the conflict, as I could see it, was between their socialist leanings and their commitment to the Union. During the time I worked for the Corporation I was involved in Socialist Youth Group activities in Belfast. We would go down to meet people in Dublin like the Behans and I would talk to my work mates about them. They would argue back that those sort of people could not possibly be labourist or socialist. I'd ask them why and they would tell me it was because they were Catholics. The Pope told Catholics what their politics should be and the Pope was not a socialist. Whether it was an excuse or a genuine belief I don't know, but it was the one reason they gave me for not looking to the South for support and solidarity.

Sam Thompson, the playwright, was employed as a painter whilst I was working there and I used to discuss plays and politics with him. I was very much into Seán O'Casey at the time, although my memory was that Sam wasn't over-enamoured with Seán O'Casey; perhaps it was a case of professional jealousy! Sam didn't stay very long; he got the sack over trade union activities. The politics we discussed would have centred around socialism and the Soviet Union and not so much the actual Northern Ireland situation. Whether or not that was because we were running away from Irish issues I don't know. Political debates were always more international rather than local in tone.

My family never had any doubts as to their nationality. It just was not an issue. Even my most Orange aunt had no doubts at all that she was Irish. It came as quite a culture shock when I met people on the radical fringes of politics on my trips to Dublin. Their whole attitude was different to mine. I had Protestant, puritan attitudes and an inherited code of respectable behaviour. I found that in the South of Ireland none of these attitudes applied to the people I was mixing with! At the time when De Valera and Cardinal McQuaid were creating the Catholic ethos, my friends lived in a different world. I had always thought that 'The Lark in the Clear Air', 'Kitty of Coleraine', 'Star of the County Down', all those tunes, made up Irish culture. I thought I knew something about Irish republicanism; I'd heard about Wolfe Tone and James Connolly, but it was only when I met people connected with the Irish Workers' Party that I came into contact with what might be called a republican culture – the hooleys, the theatre, the art world, the drinking, all the things my mother would have been suspicious of as a life style, and which were, you might say, broadening experiences for me. She, in an extreme Presbyterian manner, was a deep and sincere Christian who had an equally deep and sincere suspicion of ostentatious church-goers, bible thumpers and institutional religion.

After my apprenticeship finished at the Belfast Corporation, I was asked to stand as a shop steward. Nobody else really wanted to be a shop steward because in those days you could be told on a Wednesday that you were being let go on the Friday. Friends of mine advised me not to stand. They would come up and say, 'row in, row in', from a protective point of view because they knew that if I agreed to stand I would get the sack, which duly happened. I was made the shop steward on the Tuesday and I was sacked on the Friday! My only regret about that incident was that six of my colleagues who shared a taxi with me were sacked as well to make it look non-discriminatory.

I ended up going to London. There was a great demand for labour at that time; it was a boom period in 1957 and I ended up in a Czechoslovakian Merchant Bank in the City. In those days you were recruited on the basis of your handwriting, but afterwards I went on to study and pass my banker's exams.

I joined the Connolly Association and took part in the very first civil rights marches in England – this was before they took place in Ireland – and I began speaking from Connolly Association platforms. The Connolly Association had quite a few Protestants from both parts of Ireland involved in it. Some would have been trade unionists from working class backgrounds, but there were others with a Protestant ascendancy background from the South of Ireland, people who had attended public school and universities like Cambridge. We campaigned against the injustices of the six county state, the Special Powers Act, gerrymandering, all the basic civil rights demands. We also worked very closely with the British Labour Party, with a group which was known in those days as the Movement for Colonial Freedom. It was a kind of sub-committee on Ireland which tried to involve as broad a spectrum of the Irish people as possible, although we weren't totally successful in that. I chaired one of the committees which met in the House of Commons with Lord Brockway as host.

When Civil Rights agitation broke out in Northern Ireland I wanted to come home. It wasn't just for that reason though, for by then I had married, I had two sons and I didn't want to bring them up in London. I thought they would be better off back in Ireland, so I came back and immediately got involved in the Civil Rights Movement. I also went back to work for the City Hall in the City Surveyor's department but this time on the administrative side. Again, I have to say as a point of honesty that not everyone employed in the City Hall was bitterly anti-Catholic, but the atmosphere there was very tense. I have fond memories of many of the people who worked in the department; two socialists from the Shankill, one a storeman, the other a messenger, are among those who come to mind. No one could have been more humorously destructive of unionist notabilities and unionism than were 'characters' such as these two.

I became a member of the Belfast Executive of the Northern Ireland Civil Rights Association and subsequently became their Public Relations

Officer during the anti-internment campaign, and for a while I edited the Civil Rights paper. Then, of course, the Civil Rights Association got into difficulties; the splits took place and the military campaign began. We began to walk a tightrope, very conscious that we should not be provocative or confrontational but at the same time always wanting to carry out our agreed programme in the way that we had decided. Our aim might have been a utopian one. We wanted to focus the issues on the democratisation of Northern Ireland and to achieve it on the widest possible basis by involving forward thinking people in the Labour movement and liberal Protestants. In so doing we believed that Northern Ireland could be transformed. Paisley, of course, accused us all of being crypto-IRA members but that wasn't the case. I make no secret of the fact that I was approaching civil rights issues from a socialist republican perspective in those days. I wanted a united Ireland and I thought unionism was only maintaining itself by creating a class of poor whites and an aristocracy of Protestant labour that by no means included large sections of the Protestant working people. It was this that I believed was dividing our people. The so called 'unionist family' had obviously some very neglected, if not abused, members. I believed that was the real basis of partition and I wanted to work politically, rather than militarily, to end it. I certainly had no time at all for the kind of politics that confuses people into denying their own nationality. I saw the civil rights as a means of reuniting the people of Ireland into a more democratic system of government. I make no apologies for that. This would still be what I would like to see.

Others were more impatient, younger and thought that they could leap over hurdles and get to the goal quicker. Some of them were motivated by a reactive sectarianism. They were more focused, probably justifiably, on the injustices they had suffered under a Protestant unionist regime, more so than they would have been on the real government which was over in Whitehall and Westminster. I would say that NICRA never lost sight of the fact that ultimately all the abuses and all the problems emanated from Westminster and Whitehall. That is where they still reside. The military campaign, whatever the arguments for it, certainly did make it exceedingly hard for NICRA. It made it especially hard to rekindle an awareness that unionism was not synonymous with Protestantism among sections of the Protestant population. Ultimately though, I think that everyone in NICRA wanted the same thing, we just had different ideas about how to get there.

For a while after NICRA ended I just dropped out of politics and concentrated on studying to qualify as an economist. More recently a group of us who had been involved in civil rights decided to get together again and we formed the Campaign for Democracy in 1991 during the bicentenary of the United Irishmen. The Campaign has a strong Protestant input into it. The idea is to campaign beyond civil rights into the area of democratic rights. We believe that people here should govern themselves and have the political institutions that will enable them to do that, not talking shops or institutions which are circumscribed and limited. We don't believe that such democratic institutions can be achieved within the present United Kingdom constitutional set up. We know that they can't be achieved within a Six County set up either. We believe the only solution is a new Ireland with all-Ireland institutions that are agreed and governed by a constitution that satisfies everybody and in which everybody has their input. That constitution should follow the principles of the United Irishmen but updated to suit modern conditions. It would be secular, pluralist and have an all-inclusive definition of Irish nationality. It would enable the people of Ireland to be self-governing, so far as that can happen in an EC context, and it would be democratic and anti-sectarian. Part of what we see as important is to bring the Protestant anti-unionist heritage back to the Protestants and at least give them the knowledge of its existence so that they can make a choice. I don't think they have a choice now because most of them have been indoctrinated by unionism over 70 years. I think that if I had had only my schooling to rely on then I would have been the same. It just happened that in the environment that I was brought up in the unionist hegemony wasn't complete; there were huge gaps in it and I was able to learn about our other traditions.

I do find it interesting that in the present political environment the younger of the traditions, nineteenth century unionism, is seen by more and more people as something of the past, whereas the ideas of the United Irishmen, which never had a chance, are still relevant and have the elements of the key to the future.

11

Donald Graham

Local Government Officer. Born 1954.

I was born on the one and only day in Northern Ireland, the Twelfth of July, the third child of a family of ten, so there weren't any luxury items in our house. Where people had wall to wall carpets, we had wall to wall bodies. It was tough on my mother who had to look after us all in a three bedroom house, but great for us as children. We lived in a working class area on the edge of East Belfast, a place called Knocknagoney which means 'Hill of the Rabbits' in Irish. It was a brand new estate and we were among the first tenants. The estate was made up from the 'respectable' employed working class with Shorts, the shipyard, Fords, other engineering works, the B Specials and later the RUC reserves being the main employers. It was a good environment to grow up in; we had a garden, hills either side of us, the forests and lots of friends to play with.

My father was certainly loyal to the British crown. He had been a soldier since his late teens and when he was demobbed, he became a minor civil servant and joined the Territorial Army. What was more unusual was that he was from Donegal and consequently we spent a lot of time during the summer in southern Ireland. Unlike other Protestant families, we never had a problems crossing the border to buy butter or going to see where the harlot of Rome lived! I would describe my family background as unionist, not overtly loyalist, but certainly my parents believed in the link with Britain and supported Stormont.

I think that the school that one attends in a place like Northern Ireland is especially important. If you go to one of the middle class schools like Inst or Methody or the Royal Academy out in Ballymena, you are obviously well-connected; again if you play rugby, all these are the kind of routes for being 'one of the boys'. My mother was very, very keen to have us all educated as the escape route to a better life but because we came from a working class background, we never had those contacts with people who can make the path through life easier in terms of career opportunities. I was never one of the boys and my address didn't go down too well either. By the time I was a teenager the character of our estate had changed radically; it was looked upon as a UDA area, quite threatening to people. There were major fights between tartan gangs. I wasn't in a tartan gang but I certainly wore my heavy boots and the old denims at the weekend. Nor did I walk around on my own in those days. I remember that after the youth dole office, originally sited near the Belfast Tech, was blown up, we had to collect our dole with the adults in Corporation Street. The clerks used to give people cash rather than the cheques that are posted out today and everyone collected their money in groups. All the older guys were there with their dogs so you made sure you had your steel tip boots with you, that's for sure!

After I left primary school I went on to Bangor Technical College which was very entertaining and very uneducational. Bangor was still a small town in those days; all the Protestants from the Shankill Road hadn't been shipped out and Kilcooley hadn't been created. It still sticks in my mind that there were six Catholics in my class in Bangor; I think it is quite remarkable that I can remember that, that it was noticeable to me, but up until that point I had been educated in a purely Protestant environment. However I was 'exposed' to contact with Catholics in Donegal and during the summer played with a large Catholic family from Dublin who had exactly the same number of children in their family as we did. Within my circle of friends on the estate, very few of us went on to further education. I was one of the exceptions. I remember that there were only two of us who took up reading books from the library on a regular basis. Not that I was a bookworm, I hasten to add; I played football five nights a week too! But I did begin to pick up bits of knowledge in my own time. The first political book I read was a biography of Khrushchev; at least it was a move away from Biggles and thriller novels!

By the time I was 18 this period of the 'troubles' had broken out. It was a very frightening and intimidating time; people were getting their throats cut, being picked up and brutally treated, butchered and killed. I knew several people that had happened to, some Catholic, some Protestant. It's hard when you are looking back with hindsight and perhaps using concepts and views of events which you may not have been fully conscious and aware of at the time, but I do know that I felt angry with unionism. I didn't really understand what unionist politicians were doing, why they came round our estate and made lots of promises which they never delivered. I remember one time we were promised a swimming pool which of course we never got! I couldn't understand why people thought these unionist politicians were the best thing since sliced cheese. When Stormont folded, Bill Craig had this massive show and me and my mates went up, and I remember seeing several of my teachers from school there. I must confess that we had gone more on the look out for talent, one of many failed forays, but it was an eye opener all the same. I still would have had a Protestant view of the world. I remember being very annoyed whenever Máire Drumm came on the television. I didn't understand what she was saying; she just seemed to be so offensive and strident. I just used to think, 'Who is this bloody head banger?', you know, 'I wish she would shut up. When is the movie coming on?' My comprehension of political and social issues was reactive; I didn't place them in a broader societal context.

That was a gradual process. I went to study Sociology and English Literature at the College of Business Studies in Belfast city centre when I was 18. It took months for me to figure out what was going on in Sociology. It was beyond me. All those debates around Durkheim and functionalism and Marxism were forcing me to look at other people's world views as opposed to the narrow insular world view of Northern Ireland and the even more insular world view that one finds on a working class loyalist estate. I think that Sociology helped me to comprehend; it gave me more a systematic view on life, or tried to anyway; it made me raise vital questions.

Going to Queen's University was a big mistake because it meant I was still enclosed in this world of Belfast. I always had this view of Queen's that I would enter this rarefied atmosphere where people didn't think in a sectarian way. I remember going down to the toilets in the library the first day that I was there and on the back of the toilet was all the usual graffiti, 'No Pope Here' and references to 'fenians'. That shocked me. I thought Queen's was above all that, when of course it is very much an institutionalised part of it. I joined the Labour Club in Queen's. Politically it wasn't that well thought out on my part, I just identified with debates which centred around social issues. One morning I learnt how the establishment of the welfare state had been imposed on the unionists by British central government and if it hadn't been imposed, we wouldn't have had it. That just confirmed everything I had felt about unionism. I could never understand attitudes like Northern Ireland being this stand alone institution which must be preserved at all costs and Protestants being a hard working, abstemious, disciplined and very independent people. You only have to step backwards for a moment to see that basically too many Protestants have become a group of people who are sycophantic and can see nothing beyond an allegiance with Britain. Northern Ireland is an open air bru on a £6 billion hand out a year. The problem is that all those Protestants who are on the dole don't appreciate it, that's all!

I travelled in Europe and Canada during my summer holidays, which is how I ended up applying to do an MA at McMaster University in Hamilton, Ontario. It was there that I joined the Canadian Party of Labour, one of the few parties to stand up for self-determination for the Quebecois. I became involved in the intense debates of the day, read Marx, began to understand dialectics and started to write a column for the paper, *Daily Worker*, on Irish issues. Although I'd begun to understand imperialism, of what it sought to achieve in terms of wealth, place, power and people which had helped me to place it in an Irish context, my politics would still have centred around class issues. At that time I thought class was the issue and not nationalism, that Protestants and Catholics had to overcome this false consciousness and get together. All very rarefied of course!

But when I returned to Belfast I did have a much broader political perspective than when I had left. I returned to live in the same area for a while, still played BB football with teams of UDA and UDR members, but I kept very quiet about my political opinions. It would have been futile to have debates anyway, but then it might be futile to have a debate with any football player when your purpose in hand is to win the match!

My first job was as a Research Officer for the Fair Employment Agency. Essentially four or five years after the British passed the Fair Employment Act, the Agency had completed very few investigations and officially it couldn't find any discrimination. What was happening was that companies like Shorts were denying us access to their employment records and the shipyard were telling us that, if there were any Catholics in the yard, they must be deep sleepers. On this basis we would conclude that there was no absence of equal opportunity. Of course the laws were weak but I never felt that was as much of a problem as the attitude which the Agency took, which was one of 'educating' people about their responsibilities. Our powers to investigate were seldom used to full effect and whenever they were used, the investigations were so drawn out and long winded. It was quite usual for the draft reports that the officers had prepared to be binned and rewritten to suit the internal political prejudices prevalent at the time among FEA members.

In the end there were four of us who accused our employer of malpractice and maladministration. We wrote to the Minister of State to say that we were not being allowed to apply the law. It became a very angry and bitter dispute and it also became very personal, as these disputes inevitably do. We had all jeopardised our jobs, but we had also put ourselves at physical risk. One member of the board accused us all of being 'a bunch of Provies' and another said we were taking advantage of the hunger strike. Given the sectarian assassination campaign, such comments exposed us to serious violence. We were threatened with internal disciplinary action and political victimisation. I don't think anyone saw any room for compromise at the time and two of us resigned, as did two Agency members, Inez McCormack and Des Bannon. The latter submitted a dossier to the Secretary of State outlining failures of the organisation and its chair.

The unionists used to criticise the FEA as a sop to Catholics and they were quite correct. It *was* a sop to Catholics, trying to draw them into the political process, trying to achieve an accommodation, but it wasn't much of a sop because it never delivered! The ultimate bankruptcy of the FEA was confirmed to me when representatives of the agency went on a guided tour of America opposing the MacBride Principles. In the UK no other equal opportunities body has gone to bat for its government or for a particular firm against a campaign which was trying to generate internal debate and achieve progress on fair employment issues. It was the MacBride Principles which were the driving force behind the change in legislation in 1989, remarkably so given they were an external force. The new laws which were brought in obliged employers to return their employment profiles, which previously they had refused to do. Key investigation powers in terms of hearing individual complaints and appeals were taken away from the Agency, a tribunal was set up – all very basic steps which we had been urging the government to take on board.

Discrimination remained a touchstone in my life. I went on to work for Shelter Northern Ireland (a housing campaign group), but it seemed to me that the people I was working with were not interested in the issue of discrimination in housing being raised. I wrote an article on Poleglass for *Roof*, the journal of Shelter in Britain, on how the Department of the Environment had intervened to stop the development of Poleglass, a housing estate for Catholics, in response to Ian Paisley and the UDA. I went in to work after it was published to find copies of my article all over the place. My colleagues had had a private meeting the night before to discuss my future and had phoned the Editor of *Roof* in London, asking him to stop printing these articles I was writing on discrimination. He refused, of course, and the Director of Shelter initiated a formal investigation which led to the withdrawal of all central funding from Shelter Northern Ireland. They remained very supportive to me and later funded research I carried out for other organisations. The tragedy was that an incredible opportunity to provide a service not controlled by the DOE to all community groups and tenant activists on housing was lost. That is still of some regret to me, especially when I met and worked with so many great individuals in North Belfast from Protestant and Catholic estates. What impressed me was these people, to whom I was a total stranger, allowed me to work on the ground with them, put forward ideas, attend meetings with officials and 'put the boot in' on their behalf. They all had one basic common theme: how can the living conditions of their own communities be improved; what would it take? An incredible amount of effort was and is no doubt still put in by individuals engaged in what is often a thankless and frustrating task, their only reward being a hard time from everyone to get a result, for not getting a result, for simply being there. Gimme shelter, they deserved it; I hope I helped. Anyway, I wear slippers now!

After these experiences, I began to work from a resource centre in Belfast engaged in various pieces of research for the Campaign for the Homeless, including a draft Homeless Persons Act, which I regard as one of my better pieces of work. I was invited by a number of community groups to become involved in housing issues at a grassroots level, in both Catholic areas – Unity Flats and Divis – and Protestant areas – White City and Tynedale. There was a dramatically different atmosphere between the estates. I wouldn't want to do the White City tenants a disservice, but I think they had more confidence and respect in the state's institutions to deliver what they wanted, though they realised it was still going to be a struggle. But they simply weren't living in a similar environment to tenants in Divis, nor were they seen as a political threat by the Northern Ireland Office. In Divis at that time the 'battle of the Irps' was on. They were all shooting at each other; there were snipers on the balconies, claims that the British forces were looking to assassinate people. Divis had been caught up in political conflict since it was first developed. The tenants were challenging fundamentals about the destruction of a community; they were challenging sectarianism in decisions over the allocation of financial investment; they had gained an international profile. White City, by comparison, was as 'safe as houses' although still an important and vital struggle for better conditions.

Since leaving Belfast to work in local government in England my views in relation to Northern Ireland have changed. I can see how the administration of local government here could be more successfully managed if people were empowered politically but I also realise the dearth of skills there are in Northern Ireland. Since Direct Rule from Westminster there just hasn't been that opportunity for people to develop independent political and administrative skills within this context and there hasn't been for a quarter of a century. Accountability remains an alien concept although we have managed to spell democracy; maybe that counts! People do need to learn and apply the political and administrative skills within a truly open and accountable framework to run their own lives but the big question mark remains over what would pass as fair and impartial administration. The way Belfast Council behaves itself is so ridiculously sectarian. If any Labour administration behaved in such a manner in Britain, the *Sun* would have a field day but, because it is Northern Ireland, it doesn't matter.

What is remarkable about Direct Rule from its inception is that it has kept the fundamental inequalities, which derive from historical patterns of employment and historical investment strategies, unchanged. After 25 years of Direct Rule we live in a society which is totally reliant on the public purse for supporting infrastructure, industrial investment and public sector employment whether it be the civil service, the RUC, the Housing Executive or the Health and Social Services Boards. Where is the evidence of active involvement and direction by the British government to reverse discriminatory patterns of employment? It has had the opportunity. It has had the economic muscle. It pays the piper. It did nothing.

That for me is the real telling point. British policies have not been about change but the management and manipulation of an accommodation process which leaves things as they are. We still have to confront the fact that Northern Ireland was established as an overt discriminatory statelet whose primary purpose was to maintain and protect Protestants. I think it is important to remember that a lot of people are very happy with the way things are! Respectable skilled Protestants did very well. They guaranteed their sons' and relatives' employment in the shipyard and Shorts and the public services which developed tremendously under Direct Rule. Mind you, this development has also helped secure middle class Catholics in fields such as the legal profession, social work, education and similar fields. The jury's still out on whether working class Catholics have shared significantly in this largesse. Those who were not fortunate to have such connections made do. When Protestants talk about their birthright, really they sold it very cheaply to the original unionist landed aristocracy. That puts working class Protestants on the defensive, particularly those who didn't do very well out of it. There has always been a strand within the Protestant working class grasping for some kind of socialism; my one regret is that they still see themselves as unionist. I feel that there is always a potential there which is never realised and I think that as a group, Protestants sell themselves short and don't get very much for it.

Given that there is over a million Protestants living in the North of Ireland, I think we would have a radical impact on the construction of an Irish society, a tremendous impact, all to the good, and I would hope that through that unity we could cast aside all those unionist hacks who have done very well at our expense all these years. No surrender!

Counter Culture

There's a lot of notions here about our unique and colourful orange and green culture. Frankly I think that we're part of a transglobal multi-national consumerist culture that recycles cultural artifacts around the globe (phew!). I'm more excited by the counter or resistance culture, one which demystifies, provokes and challenges our world.

12

Rick O'Shea

Cultural worker. Born 1950.

Locations matter a lot in Belfast and just by describing an area as the Shankill or Sandy Row or the Bone gives a fair indication of where one's politics lie and indeed one's whole outlook on life. I was born into a house of 'good' proletarian stock off the Lower Newtownards Road, the essence of loyalist territory. Our area had all the jobs – manufacturing, linen, rope works, shipyard, engineering – but in terms of the people around me, their existence and their living conditions were really quite poor: traditional two-up, two-down slum housing with no amenities, just a cold outside toilet. You had to be a keen whistler!

I remember the Twelfth celebrations as a focus for street parties during my childhood. I walked miles with my mates, hacking down trees and proudly trailing them along the main roads to our street bonfire. Being the one with an artistic bent, I was also called upon to paint sectarian slogans on the ground, like 'Fenians Stay Out Or Else' in honour of the occasion as well as painting the kerb stones red, white and blue. There certainly was a decency in people in the street but no adult ever tried to stop us. I 'felt' I knew what the slogans meant but wasn't totally aware of all the implications. Lundy, the traitor, was an important figure and a dummy was fashioned after his likeness. He was paraded round the houses to collect money for the street party and finally placed on top of the bonfire. As I watched him burn, little did I know that some day it could have been me up there, metaphorically speaking of course!

I was always aware that 'something' lurked beyond the fringes of my area. That something was symbolised by the Short Strand and more specifically, the 'fenians'. Geographically Short Strand was easily defined, a small self-contained area on the edge of our own. The dividing line, Seaforde Street, was a street which nobody wanted to walk down. At the top of it stood the 'dark' Catholic church surrounded by railings. My primary school was situated practically alongside this street and yet for me it was a neighbourhood surrounded in mystery and taboo. I find this difficult to describe in words; it was, in effect, an irrational feeling towards Catholics, one which can't be explained merely in political terms or in discussions about difference. As a child I wouldn't have understood such sophisticated arguments anyway. It was more akin to some sort of brain washing and similar I think to the attitudes of superiority which white people have about blacks or the fear and loathing people have against Jews, a dark side of human nature common everywhere but at times exploited for political ends, a festering process whereby the power of myth and imagery, delusions and paranoia reduced Catholics to inferior, almost demonic beings.

There were the various stereotypical views about Catholics being work shy, not much point giving them better housing because they would only reduce them to slums, keep coal in the bath, and how they were encouraged by priests to have large families to outbreed us, all this in contrast to Protestants who supposedly believed in the inherent dignity of hard work and that through work one achieved salvation. The way Protestants viewed the Catholic religion as akin to devil worship compounded this. I remember as a lad coming across the Roman Catholic catechism and my friends and I thinking, 'Wow, this is devil stuff; look what we've found!' And of course whenever anyone got inside a Catholic house, there would be revelations of strange flickering electric candles under spooky pictures of Jesus with an exposed bloody heart, yuck! Jesus crucified on the cross and little porcelain bowls at the entrance of the house with 'holy' water further enhanced this idea that Catholics were crazy devil worshippers. Then there was the prevailing belief that Ulster was more enlightened and freer than the priest-ridden 'free state'. Looking back, I find it so ironic considering that Protestants vote for the most fascistic of representatives. Can you imagine the country run by the fundamentalist DUP? Education under the total control of their clerics; there goes the Darwin theory, abortion would carry a prison sentence for women, so would homosexuality, and no Catholics need apply.

I initially met Catholics when I went to visit my granny. She had been retired to the country, which at that time was the post-war asbestos prefabs on the Annadale Embankment. People considered this to be the country because there were trees there and the bus service was dreadful. We had to walk three quarters of a mile to the nearest bus stop. Some Catholics had also been rehoused there and I played occasionally with them, though not to any great extent. My impression was of the Protestant religion being more liberal, less fixed, but I think that had more to do with my parent's attitudes. I actually attended several Protestant churches and thought nothing of it. It didn't occur to my mother that there was any problem in my attending the Church of Ireland, the Baptist church and the Presbyterian church all on the one Sunday! In the end I knew that I would have to choose, or rather that one would be chosen for me, that being the Church of Ireland, which was my mother's church. Of course as children the churches would do their best to keep our attention with wee stories, giving us book markers and coloured religious story books, all of which fascinated us as we rarely had anything other than our school books. But we were very good at behaving badly and getting away with it. For a lark we would visit the little mission halls 'to be born again.' During the service we would put our hands up 'to be saved' and an old man would take us aside and 'save us'. We would be pious for a couple of days, no cursing, never 'taking the Lord's name in vain', believing in God, no going to the pictures, but this soon wore off and we reverted to our own boisterous selves.

Like any number of Ulster's working class families, a parent's aspiration was for their son to get a good trade behind them and get an apprenticeship. College was out of the question; my parents could never have afforded it or indeed even understood it. Nearly all of my friends went to secondary schools rather than grammar schools. Repression rather than education was the order of the day and certainly there were very few books in our house or even a place to do your homework in peace. I remember one interesting little episode which was an indication of children's aspirations. A library was opened in the area. It opened in the afternoon after school and hundreds of children besieged the librarian on the steps, demanding to become members. We were all told to come back the next day of course, but I remember that when we finally got into the library, we were all gossiping and shouting and playing around, so excited to have been given this facility.

The traditional career route was to the shipyard, if you were lucky and labouring in the mills if you didn't have the family connections. Your father or relative 'spoke for you' and that's how you entered your trade. But I had this other idea that I wanted to go into the printing trade. This was seen as a very good trade, a trade with prestige attached to it, almost like clerical work, which meant that you didn't have to get your hands dirty or work in the cold. The company where I began had a Protestant work force; I can only remember one Catholic who worked there who had previously worked for the *Irish News*. He was always looked on with a bit of suspicion. The owners of the company were from traditional staunch Unionist stock, the old Ascendancy, not the sort who usually have Catholics about them! Some of the work force were also members of the B Specials, so when the Civil Rights movement began they had their own experiences and perspective on the political situation. I think also that of my friends and fellow work mates most didn't really understand what was happening. They had a very blinkered view.

I don't think that understanding has been enhanced through time either. It alarms me to hear the same questions being asked on long standing radio programmes like *Talk Back* and the same hackneyed answers being given too! We seem to be caught in a time warp. People quite rightly complain of censorship but I think that at the heart of the problem is the television and radio's notion of 'balance', that somehow there are two sides to each issue, right and wrong, Protestant and Catholic, and that truth lies somewhere in the middle. In this divided society people communicate to each other through what is mediated to them through newspapers and television. When you are from the Protestant community what you see and understand is disruption, violence and sedition rather than any clear picture of the reasons why that violence and discontent has occurred in the first place. All the debates are focused on the same old issues; we can't break out of it; all political social and cultural agendas revolve around endlessly going down the same roads, the same old arguments. No wonder the middle classes have tended to steer away from what's going on; it just bores the arse off them – although they also have a lot to answer for!

The company I worked for relied for a lot of its work on printing statutes, rules and ordinances from the old Stormont regime. When Stormont fell in the 1970's it presented no problem for them to print some Northern Ireland Office anti-IRA propaganda, a risky thing for them to do as they could be blown up by the IRA. They would have been seen as a legitimate target after all. But as far as most of the workforce were concerned it was just another job to them – but keep it hush hush.

Still, I wasn't the only one about who questioned what was happening around me. Don't ask me why I should feel this way because I really don't know; perhaps certain people have this questioning streak, a certain cantankerous edge to them. There were others who knew something wasn't quite right either. They were generally quiet, intelligent people who kept their heads down. You really had to probe to get anything out of them. When the opportunity came they got out of Northern Ireland. I always wondered at their willingness to emigrate when they had a reasonable job, a wife, kids and a mortgage. A number of my work mates saw Ruskin College as a way out. I wanted out too. I wanted to be a typographer. I loved designing but when the order of the day was to make everything 'as big and bold as you can make it' it left little room for creativity. I had day release to study for my City and Guilds but this didn't allow much in the way of creativity. I envied the full-time middle class students who could spend all their day being creative. I never knew that I could apply for grants. Anyway, I was told to 'get a trade behind you and you can go where you like'. I gradually became more and more fed up and just about managed to serve my time. What a laugh now, going through five years of low wages, boredom, treated quite literally as a 'galley' slave, attending two night classes a week only to see the job vanish inside a computer!

What really struck a chord with me was the alternative counter culture of the sixties. First the 'underground' music, then bits of it began to surface on television. To me it was a rejection of the confines of loyalism and republicanism, something I could never get a hang on. It looked exciting; I wanted to belong. I fell in with a group of hippies. The 'tribe' who produced the underground magazine, *EGO*, used my printing skills and quite literally produced the magazine underground! I used to typeset it, laid it out and would nip into my employers' printing works just to print it and slip it out under my 'great' coat to sell it on the streets. I would take more and more days off work until finally there was a gentleman's agreement that I would have to leave the company. After that I recall bullshitting some sales rep into letting us print the magazine on one of his small offset machines. However, a car bomb in Bedford Street blew the plate glass window in around us, but we still managed to finish it!

This was the first time I came into contact with Catholics but these were not the Catholics that I had imagined from my childhood; these were long-haired hippies, highly educated Catholics who were libertarian rather than republican minded and who aspired to an alternative lifestyle. We were a large, highly politicised group of people, not just into peace and love but anti-capitalist and anti-sectarian, raising both women's and gay issues. I remember this crazy bunch of people meeting the head of the Community Relations Council en masse and convincing them to give us money. With a small seeding grant from them we established the Belfast Arts Lab in Upper Donegall Street, a cultural meeting place for young people. We had our centre for information based on the BIT centre in London, our theatre space for workouts, our 'university of the streets' where we would educate ourselves through self-help, the beginnings of a sound studio, a place for the Claimants' Union to meet, a place to make 'hippy' crafts like candle making; we even had enough money to buy our own cheap printing press.

There was a real need for a people's press at that time. During the late sixties and seventies, there was a proliferation of small local magazines, community news sheets, women's broad sheets, pamphlets, posters and fliers, thousands of which are now housed in the Linenhall Library's political collection, far more so than today despite the advent of all this user-friendly technology. I think the ideology and tentacles of Thatcherism and her state succeeded in penetrating, co-opting, neutralising and professionalising what was once militant self-help grassroots politics.

It wasn't until I started printing some of their literature that I came into contact with republicans. Of course it is hard to say whether I met any Provisionals but I certainly met Official Republicans. They had moved away from militarism and had attracted many radical political idealists, quite a different movement from that associated with them today. Culturally they were quite interesting, more international in their approach to films and theatre, and they were involved in a number of community campaigns around housing, the proposed new ring road and redevelopment, which was a big issue devastating working class communities in the inner city. At that time I associated the Provisionals with old style nationalism and reactionary conservative politics, and of course their brutal bombing campaign, a world away from the socialism

I saw in the Official Republican movement, though of course people see things differently when they're living 'amongst it'. That has changed through time and I wouldn't see Sinn Féin in that light today. Any concept of Catholics as devil worshippers had evaporated by then but no matter what Protestants think of their own clergy, I still find it bewildering when left-wing diehard republicans broker peace deals, etc. through priests, even though allegedly they abhor the Catholic church and all it stands for. Using priests as conduits gives them great credence and yet history has proven that the Catholic church more often than not sides with the dominant powers, in our case the British, and has constantly tried to compromise republicanism.

I guess what really matters to people in their lives are not the grand political movements but the groups of people one is drawn to and works with. To me that's the important thing in anyone's life. I'm a bit of an idealist and had the privilege to come across others who didn't care much for money, degrees, careers or houses but in their own way wanted to do something different to build a better society. One such group were the people who supported and ran Just Books. In the late 1970s we had this crazy notion of opening an alternative bookshop at the height of one of the worst bombing and sectarian assassination campaigns in Belfast. We were told that it would be blown up, no one would come to it. Premises were chosen between the Shankill and the Falls and the shop did open and ran for over fifteen years, finally closing just before the first IRA and loyalist ceasefire was announced in 1994. It started as a city centre bookshop selling local pamphlets, all manner of socialist and anarchist literature, anti-nuclear stuff, books on drugs, political comics, posters, records, T shirts and postcards. It also ran exhibitions, had a small café/meeting place, a printing press and a keen interest in using video. These combined produced a powerful communications tool, all of it managed on non-hierarchical lines. I think it was an amazing group of people, very resourceful and multi-skilled in campaigning, inclusive in the sharing of resources and skills to other groups within the progressive movement and yet a group which despite everything, still maintained their integrity.

The collective supported campaigns which would be seen as part of the republican agenda, particularly prisoners' issues and those based around justice and equality. Whilst fully supporting efforts by groups like Equality which were campaigning against job discrimination, I do remember debating the sectarian nature of the workforce in Shorts – I think at that time Catholics represented less than 5 percent of the workforce – and whether we really wanted to campaign to have equal opportunity for Catholics in Shorts when 'the great working class' in the factory were engaged in manufacturing weapons of mass destruction to be used on their fellow workers, missiles which were subsequently used in the Malvinas war to slaughter Argentinians.

What I think was really important was that the collective actively campaigned beyond the confines of the anti-imperialism. The anti-nuclear movement, feminist concerns like free contraception and abortion, against uranium mining in Donegal, support for workers' strikes, north and south, various community initiatives and after convincing the gay community to loan their city centre club, the 'A' Centre which brought together a couple of hundred young people together each Saturday for a feast of punk music, poetry, alternative comedians, banned films, vegetarian food and general mayhem. I remember the cops were always parked outside the Centre, just waiting to pounce, their mouths open as they adjusted to the spectacle. One of them collared a young man that he obviously knew. He asked him what he was doing in 'this place', inferring that this young man was a loyalist and a Protestant and shouldn't be mixing with 'those fenians'. The young man replied that he had left his religion outside the door. I hope he also forgot to pick it up afterwards! Really for such a collective to exist in the city centre for so long was quite unique. The Just Books collective viewed loyalism as a very reactionary ideology and a huge barrier to any progress, yet it had to admit to itself that it had drawn from the Protestant community the most radical anti-authoritarian men and women who thought 'Brits Out, Ireland Forever' was as good a place to start changing society as any; but it was only a beginning and a narrow one at that.

I've lived in a Catholic working class area since 1972, which today would be seen as a hard line republican area. I think as Protestants begin to become familiar with the 'broad church' of republicanism and become sympathetic to aspects of it they realise that they can't talk or share anything about it in their own community, especially working class areas. Loyalists aren't very tolerant of non-loyalists so they button up or they leave. One of the consequences of this is that it is almost impossible for any new generation from the Protestant community to unmask the reactionary face of loyalism. Some loyalist leaders will at times give it a more working class socialist slant, but in times of crisis it's 'mirror, mirror on the wall, who is the most loyalist of them all?'. I've generally found that there is less sectarianism in nationalist areas; however it might be different if I stuck a Union Jack out over the Twelfth!

I've noticed all sorts of differences living in a Catholic area. Repression and harassment by the security forces are the obvious ones, quite different from that experienced in Protestant working class areas, but added to this is a low level harassment: the attitudes of state departments over housing, the environment, resources and amenities, treated like dirt by the cleansing department. For instance, all this hype about the River Lagan walk way where everyone will be able to enjoy walks by the river. Well, it has all been tastefully cleaned up, new railings and seats, ornate lighting and a nice paved public footpath. If you looked at it from a certain angle you'd nearly believe you were on the Seine, complete with riverside yuppie housing! Well, that is until you reach the part where I live. All this costly development abruptly stops and the shit begins: the remains of a crumbling lock, oily rotting planks of wood, weeds, garbage on the river verges, a children's death trap. The bank opposite, where no children live or play, has its trees and grass cut regularly, yet not ours. There is no rational explanation!

I've worked on a number of films and also produced a couple of albums and singles. The first EP was quite successful; it reached number 4 in the independent charts, but then it was banned; all the copies were seized from record shops in Britain by the Special Branch. Pissed me off! The songs were the usual preoccupations about this place: anarchist rants on the police, the media, prisons and the printed cover was choc-o-bloc with news and information. It was the punk era and music was one of the few mass media areas left to put anti-authoritarian ideas across to a wide audience; it still can be too.

There's a lot of notions here about our unique and colourful Orange and Green culture. Frankly I think that we're part of a transglobal multinational consumerist culture that recycles cultural artifacts around the globe (phew!). I'm more excited by the counter or resistance culture, one which demystifies, provokes and challenges our world. Of course the most dynamic trends in counter culture feed back to mainstream culture where they are given a few essential lobotomies, repackaged and sold back to us!

The prevailing notion of a culture here which is divided into orange and green is another variant of the social engineering which has been endemic since the founding of the state. Instead of accepting that the state just doesn't work, various hypotheses, some truly pathetic, others wacky, some dangerous, are implemented. Community relations and local economic regeneration programmes offer ideal hatching conditions for these hypotheses which are then discharged into the wider community in the form of grand plans and ubiquitous grant application forms. A huge cottage industry has grown up in services to people in disadvantaged areas which are 'targeting social need'. It's virtually impossible for any articulate human being to be funded for a project unless they are 'locked into the community', community being defined in sectarian geographical terms and rarely as communities of interest. The women's movement is quite interesting in this regard. I think it was far more vibrant, militant, feminist and creative during the 1970s when the imperative wasn't rooting it in working class communities. Feminists seem intent on establishing Women's Centres in several areas of Belfast which act as advice, further education centres and 'family' support centres. Get your degree in Women's Studies and you're all set for a career in the women's movement! The recent débâcle over one women's centre illustrated the difficulty of women being grafted on to a loyalist community and quite laudably introducing some progressive ideas. However they over-stepped the mark when they invited nice Irish President Mary Robinson to visit. Some of the locals showed how warm a reception can be given in loyalist areas by trying to burn down the centre!

I always wondered why in America, where all sorts of government help strategies have been in operation for so much longer than here, that blacks for instance are as worse off now as they were during the Civil Rights days. The disadvantage is so enormous and inextricably linked to the structure of the state that throwing money at it doesn't matter. Painful as it may be for some people, what we need is that euphemistic term 'a political settlement'. People attempt to make Northern Ireland work but all their best laid plans unravel as each crisis erupts. The money given to disadvantaged areas is so small anyway and the best paid people are those who allocate the money and the legions of consultants who tell groups how to spend it. The people I know who work in this sector say it's a sham.

Do I hold out any hope for the loyalist community I came from? I think it's happy enough to sit tight; it sees itself as doing just fine. The IRA bombings have almost ceased, bit of a down turn in the economy – when has it ever been different? – but the British government is still siting new factories in Protestant rather than nationalist areas. Life can be sweet for a lot of people. Their parliament has gone but it's not a big deal for them anymore. I don't imagine if you are quite well off, have a job and a nice house, that having local power matters much. I think it matters when you are working class, unemployed, your environment is shitty, then you demand local power to change things. But anyway, all the British government statistics show that Protestants are no worse off in terms of unemployment than people in Manchester. Unionist politicians have virtual integration within the United Kingdom and their energies are directed to keeping it that way. They don't envisage grand vistas of having power in order to make positive social change. They never have! They have their little intrigues, their grumbles, they have their presence on quangos and state departments and local councils but in terms of power to change society for the betterment of all its people, they haven't the imagination to even begin.

I think what is happening in the nationalist community is more poignant now the military campaign has apparently been decommissioned. Whilst the news stands were screaming banner headlines like PROVINCE IS ON PEACE ALERT I think nationalists saw peace, not as an act of taking the guns out of the situation, but a chance, however tentative, that their frustrations and aspirations could be satisfied, that things could change. There was an almost unanimous desire for talks, for compromise and accommodation. Unionists have refused to talk around even the most mildest of reforms. Nowadays even the SDLP, a party not renowned for its militancy, has been alienated. I get the feeling that nationalists are more resentful and disdainful of the unionist community. Without the cloud of violence, that community has been unveiled to them as what it always was: intransigent, unimaginative, self-righteous and increasingly I think, nationalists see it as offensive. Actually I don't hold out much hope for the nationalist community. The media still chooses to highlight it as a violent community rather than one which has organised collectively against layers of injustice. Its views are but sound bites in someone else's thesis. I don't see much of a focus within the SDLP or Sinn Féin. There was a time when Sinn Féin saw itself as a socialist organisation, but that socialism, unlike the state, has withered away and with it a vision that was worth working towards. I suspect that some of its membership has become very disillusioned; perhaps instead of a splinter group within the IRA there might be a splinter group politically; maybe apathy will get there first. Some republicans still find inspiration from the remarkable events that have happened in South Africa but I think that if we have to look for parallels in the rest of the world, nationalists have more in common with the Palestinians or even the ethnic ghettoes in British cities. The media has always peddled this view that the struggle in Northern Ireland was an anachronism, a relic of the past more akin to the seventeenth century than the modern world; but when I look at the uneasy social relationships and unbending ethnic boundaries of some British and American cities, I wonder if Belfast is not a paradigm for the future.

I could rant on for hours about the society which I would like to live in but, simply put, it's a place where there is justice, equality and compassion and where people have the power to control their own lives. I think people all over the world aspire to that and it is always too much to ask for. I could go on and on suggesting mechanisms of how to achieve that: non-hierarchical structures, co-operation, mutual aid, but unfortunately the solutions people put forward in Northern Ireland are based on a faith in state institutions of power and authority which crush individual thought and local creativity. Someone, I forget who, wrote that there is one thing in the world more wicked than the desire to command and that is the will to obey. Whatever solution is eventually found for Northern Ireland, whether it's British, Irish or a fudge of conflicting identities, I'll lay odds it will follow that general pattern.

13

Musician and Sound Engineer

Born 1966.

M y parents never made sectarian comments. They were
ecumenical Presbyterians, very devout and into joint services, the
sort of people who wished that everyone could be nice and civilised to
each other. My granddad was sectarian. On a Sunday he'd go on about
how the Catholics in the town got more 'O' levels than the Protestants
and how this wasn't right. He was the sort that if he'd ever had a wee
farm he would sell it for £10 to a Protestant rather than a £1m to a Catholic.
If you couldn't keep the land in your family you kept it in the same
religion; you didn't let it fall into the enemy's hands.

I had a comfortable childhood in Newtownards. Although the primary
school and grammar school I attended was totally Protestant, Catholic
families lived in the same street as we did and I definitely think that
makes a difference. More or less everything in my life revolved around
the church in my younger years – Sunday school, the local church youth
club, the scouts. My mum was in the choir and my dad was an elder. I
hated church. I hated Sunday school. I hated that I had to get dressed up
on Sunday as opposed to any other day. I thought it was hypocritical. I
would rather have been out playing with my mates. My granddad was so
religious that we had to hide the Sunday papers because Sunday papers
were wrong and colour supplements were especially wrong and the
television couldn't be turned on either. Sunday was a nightmare day. It
wasn't a day to look forward to at all.

By the time I was twelve I was your standard, boring kid. I wanted to
join the army; I was into *Victor* comics, plastic boy soldiers, model

aeroplanes, and I wanted to get a gun somewhere and charge about being a hero. It was 1978 and punk was happening. I thought: this looks fun, this looks different. By 13 I was wearing all the clothes; I was listening to the Sex Pistols at scout camp. My friends from the street and I had this exclusive club; we were all into rebelling, having something that belonged to us that our parents wouldn't be into. I was all set for 'O' levels, 'A' levels and university, but I just got more and more into punk. I started up a band when I was 14 and then CRASS came along and took punk one step further. It wasn't just a fashion show any more; it was about political ideals.

There were two types of punk circles in Belfast, the chaos punks and the CRASS punks. Chaos punks were nihilists, thought everything was worthless, everything was shit, nothing was worth believing in; they were into getting drunk. CRASS were a big phenomenon in punk circles. The music they were playing wasn't much good but what they were saying was very important. They weren't strictly anarchist in the usual sense of the word; they weren't wildly accepted by anarchists of the time either because they were pacifists and that was frowned on by anarchist circles and by the chaos punks. CRASS were against the whole establishment. Their lyrics were clear and well thought out – intellectual in a poetic way, not rebellion for rebellion's sake. I saw CRASS at the Anarchy Centre in Belfast and it was one of the best gigs I ever went to. The Anarchy Centre was amazing and that's when I got interested in the politics and started going to Just Books and the café and print shop there to get books and magazines on anarchism.

My schooling just went by the wayside. I was into the band, into glue sniffing, and formal education wasn't part of my vision. I beaked off for a year and the school told me not to bother coming back, but I got so many 'O' levels they changed their minds. I didn't really want to study for exams but I couldn't think of anything better to do. I didn't realise that you could leave home at 16; I thought you had to be 18, so I went to Bangor Tech to do Sociology and Economics. I think I'd got some idea of going to the London School of Economics, where all the radicals went; the problem was that if I had gone, I would have been 20 years too late!

It was a major hassle being a punk in Ards, plus we had a couple of Catholics in the band and you can imagine how that went down with the locals. Our local hard men were the Red Hand Commandos. We used to

call them the Red Nose Commandos because they were the typical alchos
you find knocking about Ards. I got a couple of kickings from them and
they broke my arm with a pool cue. Anyhow, the band did well, had two
tours of England with DIRT and ANTI SECT, bands that were big in punk
circles, and we toured Belgium, Holland and Germany.

When I look back, I realise that what attracted me to the punks was the
whole anti-sectarian nature of it and the fact that punks were outcasts
from their own areas. Everyone came together and were brought together
because they were outcasts. Politics and religion were rarely talked about.
In the band we would have been against the Southern state because it
was a capitalist state and against the huge influence that the Catholic
church wielded. No one wanted to be ruled by Dublin or London. London
was imperialist and capitalist, Dublin was capitalist and ruled by Rome.
We weren't into party politics; they were all, even Sinn Féin, into the
electoral stuff and we didn't think much of elections. No one bothered
that much about the national question or about their nationality, whether
they were British or Irish. The message we took with us in our songs was
a vague anarchist message. All of us, except the drummer, would definitely
have supported the banning of plastic bullets. The drummer wasn't really
into that; he wasn't into politics. He was from a loyalist background and
his dad was in the DMSU, a special police unit, the one after the SPG;
anyhow, they were bad people. So basically myself and the bass player
would have been into the idea of a united Ireland, the singer was still
getting her head round the idea and the drummer drummed.

We did some direct action – gluing up banks, writing graffiti on banks
because we didn't like banks, super-gluing credit cards into the cash
machines; it wasn't very well thought out – smashed a few butchers'
windows for animal rights, all small-scale stuff. Bishopscourt was quite
big with the punks. It was a small base as far as NATO was concerned but,
nevertheless, it was an early warning system against Cruise missiles like
Greenham Common. We had excursions into Bishopscourt to wreck the
cabins and pumping stations, smash things up generally and paint slogans
on the runway. Then there was 'Stop the City'. The basic idea was to get
as many people to London and close the city down as a protest against
international capitalism. The ones who had their heads screwed on were
moving constantly, smashing the place up, keeping mobile, whereas the
ones like me who didn't know stood on the spot and chanted pathetically.

I was there for five minutes with my whistle to scare the police horses. I blew a whistle once and this meat wagon pulled up and I was straight into the back of it and had the shit kicked out of me the whole way to the police station.

We were into the All Night Party organised by Rathcoole Self-Help Group. That was quite an interesting group of people who had communist or anarchist ideas that had been Rathcoolised as it were. The All Night Party was going to put forward Hagar the Horrible for election. It was a piss take of the whole political system. Year in and year out the Rathcoole estate elected Official Unionist and DUP councillors who did nothing for them. There were 14,000 people living there at that time and they had six shops; it was a wasteland, but people kept voting for UUP and DUP. Hagar the Horrible beat one DUP councillor, the second choice UUP and the Alliance Party. I think he finished third. He got a pretty good turn out. I don't think anyone thought about what would have happened if he'd won – probably need a serious rethink about his politics. I also started to help out in Rathcoole doing advice work, benefits take-up campaigns, regular hassling of the Housing Executive, anybody really who was in authority. We tried to organise a festival and get the Newtownabbey Council to finance it, but when they heard who it was and remembered the whole Hagar the Horrible campaign, all the doors to finance were closed. We stormed the Council offices in protest and they said we should all be whipped out of the borough.

I helped to set up the Centre in Belfast where we put on gigs, poetry evenings, café, screen printing, a news sheet, putting into practice non-hierarchical ideas. I got interested in producing records; I continued to be involved in bands, made records on American labels, did a couple of tours of Europe, which is brilliant for touring. They have these youth centres which are very political and yet government funded. I could never understand how it all worked. Europe must be a more tolerant place.

Then when my son was born I needed some money and I started working in an organisation for the homeless. At the time I thought it did wonderful things for the homeless but I discovered that the place was a joke. The workers didn't give a fuck about anybody. They would lock themselves in the office and get blocked. Everybody was mixed up together, so there were men, women, old, young and ex-sex offenders mixed up with kids who were just out of care and had been abused all their lives. We had alcoholics and ex-prisoners mixing with young people, getting them blocked all the time. Everyone was stealing. The whole place was locked and I walked about with a big bunch of keys. I walked around in shock at the sexism and sectarianism that was all around me: that men would whistle at women in the street, Protestant kids would take Catholics, who had been in the same institutions with them, down to the Eleventh night bonfire knowing that they would get beaten up. I think I had been insulated by being in the anarchy punk circle for so long that I had forgotten what real people are like.

More recently I worked for a while on a Protestant estate. It's a dying estate. Anyone who gets a job moves out and the people who bought their houses under the Thatcher regime have no hope of selling them. There are three types of people who live there. There's the people who are unconnected, there's the UDA and there's the UVF. It goes in that order who you can talk to. There's a constant fear present that Ulster is being given away to the Catholics, that everything is being given away to the Catholics. They don't see that the IRA have actually surrendered and accepted partition.

I'm not sure what heritage means but as far as the Protestant culture goes, it's having a wee parade on the Twelfth, beating a drum and hating Catholics; that's what the culture revolves around. Everything else is English. They're little Englanders. As to Irish culture, I don't like traditional Irish music particularly. Ever since I moved to Belfast I've had to listen to it non-stop but I've never got my head round it. It's fine if someone else wants to play Gaelic football or traditional music, I've no problem with it, but I'm not that interested. I don't want to learn Irish either, but I would defend the right of people to speak the language and they should certainly be supported equitably. I understand why people want to keep their language and culture alive as part of their heritage but I wouldn't consider it part of my heritage. If it all vanished tomorrow, it wouldn't worry me that much. I wasn't taught much Irish history at school – after the famine we switched to Tudor Kings and Queens – nor was I that interested in reading about it. I was much more into science fiction and anarchism; they're not that far from each other really!

If I have a heritage at all, if heritage means believing in something that people have believed in the past, then mine would be an anarchist heritage: the CNT and the Spanish Collectives, the international workers' movement and an international punk movement, even such as it is. The ideal for me would be a united Ireland, a country like how Nicaragua could have been or Spain during the revolution, a pluralist society definitely. In the meantime, I would like to see a lot more debate about what people want rather than what they are against. After the ceasefires people were all talking about how things had changed. I didn't really see it myself. It's good that the war has stopped, more or less, but now it's all about talking. Whether anyone is going to start talking I don't know. Maybe they can begin by shouting at each other across the table; at least that's a progression from killing each other.

14

Animal Liberationist

Born 1968.

I was born in Lisburn, a year before the 'troubles' officially began. My dad was always a dreamer, a man who had big ideas but never followed them through. Our life followed a series of emotional highs and lows. I have no doubt that his head was in the right place; he was just unfortunate. When I was a child, he bought this huge mansion with 13 main bedrooms and peacocks in the grounds, but after a series of misfortunes the house was sold off bit by bit and we moved to Belfast. My father's mother was from a long line of baronets and her family had a lot of land and money. Perhaps my father still hung on to some illusion of grandeur.

My most vivid early memories are from the time when we lived in Belfast. I used to have this recurring dream. It started when my parents began decorating their bedroom and I remember a small step ladder in the room at the time. In the dream the room was a brilliant luminant white and I'd walk to the step ladder and climb to the top. When I reached it I fell off and I'd keep falling and spinning, never reaching the ground, falling until I woke up. I've since been told that this is a variant of the classic dream of insecurity. My granny was the real stabilising influence on my life. She looked after me when my mother went to work and encouraged me to be creative although from what I remember at four years old, it was never a pretty sight!

My dad's jobs changed with the seasons but my mum worked in a nursery school in Sandy Row. It was rough. One of my earliest memories is of someone painting the nursery school windows and being shot. All the other kids would tell me stories about their dad's guns stuffed down the U bends in toilets. When I was five someone in our street got his hand blown off; he'd picked something out of the gutter. It still disturbs me now that I can remember the events and yet have no memory of shock or trauma or even that such events were out of the ordinary. Even when I got lost in a petrol station after it had been blown up, my distress was caused by the fact that I was lost and separated from my sister. This was the normality of my life in Belfast.

I remember lots of soldiers and security measures during those years of the early seventies. I didn't think of this as strange; in fact I used to wave at soldiers in the backs of their jeeps. I was told that if I waved they would wave back — and sure enough they did! I suppose I should have been warned to make sure I didn't wave in a manner which could be vaguely construed as a throwing motion in case I was shot. Actually, I do remember a short information film being screened which warned children against crouching on street corners with toy rifles. Nothing was mentioned about waving but I suppose the outcome was the same.

My parents decided to move down to Fermanagh. Growing up in the country was great. I spent lots of time on farms, in fields and down by the river beside our house, but it was a culture shock. We were the outsiders moving into a small tight-knit community. People spoke a different language, there were no double deckers, no trains, and most importantly, at the time anyway, our colour television wouldn't work there. My mum got a job teaching infants and it was weeks before anybody spoke to her or me. My name being Kevin was one of the things they objected to most. I could never work it out. I was called Kevin because my mum, being English and coming to live in Ireland, thought she would give me an Irish name so that I would fit in! I've always been conscious of my name, even in later life. Whenever I was stopped by the RUC I was always the one to be breathalysed, but I never knew what the problem was when I was young.

It was a tight community, a village sealed off top and bottom at midnight. You kept, or as a child, you were kept to your own. Catholics were in the minority in the village. I didn't really have much contact with them which was lucky because from what I was told they were gathering information on me, couldn't be trusted and would shoot me in my bed. I made lots of friends. I love music and I played a flute in a marching band. Church music and hymns – we didn't play loyalist songs, although we would march on the Twelfth. Mostly we marched to church on Sundays in our uniforms and big hats. The Orange Lodge was strong in the village and the Lodge members would come out to the house trying to get me to join. I went along to one junior lodge meeting but it didn't make sense to me, all the ceremony and rigmarole, the mumbo jumbo. That was just to get in the front door! I told them I wasn't going back and they would call round on a regular basis telling me how I had let them down. After that I joined Christian Endeavour as a junior leader and as a Sunday School teacher. We would go off to camp and I would teach the Bible. One of the reasons I got involved with Christian Endeavour was that it was on the same night as the junior Orange Lodge meetings and I felt obliged to choose one activity.

Division was the order of the day and I never questioned it until I went to school in Enniskillen. There I was introduced to running battles between the Catholic and Protestant schools in the town square. I went to a 'mixed' school, both Catholics in attendance being in my class. I got on well with these two. I got a bit of stick occasionally about my association with them. Not that my attitudes or conditioning changed – I was told that they were okay Catholics because they had gone to our school against the priest's advice rather than go to a Catholic school.

I knew local people who were killed, either shot or blown up. This only served to strengthen my prejudices. It was depressing. I know my dad became narrower in his outlook. Despite comments, he failed to see that this was happening to him and denied it. I witnessed some non-sectarian deaths, one of which was a boat accident in which I was involved. That had a profound effect on me.

I was bullied for the first three years at school for no apparent reason. The bully later went on to join the UDR; obviously he thought this was the perfect vocation for himself. I began to look for answers to what I was seeing in the world around me but I was still very shy and lacked self-confidence. My school was full of over privileged rich kids and I began to detest their attitudes. It was the sort of school where if you have money you fit in. It didn't matter about academic ability; in fact being good at sports was more important. All the head boys were rugby players. I dropped the uniform and had my ears pierced. The girls could wear earrings and I objected to the fact that I couldn't. I was considered disruptive. I think it was an adolescent mix of wanting to do my own thing and trying to be noticed. It was a difficult time; my parents were trying to push me in certain directions and I wanted control over my life but they just thought I was going astray. I was invited to remove myself from the school roll book, which I did. To be fair to the school, after I had joined the local Tech, they invited me back.

I started going out with a Catholic girlfriend which gave people something to talk about. Both of us had problems and used to get a hard time about it. One day I was caught without any of my mates. I was lucky that the incident happened literally across the road from the hospital which speeded up my admission. I spent lots of time away from home with my new found freedom – a car, but I knew my life was heading nowhere. I desperately wanted to get away.

I left home when I was 17 and travelled. I went to Germany, dossed about in Hannover and then went to England. I did a lot of soul searching. Really being away from home helped me to tranform my view of the world. It also put the North into a new perspective. I realised that I was seen by others as part of 'orange' culture but that I had never really felt a part of it myself. My involvement in it I can only descibe as protective colouring.

Whilst I was in England I became very interested in the Animal Rights Movement, became a vegan overnight and got involved. When I got back to Belfast I joined the Animal Rights Movement here. After a month all the main people in the group, eight of them, were arrested for criminal damage and attempted arson and three people were subsequently jailed. There was no group left and it was left to me to carry things on. I was thrown in at the deep end; I had to be self-confident, drag the stall out, talk to people, get people organised.

At that time I thought animal rights was a moral issue but as time went on I began to differentiate between animal liberation and animal rights. I think animal rights is too narrow an issue. I can relate emotionally to the angry desire to destroy everything connected with animal abuse quite easily but that is the crucial moment when analysis is important. Various well meaning people counter their anger by writing off letters and sending petitions to their MPs. For me, it was thinking about animal abuse which made me look beyond to other forms of abuse in our society and the issue of animal liberation became for me one of human liberation. It dawned on me that the same power structures and hierarchy that were responsible for oppressing people were also responsible for the oppression of non-human animals. I lost faith in single issue politics. Even a casual glance at history shows that reformist politics, which seek to pressurise governments to reform their practices and laws, lead not to genuine change but a dead end.

I started seeing common traits between animal liberation and the political situation in Northern Ireland. Blood sports like dog fighting and cock fighting have been criminalised but terrorising animals on horseback, the hunt, still exists, even though most of society oppose it. It's a sport for the elite. The hunt is a microcosm of our society from the red jackets on horseback, the master, through to the terrier men. The terrier men are the lower classes, the bully boys who dig up the fox and do the dirty work. Whenever there is a threat to the hunt the police turn up fully armed to protect them. They question the saboteurs, not the huntsmen; they take our names no matter what the situation is; they take our shoes for forensic evidence; they harass us; they put us under surveillance. People think that they just throw loyalists and republicans into Castlereagh but that's not true. Animal liberationists have been lifted for conspiracy and taken to Castlereagh where they have been strip searched and interrogated.

If you make a complaint, if you argue that it's the system itself which is abusive and exploitative, that the system we live in is responsible for all animal and human rights abuses, then your argument is nullified. You are told that it is not the system which is at fault but just a fault within the system. When the state realises that you're not just a dog lover or someone who wants their dissent sold back to them in the form of T shirts and badges, then they call you a terrorist and put the whole propaganda machine into operation against you.

Words can't express the contempt I have for the bloodsports fraternity and all they stand for. A social event based around chasing and ripping apart an animal is an anachronism. Hunting is a throwback to feudal times. The violent backlash from the hunt towards hunt saboteurs is because it's not just their day's sport which is being threatened, it's their entire way of life. I travelled to England to meet people involved in hunt sabbing and Earth liberation there. I brought a lot of ideas back here. Sabbing is a good example of direct action. Ordinary people who, in the abscence of legislation, go out and oppose hunting with a view to saving animal's lives.

Where am I now? I like to believe I'm thinking for myself. With regards to my politics? Well, as an activist in the North of Ireland, I see the RUC on hand to protect those who would seek to maintain the status quo. I believe we need to bridge gaps and heal wounds in our society. Personally, I find that dealing with my own alienation and conditioning is a hard and unromantic task. We are all brought up to be the building blocks of the state. Challenging the state within us and reinventing our everyday lives is the only possible foundation upon which we can move forward to a meaningful class consciousness, a consciousness where we are strong enough to destroy the dominant class and their systems and move forward to a self-managed society. Far easier said than done! Chucking a brick through a pane of glass is piss easy in comparison.

Looking back on my life in Fermanagh nowadays is like looking back on an alien world, a world where people have chosen a comfortable lifestyle – people who don't want to rock the boat, people who don't want to ask questions. I find it strange that people can't see the divisions for themselves and that they can accept injustice as just being a part of life. Nowadays I live in Belfast and because my politics are completely contradictory to that of unionism I've found I'm more at ease and am generally more accepted within the nationalist community.

15

Sculptor

Born 1946.

For the first eight years of my life I lived in my grandmother's house in the Lower Shankill. The houses had been built in the 1830s and 1840s, just beyond Townsend Street, which was where the original town of Belfast ended. They lacked the facilities that typified the period: no electricity, no bathroom or inside toilet, no kitchen or scullery, just a gas cooker outside the living room door. We shared the house with another family. They occupied the ground floor and we had the top two floors which consisted of a living room, a parlour and three bedrooms. There were nine of us living there: my grandmother and grandfather, two uncles, an aunt, my mother, father, sister and myself. The lower Shankill was a very clannish area; I had aunts, uncles, first cousins, second cousins, all living within an area of 12 streets, and third cousins who lived 20 streets away.

I had a weird childhood. I'd been born premature and was revived from the dead. In fact, I was so small that I couldn't be handled, so I was wrapped in cotton wool and put in a box. For the next seven years I was in and out of hospital all the time, having operations. I sometimes wonder if this didn't affect my way of thinking, if it didn't account for my twisted point of view! I hated the operations and having to be strapped down onto the bed so that I couldn't use my hands. I always used to fight and I learnt how to mentally stop the tablets that the doctors gave me from knocking me out. When they realised what I was doing they started giving me injections, but it still took three doctors to hold me down on the bed. They were strange experiences to have especially when you are a child. Nowadays when I hear stories such as how a mother can lift the car her child is trapped under, I think of this energy that we all have; it is in all of us given the right circumstances.

As children we were lucky because we had a place we used to call the wreckage. It was an area where about ten houses had been bombed during the Second World War. The houses had been cleared but not rebuilt, so it meant we had a little piece of green to play on. We made our own fun and girls and boys played together. Most of the time was spent on the street playing games – skipping rope games, hide and seek, 'kick the bucket', 'wild boar', 'stick in the mud', 'one, two, three red lights', handball against the gable end and street songs which I still remember like 'I'm a girl guide dressed in blue, these are the actions I can do'.

My grandfather could read and write, which meant that lots of people who were illiterate would come to see him for advice when they had troubles or were going to court. I learnt a lot from just watching him at work. My father was a machinist in a large firm, my mum worked in the mills, my aunt in Gallaher's tobacco factory. My whole family worked, which isn't surprising; Northern Ireland was created to give Protestants work; it was a Protestant state for a Protestant people. I think that if people have work they are willing to put up with a life of hardship and poor housing conditions; it's only when work ceases that they begin to ask questions.

Ours wasn't a religious household and none of my family were in the Orange Order, although of course there were members of bands and the Order who lived in our street. We had an arch every Twelfth of July and as only a few houses had electricity, we clubbed together to put electric lights on it. The Twelfth was a spectacle but there were other spectacles too which I remember even more vividly, like sitting at the bottom of the street watching the motor cycles drive up the Shankill from the ferry for the race, the seven mile straight, and the big street party for the Queen's coronation when we all got given a coronation cup.

We moved out of the Lower Shankill in the fifties to a new estate on the edge of Belfast. This was the first time that I came into contact with Catholics and knew them as friends and neighbours. Children don't react the same as adults, so we didn't know that we were any different, but it was strange for the older generation. My father always voted Labour. In those days the Labour Party was a big thing, very different from today, and he always thought that working class people should rely on themselves to get things done. It wasn't so difficult for him to live beside Catholic neighbours, but lots of people who moved up there at the same time were staunch loyalists and found it strange living with people from a different background. However, times were changing in the fifties and sixties and Protestants were beginning to understand that Catholics were living similar lives to themselves, despite the fact that their politicians were telling them differently. When the 'troubles' began in 1969 our estate wasn't affected until about 1972 because people had built up strong friendships over 15 years. What seemed to happen then was that a new wave of Protestants moved into the estate after they had been burnt out of their areas with the pogroms. They were uptight and started a campaign that Catholics shouldn't be on the estate. Catholics moved back into their ghettoes again, although my family would still have visited those who had been friends and neighbours.

The estate had been built in the centre of a middle class area and the school that I attended was very, very different from the one on the Lower Shankill. There I had been taught to read and write and very little else; there weren't any resources or facilities. I barely knew that musical instruments existed. At my new school I learnt to play the recorder and I joined the choir. There were no such things as choirs in schools on the Lower Shankill! We had sports days, played football and rugby on the playing fields. It was a real opportunity and all of my brothers and sisters did well academically. I had that opportunity but I was so contrary! I decided that they were teaching me subjects that I didn't want to learn! Then I discovered libraries. That was really wonderful. The first book I picked up was about the Greeks and Greek civilisation which fascinated me, and then I found all these books on psychology that really blew my mind! I taught myself so much. Luckily my father was very enthusiastic about it; I think he thought that self-taught was more important than school.

After school I could have got a job in an engineering factory but I didn't want to. I worked for a couple of years as a van driver's helper with the *Belfast Telegraph* and then as a film projectionist, but I got fed up and eventually ended up in the engineering factory. It was situated in a Catholic district although most of the people who worked there were Protestants. I was a machinist working on textile machines which went off to third world countries like India.

It was a private firm with its own rules and regulations, very regimented. You had to make a certain amount of money for the firm before you made anything for yourself. The reason for this was because the firm was giving you a job! The union was weak and the workers had little say. The firm was run for the owners to make millions; that was the be all and end all of it. Every worker was a number. You weren't a person. You didn't have a name. Take, for instance, when you went to the toilet. You had three minutes. They took your number and they would come round when your time was up. The toilets had half doors so they could make sure you weren't staying there for any longer than your three minutes! There were no fans to draw the dirt out of the factory so in some parts of the work space the dirt would be a foot deep. There were no washing facilities; not that it mattered, because you weren't allowed to wash on the firm's time anyway. Someone just brought in a bucket of cold water at the end of the day before you went home.

In those days if you spoke out against a private firm you were dismissed. I joined the union and became a shop steward and we organised a strike because we wanted to change the way boys were treated. At the beginning you were classed as a boy, which meant you did the same work as a man but got paid half the wages. It wasn't an apprenticeship; basically it was slave labour. All the boys came out, about 5,000 of them. The management didn't mind us going out because they had run out of an order. We were out for six weeks. On the fifth week an order came in and the management sacked the 5,000 boys. We could go back and apply for our jobs again, which is what most of us did! I was really on the fringes and I went back to work like everyone else. The management wouldn't take the main people who ran the strike back on again though.

In 1972 shop stewards from Shorts missile factory came round the factory looking for people to join an organisation called LAW, the Loyalist Association of Workers. I became a member. At the time I thought that it was going to be a socialist organisation because it was being organised by union members. The idea was to infiltrate the factories, the power stations and all the important services to gain control.

At that time also, Bill Craig was setting up his new political party, Vanguard; lots of things were being worked out. I went along to see what Vanguard was all about. I was a motor cycle enthusiast and one of the shop stewards asked if I would join an escort for Bill Craig when he went about the North organising his political rallies. It would look spectacular with us in our leathers and our Vanguard printed arm bands. It was all for show but I did that too. We escorted Bill Craig, got our petrol paid, free meals and free digs if we stayed overnight. At first the rallies were very small but they got much bigger as time went on. The meetings had a swearing-in ceremony and you had to stick your hand up in the air, like a Nazi salute. That came out in all the papers at the time and it was scrapped because obviously Vanguard didn't want to be labelled as a fascist organisation although, of course, essentially they were fascists.

At the start Vanguard wanted to get lots of working class people and farmers involved but that changed as more right-wing business people came into the organisation. It was like a pyramid being built, the working class at the bottom, then the business class, all the way up to Bill Craig at the top of the heap. We were on the fringes of the organisation but we got to hear different things; for instance, I heard about the Ulster Workers' Strike about a year before it happened. Later on I was asked to join another organisation – I can't remember the name now – so I went down to Bangor to see what it was all about. This guy who later became a Vanguard politician was in charge of showing us how to shoot on a range run by the B Specials. You know when the B Specials were disbanded they still got to keep their shooting ranges, their weapons, their organisation and their B Special Clubs.

I didn't join up to that. The UDA was being formed about then out of the Woodvale Defence Association and I went to the meetings, though I was still only on the fringes. It was vigilantes at first and then it became an organisation. I did barricade duty during Operation Motorman, letting people out of the area who had special passes. I didn't know at the time what they were going out to do but it clicked afterwards. It was a grim time. There were lots of murders and I became very disillusioned. I'm someone who is into people talking; they can argue and scream if they want to, but not killing. I don't believe anybody should be killed for their views.

Looking back, all I can say now is what I heard at the time. They were going for independence. Rhodesia went for independence a few years earlier and this had spurred on the idea of an independent Ulster. Once the Ulster Workers' Strike happened and they got rid of Sunningdale I just think they didn't know where to go from there, didn't know what to offer in its place. A lot of people, like David Trimble, the Ulster Unionist Party leader, started their political careers in Vanguard. I always used to think that Vanguard died, but it didn't die! It just took a new form!

It's interesting listening to the PUP and UDP nowadays with their socialist leanings allied to loyalism. Listening to them on the television is very different to listening to them at their meetings and as I don't go to their meetings, I can't really comment that much. There still is that siege mentality which I can understand. Ultimately I don't think that they will go very far; they won't get a share of the vote because the Protestant working class are very conservative and the Ulster Unionist Party is broad enough to encompass everyone.

As I said, those months leading up to the Workers' Strike were grim times and I got out of Northern Ireland and travelled the world. That opened my eyes to all sorts of possibilities. I think people should go away and see things from the outside. I went down under, met a third generation Irishman in a bar and he gave me a job, my own car, a salary. I got into wine, house parties, mixed with self-made millionaires in their mansions; it was an amazing time for me.

When I returned to Belfast I went back to the engineering factory, but I couldn't stick it. I worked for several other firms, even worked for the Russians on an order for the Siberian oil fields. It was for an American company which was using Irish people because they had restrictions against Russian orders in their own country. That led to reports of KGB agents in Belfast; I don't know if there were any Russian agents; there might have been! Eventually I gave up on straight jobs and left to make my sculptures.

One day I was walking through Belfast city centre and someone gave me a leaflet which said: 'Come to our May Day celebrations in Rosemary Street'. I had always been interested in left-wing ideas but at that time I knew no one with similar ideas to myself. I didn't think there were any other eccentrics in Belfast; I thought that I was the only one! So I went to the meeting and said that I was interested in socialism and that led to an amazing set of adventures. I became involved in an unemployed group and claimants' rights. I began to travel Ireland, lived in Clare, Cork, South Armagh, Rathlin Island.

Wherever I travelled I never had any problems as a Protestant, not even in South Armagh, probably because I didn't class myself as a loyalist. I was a bit wary about going over the border on political campaigns though. One of the first campaigns I got involved with was over Reagan's visit to Ireland. We decided to demonstrate against Reagan, so we had 50,000 fake punts printed up and we travelled down to Galway where Reagan was to speak. On the way down we would stop in every town and give out these fake punts. People were amazed because they thought it was real money. Halfway down we came to this wee town and I jumped out. I was dressed up as the CIA man handing out the money from this black bag with CIA printed on it – as CIA men do! I hadn't the bag buckled right and there was this traffic cop – I can see him now; he had his hands up in the air, directing traffic. All this money dropped out of my bag at his feet. He kept staring at it with his hands in the air and all the traffic banged up behind him. We managed to get away, but ten miles down the road the sirens went and the cops stopped us. Our driver, another eccentric from the Protestant tradition, was a good spoofer. He said we had only £500 left. It was laughable really; our driver had a Reagan mask on and a big red cloak. They confiscated the £500 though of course we still had £30,000 stashed under the seats. We just stopped at the next town and started all over again.

We made friends in Galway and had a holiday on this big landowner's property. We enjoyed the holiday so much that we decided that we should move down permanently and squat on it. For six months we had an experiment in collective living. Then we moved on to Cork, took over a mountain which the Hare Krishnas owned and tried to become self-sufficient. It was an adventure. I learnt a lot about how communities and organisations work, how strong people can take over if you let them, relationships between men and men and men and women – I won't get into that last one!

Nowadays I still do my sculptures, I still travel and I have become more and more interested in the different realities of the mind and the subconscious. In a sense, I have always been interested in it since my childhood when I lay on the hospital bed for a couple of months at a time; maybe that's when I got all twisted! I am still fascinated by myths. I've been studying myths and mythology for thirty years now ever since I first picked up that book on the Greeks. In all cultures myths can be related back to the same human experiences, even though they happened to different people in different times. I don't know whether it's because they have the same origin or whether it is because we all think in similar ways.

In the last ten years I have really become interested in the Celtic magical tradition, studying the inner meanings of the Celtic texts. They are timeless really. I have learnt how the Celts could travel to different levels of the subconscious by means of an inner journey, and come to understand the importance of ecology and living in harmony with the environment – how everything in the world is unity. I do visualisations; I go to the ancient Irish sites with others and, even though I am still a sceptic in the sense that I ask too many questions and there aren't enough answers, I have had so many strange and wonderful experiences that in the end I have to accept that, if I apply my logical mind to the mysteries, I can't understand them but something weird and wonderful does take place. Of that I have no doubt.

Scenarios for Ireland? All these talks may not go anywhere so the Americans are going to take us over; we'll become the 51st state. Then they'll turn us into a theme park for American tourists. They'll all be able to come over here and look at the wee white washed cottages with the thatched roofs and say: 'Gee, my ancestors came from here'. I'll probably be dressed all in green as a leprechaun saying: 'Ah begorrah, top of the morning to ye'. Is that really so far-fetched as any other scenario? Socialism isn't going to go anywhere;

socialists are always struggling for their corner. I had a lot of strength for a long time, but it burns you out eventually. I'm not quite burned out yet, but I think I will leave future scenarios for Ireland to the younger generation.

Sisterhood

The feminist movement helped women to analyse and explain a lot of what they had seen as their own failures and to realise that they were not failures at all but the consequences of being part of a system which was not geared to accommodating them.

16

Iris Adare

Humanist. Born 1939.

Today people think that I am pretending when I say that I feel at home wherever I am and that I don't remember the ideas we have today of differences and of borders as being particularly significant when I was growing up. Even later as an adult I mixed in circles where being a Catholic or a Protestant simply wasn't an issue. I don't know how to be convincing about this.

I grew up in what's known today as the Lower Ormeau Road, not that it had that designation in those days; there was never a Lower or an Upper Ormeau Road. It was a mixed area. There were Catholic families in the street, Jewish families, two ladies whom I suspect were lesbians and an Hungarian Jewish chef who used to tell me stories of his life in Budapest and how it was divided into two cities. Many families took in theatricals who came to entertain in the theatres and the Opera House and our family took in a lodger from Dublin who came to work in Belfast as a brickie. Sometimes in my class at school there were children's troupes who had travelled over from London to perform in Belfast. Although ours was a working class area, I suppose that for Belfast it was quite cosmopolitan. The City Hall was five minutes walk away, the city centre was our playground and the Dublin Road was a favourite haunt. We were not only beside all the cinemas and the theatres, there was the University and the Markets area where my granny lived and where we went to buy our vegetables or called in at Murdoch's, which was more of a farmyard than a shop. They kept horses and ponies and traps until quite recent years.

I was the last child of a big family. My mother was a frustrated, ambitious, capable, energetic woman who had opened a shop on the front of the Ormeau Road opposite the Gasworks and my father was a very quiet, studious man, not physically strong, a despatch clerk with a linen company, who liked nothing better than to relax with a book. Our house was full of books, current novels doing the rounds like *Gone with the Wind*, the complete works of Milton, Darwin's *Origin of Species*, books on religion, a copy of *Mein Kampf*, all kinds of books. Although my parents were well read, it really didn't get them very far in life. They were confined by their social class. Both of them had had extremely hard lives. My mother was orphaned when she was seven and my father's mother was a widow who had brought her family up single-handed. They were part of that whole movement of people who came to Belfast looking for work at the end of the last century and the early years of this one.

We were Presbyterians. Our minister had been well educated at Oxford and whilst there he had become involved in something called the Oxford Movement which caused some agitation within the congregation. My father, uncle and brothers would argue the toss over the Creation and I remember quite clearly my eldest brother and one of my sisters stating that they were atheists; in fact my brother always wrote atheist on forms that he had to fill in. Once, when they were arguing over the Creation I walked into the room and asked why couldn't they see that it was all just an allegory. They glared at me. I still think, as I did then, that my contribution to the discussion was as sound as theirs but because I was a girl and a child of twelve years, it wasn't accepted.

I was always very good at art. I could draw naturally, which is not as common as you might think if you have ever seen some of the work that comes out of the Art College! This is where I really felt that my parents fell down. I was a good student and I won a scholarship but they simply didn't push me. My mother was a great women for saying, 'Don't try to go above your station' and that was a big source of conflict between us. It was terrible for me to come to terms with but you have to remember that many people thought the same way in those days. Maybe they saw it as a way of preventing the heartbreak that they had suffered so much themselves. Thankfully now it is quite different. As it happened I developed lung trouble when I was 16 and although I saw a number of doctors, it wasn't diagnosed until it had become tubercular and by then

I had to spend a year in bed recovering. That really put an end to my hopes of going on to college to study Art.

My first experience of real bigotry was meeting my future mother in law. My husband is from a Catholic family and she couldn't be civil with me for half an hour. She never could accept the fact that her son was an atheist and I think she felt that I had led him astray, although that wasn't the case at all. Obviously my husband leaving the church was a source of great sadness to her. My first child had suspected congenital heart disease and so he spent the first three and a half months of his life in hospital. One night the hospital staff thought he was going to die and they arranged for the Church of Ireland minister to christen him in our absence. The one and only time we asked my mother in law to mind him she took him down to the chapel and had him baptised a Catholic. Now he says all he needs is a bar mitzvah to complete his insurance policy!

All of our friends during that period of the 1950s were socialists and atheists and we avidly discussed politics. I remember people like Jack O'Grady who was an anarchist and sat around talking about revolution, Doug Armstrong, a Trotskyist who had fought in the Spanish Civil War and who opened his flat on a Sunday as a political salon. He was completely poverty stricken, a man who had spent his whole life living in terrible conditions and furthering the cause he believed in. Nowadays people would probably think, 'What a boring old fart' but to us youngsters he had everything to offer, fabulous experiences you would give your eye teeth for. We were all very idealistic. It was the time of the Cold War and the McCarthy era; Guatemala was a big issue and we were trying to convince people that America was the enemy to be watching for. Politics were outward looking and not so much concerned with what was happening in Ireland. I do recall the IRA campaign in the 50s but only in so far as I spent a Sunday night in St. Mary's with some woman singing 'Bonfires on the Border'. What was happening in Ireland really didn't figure with the same intensity as what was happening in Hungary or Prague.

I joined the Communist Party briefly but by then I had a baby and it just wasn't possible for me to get out to meetings. I'm not going to condemn the Communist Party because I know there were a lot of good people in it but it was too doctrinaire for me and some of the members you really couldn't have described as intellectuals. I was much too individualistic to accept the judgements that were handed down. I remember having fierce rows about what books I was reading. There was an ordered list and I was asked why I was wasting my time reading literature or reading books which were considered too anarchistic like Christopher Caudwell's *Studies of a Dying Culture*.

I was always a feminist from the point of view that I was a curious, intelligent child who craved knowledge and wanted to be accepted for what she was. When I was young I wanted to be a sailor and see the world and when I told everybody, they fell about laughing and told me that I had to be a boy. I was hugely upset to discover that doors clanged shut for girls in a way that they didn't for boys. Later in life it was wonderful to read Kate Millett and I just remember thinking, 'Wow, where have you been?' Socialism was all very well but there was a lot of chauvinism. The Communist Party was riddled with it. It was automatically assumed that the women would make tea and sweep the floor at Communist Party meetings, and it has been the same in practically every other organisation I've ever come across, except expressly feminist groups.

The feminist movement helped women to analyse and explain a lot of what they had seen as their own failures and to realise that they were not failures at all but the consequences of being part of a system which was not geared to accommodating them. I recognise that feminism is seen as an 'educated' woman's ideology and that it is more difficult to interest working class women in feminist politics. I know myself when the doctor used to call to the house when I was a child, he would be very hoi polloi and everyone was on their best behaviour but as soon as the door closed behind him the mimicry started. I've seen similar reactions myself among women who have been 'talked at' by middle class women. For me women are the most oppressed – I can't call women a race, but more oppressed even than the ethnic races. Women are still fighting for control of their own bodies, their place in society is still ruled by their biology. It's accepted today that it's wrong to tell a coloured person their place in society is determined by the colour of their skin and by the same token we shouldn't tell a woman that her place in society is governed by her biology.

I did finally get to study at Belfast Art College while the children were growing up. I found it such an undemocratic institution. I had a lot of English tutors which really shouldn't have mattered, but I felt that I was unfairly treated because my work was political and it was the fashion then to produce bland abstracts which had nothing to say about anything and in Northern Ireland in the seventies, there was a lot to be said! At Art College one has to do a seminar every so often and I did one of mine on Celtic design, which didn't go down well. It was ironical really. People would come to the College from Europe or America and ask to see the work which was influenced by the political situation and the tutors would come running to me saying, 'We need your stuff!'

One of my fellow artists did his thesis on 'Poetic Spaces in Van Gogh's Yellow Chair'. I did mine on 'National versus International Art, an examination'. The external examiner told me it was a brilliant piece of work but it got practically zilch marks from everybody else here. What hurt me the most was that they said it was too parochial, which is something which I had never been in my life. The paradox was that at the same time there was a renaissance in the concept of regional art, particularly in Canada which wanted to break the hegemony of New York and the dominance of artists from the Jackson Pollock stable. If you have strong feelings about what is happening in society I can't see why you should push that all aside and say: 'Such work would never get in a gallery; I'll have to throw a lot of paint over it and do a lot of X marks' – X was the fashionable mark at that time – 'and then call it "Making my Marks"'. I remember how my work had to fight against a room with ten black canvasses in it! By what metamorphosis does that become universal art and a painting which reflects Northern Irish society is not universal art? The politics of Northern Ireland are rarely represented in visual art and frankly, not only that, one does oneself no good in producing it!

Around the same time I became involved with a group of women who wanted to open a Rape Crisis Centre. We succeeded after much difficulty and I became the Centre's first worker. Immediately it was open the cases came tumbling in. It was like a concrete wall had collapsed on me. One of the first cases I attended was an horrific gang rape. I'm not putting it callously but that was a more valuable education in law to me than reading dozens and dozens of law books. I saw the whole situation acted out day after day for five weeks and it took vast resources of physical and psychological support to keep the woman in court for that length of time. The Rape Crisis Centre took over my life; in fact there was no other way I could have coped with it. Anyone would have been the same faced with such a ferocious amount of work and a public who knew nothing about rape crisis work. During my time there I saw an ugly aspect of human behaviour and was acquainted with behaviour that you just wouldn't believe possible. Inevitably I was forced to re-examine very deeply many aspects of life and societal attitudes and behaviour.

I am a humanist. People say that humanism is a search to put something in place of religion but I don't like that. For me it is a philosophy, a way to reason life for ourselves. It's not an economic theory; that is why I said I take it as a philosophy. It has a long history going back to the time of the ancient Greeks and many eminent thinkers – Einstein, Bertrand Russell, H. G. Wells, Professor Huxley and Richard Dawkins – have been and are humanists. The basic idea is that it is down to ourselves to organise society. There is no God. There is no preordained plan towards some predicted end. We can enrich life or we can impoverish it – that is the choice.

For me it is an essentially optimistic philosophy. I think the human race is a marvellous species. We have achieved both the fabulous and the terrible but we should, as we mature intellectually, be able to organise ourselves and cope with our time on this earth so that all of us can attain a reasonable level of living. The implications of humanism are enormous. A person says they work ten hours a day, seven days a week and the humanist asks what for? Why are you doing this? Why do you need more material artifacts? A person only needs more worldly goods if they have to prove something; it's a feeling of inadequacy; otherwise what use are they? I can only live in one place at a time, I can only eat a certain amount of food, I can only be in one car. Wealth doesn't mean anything unless it means power and domination. Why not wear a big placard and walk around the town saying, 'I have more money than you?' So much simpler than working your life away for two Mercs in the driveway. It is so banal, this material greed.

To me religions are mythologies and I find it quite amazing that people still believe in them. They offer people a golden insurance policy: you may have it tough in this life but believe what I believe and do what I tell you and there is a wonderful ... what? None of the religions explain what that is, though I accept that when a person is having a rough time it is tempting to believe in immortality.

Ireland? So much of it is about power, power over some other lot, a shibboleth which is meaningless. Ireland's smallness is regarded economically as a disadvantage but on another level it could advantageous. Wouldn't it be wonderful if Ireland became a model of rationality? My own personal feelings are that I am tired and bored with seventeenth, eighteenth and nineteenth century politics. My mind wants to go on to something fresh. Ideas here are suffering from all the effects of exhaustion. We have to find another refrain. Twenty five years of the 'troubles' is a very long time, a shocking length of time; it would eat up most of your life; it's natural for people to feel exhausted.

I don't know how we can find a solution whereby one doesn't perceive oneself dominated by the other. I'd like to believe that it is possible for people to rethink and reorganise another society which is politically and economically advanced and one in which people have given up the profit mode for something less unnecessary. That is why socialism is still very important to me. It's more than an economic system; it has idealism, common decency, equality and humanity on its side and humanism is important to me because it gives society an equitable moral structure, which complements the economic justice of socialism in an honourable balance.

It's almost the twenty first century. Decisions are being forced upon us by the technological revolution which we should be deciding for ourselves. Power is being redistributed into areas of the world and sections of society which didn't have it before. Institutions are going to be left behind. The labour force of human beings is going to become largely redundant. We need to reconstruct and plan society or else we will simply have a large population of people who don't know how they are going to subsist. None of this is being addressed in Northern Ireland where we sit still engrossed in endless replays of ancient wrongs. The popular word is global. The churches and religion belong to Byzantine times and yet they still hang on in there. It's where we are coming from but I think it is more important to consider where we are going – and it is urgent that we start now. It is later than any of us think.

17

Suzanne Bunting

Community Worker. Born 1949.

I used to tease my mum and say could she not have had me eight months later; that way I could have said I was born in the fifties! I had a secure, easy going, happy childhood in East Belfast, up beside Stormont, living on a working class estate. My father was a postman and my mother didn't work, so she was always there for us when my brother and I came home from school. We never had plenty of money but we were always comfortable. It was a Protestant estate; one or two Catholic families also lived there, but I didn't mix much with them and of course the schools were divided, so I didn't meet Catholics that much at all.

That all changed with the sixties. Being a teenager at that time was brilliant. The music was great and the 'troubles' hadn't started, so you were safe to travel anywhere. We used to go into the city centre and socialise in the dance halls. There was so much entertainment and Catholics and Protestants all mixed together. Of course, all that came to an end when the 'troubles' began. The dance halls closed down and people went back into their own areas again. I was at grammar school, Bloomfield Collegiate, but I became one of the drop outs. Why is it that whenever exams come along it is June and the sun is shining and you have to study? I wasn't interested in studying; I just wanted out. So I left school and began to work for an insurance company.

One night in March 1969 I went to a dance at Queen's University and it was on the bus home that I met my future husband. He walked me home and asked me out the next night. He had a few drinks on him and at the time I thought he would forget all about it, but he didn't. I'd never gone steady with anyone before, could never find anyone that I liked for more than a couple of dates, but with Ronnie it was love, perhaps not at first sight, but certainly at second sight. He had a brilliant sense of humour. We had only been going out together for three weeks when we decided to get engaged. My mother nearly had a fit: only three weeks and we were talking about marriage! I didn't want an engagement ring; I thought it was a waste of money; but Ronnie and my mother pressured and pressured until I agreed. We got the ring at the beginning of May and by September we were married.

Ronnie was studying for the first couple of years of our marriage. Politics – what else? – and Ancient History. We lived on my wages. Then, when he qualified, we were able to buy our first house and move in. Five weeks later he was arrested and interned. There were a couple of other Protestants interned, but of course he was the only well known one. I moved out of the house the night he was arrested. I knew that once it hit the headlines and Ronnie's father being who he was, that I would be a sitting duck and my house would be attacked. I got a lorry the next day and moved out. I squatted in a flat in North Queen Street, a nationalist area, and I've lived in nationalist areas ever since. There is no way that I could go back.

Ronnie had been a member of People's Democracy, but he joined the Officials in late 1970. At that time the Officials were very radical. He was a socialist and became convinced that the only way to achieve socialism was to rid Ireland of British imperialism. When we met I wasn't politically orientated, but I did become involved with the Northern Ireland Civil Rights Association and worked in the Markets area of Belfast. My family obviously weren't happy about the situation. We had been able to keep Ronnie's politics from both families and it was only when he was arrested that they found out. It got massive media coverage. Major Bunting's son interned for republican activity! It was really big news at the time.

Ronnie was interned for five months. The problem with internment is that there is no sentence; you don't know how long a person is going to be kept and some people were interned for four years. Whilst he was interned, Ronnie made friends with a lot of fellows from Turf Lodge, so when he was released, I moved out of the flat to a house there. I knew that we were never going to be an average family with a nice house and car and financial security. Just before he was interned Ronnie had been teaching in a school in a Protestant area at the top of the Shankill, but of course he couldn't go back there. He would have been killed. Basically, after four years of studying, he found himself unemployable. As a teacher he couldn't go to state schools because it wasn't safe and the Catholic church wouldn't employ him in any of their schools. I don't know whether it was because he was a Protestant or because of his politics, but they wouldn't even give him an interview. I felt that we were never going to have financial security so if I was going to have a family, I may as well go ahead, and I became pregnant with my daughter.

Our families never disowned us but the contact became more minimal. I didn't feel safe going to my mother's house because of the threat from the loyalists. It meant that from the day of the arrest onwards I didn't visit my family very often. We kept in touch mainly by phone After the children were born, I used to meet mum in town on a Friday and she would take the children for the weekend. Then she would meet me on Sunday evening and give them back to me.

Personally I was not politically involved. All through the seventies Ronnie was active with the Officials and then when the split came, he went with the IRSP, the Irish Republican Socialist Party. I didn't join anything all through that time. It's only with hindsight that I've realised why. Ronnie was such a well known person, he had such a strong personality that it would have been hard for me to have my own identity. Everyone took you as 'Oh yes, you are Mrs Bunting', 'Yes you're Ronnie's wife'. Ronnie was always on at me to join the IRSP but I never would, even though by that time I would have agreed with the politics. It was instinct really; I would just have been seen as an appendage to Ronnie.

One day I received a letter from a German friend of mine. She had read about a group called Women Against Imperialism and she asked me if I would put her in touch with them. So I checked around, found an address and went over to this woman's house to give her the letter. I decided to ask her about Women Against Imperialism, what it was all about, because I hadn't heard of the group before. We sat down with a cup of coffee and talked for about an hour and at the end I said: 'Oh, that's for me'. I just immediately identified with what they were doing. I got the details of the next meeting and went home and when Ronnie came in that evening, I told him I'd joined a group. I remember him asking me why, if I was to join anything, did it have to be this particular group. It wasn't so much that he was annoyed at me joining, more that he had been wanting me to join the IRSP; but it was what I wanted to do and that was more important.

We were a mixed bunch of women. There were 10 of us, seven from a Catholic background, two from a Protestant and one from a Jewish background. The sisterhood that was there at that time I have never known since. It was a really great organisation; I loved it and I am still friends with many of the women I met at that time. Women Against Imperialism were in favour of a united Ireland and saw British imperialism as the main problem in Ireland, but what we discovered was that the republican organisations had no time for us because we were feminist and the mainstream feminist movement had no time for us because they saw us as supporting a male-dominated struggle! The mainstream women's organisations were purely into women's issues. Of course women's issues were very important to us too, but we were living in areas of the city where women were struggling on their own with the kids and a husband in prison. They were running up to the jail every week; their children were emotionally distressed; their houses were getting raided, their sons being beaten up. Talking about women's rights like child care was a luxury; our priorities were just so different.

I was living the same life too. All through the seventies, after Ronnie was released from internment, he was involved in republican activity. I have never been a member of any paramilitary organisation, but I'm not making any secret about Ronnie; everybody knows that he was in the INLA. Our house was constantly raided. We were rapped out of bed at three or four o'clock in the morning. He was arrested on a regular basis and put in Castlereagh every month for months on the trot and held for up to seven days. People used to say to me that they were sure I'd be used to it, Ronnie had been arrested that many times. I never got used to it because, no matter how many times he went in, I never knew if I was going to get him back again. Whenever he left the house he always told me what time he would be back and if he was going to be late, he would phone me because every time he was late, I would be up to high doh; I didn't know if he had been arrested or whether he was lying dead up some alleyway. I was always worrying about him. Then if he didn't arrive home and I hadn't got a phone call, I couldn't very well ring up the RUC and ask if they had arrested my husband in case he hadn't been arrested and the cops would wonder what he was doing if he wasn't at home.

Then they would be out looking for him. Whenever he was late, I just had to go to bed because I had to get up with the children for school in the morning; but then I couldn't sleep. It was a very insecure time. I've noticed with other women that living that type of existence can do one of two things; either the woman cracks and she ends up on Valium and living on her nerves, or else she gets hardened to it, she adapts, gets stronger. I got stronger. I've never taken a nerve tablet in my life. The one thing I have noticed in the past 25 years, throughout all the 'troubles', is that women have become much more politicised. The protest marches were always 70 per cent women; the Relatives' Action Committees were mainly women. All during the hunger strike it was women who organised the resistance. Women have always been the political backbone of the struggle.

I could never have got Ronnie to leave the North. We went to live with his brother once in Wales, but I could only stand it for about six weeks. He was unbearable, miserable the whole time and phoning home every day. Our marriage wouldn't have lasted if we had stayed any longer, so we moved back to Ireland. At the time I refused to come back to Belfast and so we went to Dublin for a few months. That was even worse! It was 1975 and Dubliners viewed Northerners with suspicion; in fact some of the bars wouldn't even serve Northerners. The general population then, as it is now, had very little interest in what happens in the North. They are very ignorant of the political situation here.

It was also the time of the heavy gang in Dublin. The heavy gang was a group of Special Branch detectives and at that time they were concentrating their efforts more on the IRSP than they were on the Provies. A white van sat outside our block of flats permanently. It didn't move. There were Special Branch detectives in it watching everybody, checking everybody's identity coming and going. I got to know all the detectives. They would talk to me when I went out to do the shopping. It was during that time that I lost my second child. I desperately wanted to be pregnant again. When I became pregnant I wanted to have the baby in Belfast and so we came home again in 1978.

There was always a big swoop over August 9th, the anniversary of internment, and in August 1980 Ronnie was arrested and held in Castlereagh for three days. Whilst there, death threats were made against him by the Special Branch. They told him they had tried everything they could to put him away and they couldn't pin anything on him, so there was only one way to get rid of him and that was a bullet in the head and they would arrange it. He made a complaint to the RUC at the time and he made a statement to the Association for Legal Justice after his release. It was all down on paper. Two months later on 15th October 1980, he was shot dead.

I have no problem talking about the attack and Ronnie's death. People couldn't understand why in a cool, calm way I could talk about the attack, but that wasn't what affected me. It's almost as if you are talking about a film that you have seen. What affected me was the loss, not the attack.

It happened in the middle of the night. They sledge-hammered the door in. We had a friend, Noel Little, staying with us and all three of us were shot. Noel and Ronnie died and I was critical for 48 hours. It was touch and go and no one thought that I would pull through, but I did. I was in hospital for four weeks, ten days in intensive care, and was very heavily sedated, which meant that I wasn't at Ronnie's funeral, so I couldn't go through the normal grieving process. For me, there was no coffin, no funeral, no sympathy cards, no wreaths, no wake, no mourners to the house, nothing. He had just gone, my husband of eleven years and the father of my three children.

It took a year to recover from my injuries. I had the support of my feminist friends and a faith in myself which I had built up through feminism. Obviously I wanted my husband back but I knew that I could cope without a man and I didn't panic being on my own. I came out into my own after Ronnie's death. I joined the IRSP and for the first time people began to notice me as an individual.

During the hunger strike I was a member of the local H Block committee and I was also their delegate to the central committee. At first we thought the hunger strike might last a number of weeks, but nobody envisaged it lasting as long as it did. It was a terrible time. We knew when a hunger striker was nearing the end and used to take it in turns to sit up every night and listen to the radio. As soon as a hunger striker died everyone was out on the street with bin lids, whistles and putting their black flags out, should it be three o' clock in the morning. I had Patsy O'Hara's family staying with me at the end because they were from Derry and they wanted to get up and down to the Kesh every day to visit him. It was traumatic living with a hunger striker's next of kin when it was coming to the end of his time, especially so soon after losing Ronnie.

The raids on my house still continued and I was constantly harassed on the streets. Two years after Ronnie died I was arrested and held for four days after one of the supergrasses made statements against me. I can remember lying in my cell in Castlereagh hoping that my mother wouldn't find out that I had been arrested. When I was released without charge, I discovered that news of my arrest had been broadcast on all the television stations and reported in all the newspapers. It was the Bunting name again. Everyone knew about the arrest, including my mother.

My eldest child, who was seven, appeared to have coped pretty well with losing her father, but after I was released from Castlereagh she was on the verge of a nervous breakdown. Whenever the British or the jeeps would come into the street she would run in squealing and grab my leg clinging to me saying: 'They are not going to take you away, mummy, they are not going to take you away.' She had lost her father and the thought of losing me as well was too much for her. There was also another attempt to kill me. It's funny, but when Ronnie died and I was injured, I didn't think of it as personal. It was him they were after; but the second time they were after me and it's amazing how that made a difference. It was just two fellas who came to the door at 11.00 o'clock at night. I was in bed but the lodger that I had at the time went to the bottom of the stairs to find out who it was. He came back three or four minutes later saying that there had been two fellas at the door. He'd shouted to them asking what they wanted and they said they were selling ballots for the West Belfast Football Club. There is no such thing as West Belfast Football Club and besides, you don't rap people out of bed in a house with no lights on to sell raffle tickets! A few weeks later I was walking down the Falls Road towards Divis with a friend and a red van pulled out of North Howard Street. There is nothing in that street except for a British Army post. I heard somebody shouting 'Hey' at me and when I turned round, I saw two fellas in the van.

One of them shouted: 'Do you want to buy a ballot', and then he burst out laughing and they drove on. What happened that night, I think, was that because my lodger was a southerner, they didn't know if they had got the right house or not.

I didn't want to leave the North so I moved down to Tyrone where I had friends. The atmosphere there was very different, much more laid back. In Belfast I only socialised with Catholics. They were all from West Belfast and had similar attitudes. Catholics and Protestants mixed in the area of Tyrone where I lived. The IRSP didn't have any presence in that area and I didn't involve myself in politics. There was a Sinn Féin presence there and though they are republican too, to my mind they are more nationalist and not as radical as the IRSP. I don't believe they are a socialist organisation and I wouldn't join something for the sake of being a member.

When I eventually returned to Belfast everyone was asking me when I was coming back to the IRSP and I would reply that I was never coming back, I wasn't bothering any more; but I found I couldn't live in Belfast and not be politically involved. So I began to do prison welfare work, looking after prisoners and their families, visiting them, helping with any financial problems their families might have, making sure they had clothes and shoes and books that they wanted to read.

My experiences have left me with no faith in justice here. No policeman or soldier has spent any reasonable amount of time in jail for killing anybody. My attackers had the layout of my house. They knew which room was our bedroom. At that time there were barriers between the area that we lived in and the Protestant areas. On the night we were attacked those barriers were left up. That was unheard of; it had never happened before. It left my attackers with free access to get in and out of our area. The guns that were used had no previous history and have never been used since. Normally when loyalists carry out an attack they hijack a car and burn it out afterwards. There was no trace of cars either. There had never been an attack in the heart of a nationalist area before like the attack on us. To my mind, if the British didn't carry out the attack themselves then a loyalist organisation did it with their collusion. I don't expect the people who were responsible ever to be brought to court. I believe that I have the right to know the truth about that night, but the best that I can hope for is for the British to admit, in a general way, that there was collusion. I doubt that will ever happen.

I had mixed feelings when the ceasefire was declared. Obviously everybody is in favour of peace. No one in their right mind wants the war to continue. We all want to live a nice, safe life and we want our children to live in safety too. At the time the ceasefire was declared I immediately thought that a deal had been done under the table, that Sinn Féin and the British government had come to an agreement. As time passed nationalists got nothing. So, even though it's nice having peace and not having to live under the same threat of being shot dead, it's frustrating to think, from a personal point of view, that people died for a return to Stormont and everything is just back to 'normal'. I ask myself what have the past twenty five years been for? What did all the men and women give up their lives for? What did all those men and women spend all those years in prison for? The lives that we have all lived over the past 25 years, the sacrifices that we have all made – what for, if nothing has been achieved?

It's true that I spent the first 20 years of my life living in a Protestant area, but that was when I was a child and growing up. Since I left my mother's home in 1969, I have spent practically the whole of my adult life in nationalist areas and now I feel I have nothing in common with Protestants any more. It's so sad. My parents are getting older now and once you cross the divide, it's not just a political divide; it's a physical divide as well. I only see my parents about twice a year because it's not safe for me to visit them at home. My mum phones me every week, same evening, same time; they still love me and I love them. What it has meant to me is that I haven't had a family since 1971, when Ronnie was interned. I haven't had the comfort, that safety net of the extended family system that one still finds in West Belfast of brothers, sisters, cousins, everyone living around the corner from each other. Once you cross the divide you have burnt your bridges. You can't go back.

If I could tell you what sort of an Ireland would be possible call me Nostradamus! Ideally I would like to see Ireland united under a socialist system. I can't see the point of struggling for 25 years if all that changes is the colour of the flag. I think that the people who create the wealth in a country should own the wealth, not have it draining out of the country to capitalists and multi-nationalists. I'm not interested in some 32 county state with the Catholic church in control. The government should be a secular one. Nor would I want to see any discrimination on the grounds of religion. Protestants and Catholics should be equal.

I think that once there is a final settlement, no matter what way it is settled, it's going to take one or two generations before Catholics and Protestants will socialise again in the way that I remember during the sixties. Children in nationalist areas have grown up not personally knowing any Protestants and children from the Shankill Road and Newtownards Road have grown up not personally knowing any Catholics. It is going to be very difficult to overcome the mental block to that socialising. I think, as well, that my generation have become too entrenched in their own minds. I don't have hatred but I do bear grudges. I have problems with people that we have been at war with for the past 25 years and they would have problems with nationalists.

Recently I've looked back over the past 25 years and thought: 'I'm getting older; I have nothing to show for me from it all.' Throughout the seventies, when the children were small, I was practically a full-time mother and housewife. Then when Ronnie died I was a one parent family looking after the children on my own and being involved in politics. My life has been one of give, give, give ... giving to Ronnie, giving to the children, giving to prisoners, giving to politics and I haven't taken much time for myself to do anything that I wanted to do. Now that the children have grown up I am beginning to start working again and thinking about my future. It's funny really, the women friends that I had in the seventies, those who were not active republicans, these days they all hand me their business cards. My address book is full of these wee business cards. They've spent the last twenty five years building up their careers, owning their own house, having a nice car, a good wage coming in; often they have their own business. But you know, I really don't regret how I lived my life. If I was to turn back the clock I would still do the same thing. I remember once, when I was being held in Castlereagh, one of the Special Branch men told me that I was the biggest bigot he'd ever met. He said that I could only see one side of the story. That surprised me because I've always known both sides of the story; it's just that I happen to think the one that I believe in is the right one.

18
Women's Development Worker

Born 1968.

In the early seventies my parents moved away from the Ormeau Road in South Belfast back to East Belfast where they had originally come from. It was a time of people taking up sticks and flocking places and we moved quickly to a house that was vacant and where we felt safe. I was the youngest in the family; there were 15 years between myself and the next child, so all my brothers and sisters were working or had moved away from home. I never experienced having to wait for anything; in fact I was spoilt rotten.

Our family life had a strong Protestant ethos. Although my father wasn't a church goer, he would have adhered to Presbyterian traditions. We chilled out on Sunday. It was a day of rest and contemplation and preparation for the week ahead, so I didn't go out and play on the streets nor did we bother people by visiting them. Mum's family were a mixture of Presbyterians and Brethren. She was a believer in religion in your own home and reading the Bible and always complained about the hypocrites that drove to church in their big hats. I think basically what she was saying was that they had no social conscience.

We had a fast food business so I never missed a Twelfth of July. We were always cooking hamburgers and selling cans of drink and from the age that I could count I would have helped out. The first time that I went to a Twelfth of July parade I started to cry. I was very young and the drums frightened the life out of me, but as I got older I thought of it as a bit of a bore really. It all seemed to be about acknowledging people, going 'hello' and 'all right there', and we never knew anybody who was marching. I had a friend who was in the Junior Orange Order and she got to play an accordion and I asked my dad if I could join. He told me they were not our kind of people and how, when he was younger, the Orange Order used to tell lies about history, insidious stuff like De Valera's mother being a nun.

Both my mother and father's families had cut their ties with the Orange Order years previously. They told me two stories as to why this had happened. In my dad's case, his father had a falling out. He came up from Armagh to work in a Belfast linen distribution warehouse at the time that Basil Brooke was talking about only employing Protestant lads and lassies. My dad explained how that translated down into street politics was that Protestants made better workers than Catholics. My grandfather was a canapscious man and he just couldn't see how that was the case. His views on issues like mixed marriages would have been in line with the unionist thinking of the day but he had a strong sense of what was right and what was wrong and Catholics worked just as hard in his place as did Protestants. On my mother's side, her brother married a Catholic. She also had an invalid brother who played in an Orange band and it was his life. He couldn't work but he was very musical and he lived for going out with the lads in the band. They kicked him out because his brother had married a Catholic. I think the family made a conscious decision then that there were a lot of tossers in the Order and they would stay out of it.

The first time I heard the word 'fenian' was when it was addressed to me as a child. My mum loved the colour green; I'm afraid so do I and so does my sister! She bought me this emerald green dress coat and I was walking up and down the street in it when one of the neighbours asked me if I was a wee fenian. I asked my mother if I was and she told me to say that I was a good Christian. In all we had good neighbours; there wasn't any malice meant towards me in that remark, but I never wore the coat again.

We all loved politics in our house and were broadly Labour. Members of the family would have been associated with the Young Socialists and my dad had fought in WW2 and his pacifist politics came out of that time. I just remember it as a family where we would watch the TV and shout at everybody. We didn't have set views or canvass for political parties. We were observers and sceptics. My father wasn't a unionist; I would even go as far as to say he was a nationalist in a very old sense of the word. I think he saw unionist and nationalist politics as outdated and that we should move on to a socialist Ireland. He wasn't anti-British but felt strongly about his Irish identity. We had a sneaking suspicion that my mum was still a unionist but we were not sure; she would never tell us. We were a family of floating voters who hadn't found the party of our dreams.

The only thing I was interested in at school was History. I was always the devil's advocate, standing up for whichever side was getting the battering in discussions. A number of the girls at school came from rural backgrounds and if I criticised the British establishment's role in Irish history it wasn't at all popular. It was around the time of the Anglo-Irish Agreement and they used to come into school with their 'Ulster Says No' scarves and get into heavy debates about Ulster and the future. I made what I thought was a reasonable comment once about the Twelfth of July celebrations, saying I didn't think it should be a national holiday. I didn't say that we should ban the Twelfth, just that we should have another national holiday which everyone could enjoy. Some of the girls didn't speak to me for months after that. They thought that, whenever I came up with different ideas, I was literally chipping away at their identity. After a while I thought that it wasn't worth debating with them. What was the point? They were taking everything I said so personally.

I'd always been a placid, easy-going child and a model pupil, but around the age of 15 I got very disillusioned with school and thought the whole world was corrupt. I left with terrible A level results and resat them at the College of Business Studies in the city centre. That was the first time I was educated in a mixed environment, both Catholics and Protestants and girls and boys. Although there was lively debate at college, students did go home to their own places at the end of the day and they kept tight lipped over a lot of issues. At the same time Belfast city centre was opening up, with the golden mile and pizza parlours and entertainment venues. There was a much more relaxed atmosphere and my social life opened up in a way that it didn't for my friends back in East Belfast who were not travelling outside of their communities but going to local discos and clubs.

I wanted to go to university, but not to Queen's, where I would have had the same friends and would have socialised in the same ways. I think I also felt that I would always be perceived as a unionist at Queen's because of my Protestant background. I wanted to have the experience of getting involved in student politics but not the party politics that there is at Queen's.

So I went to Dublin, to Trinity, partly because my parents were elderly and it was easy for me to come home by train in an emergency but also because, on the few trips that I'd made to Dublin, I'd thought it was a great place. It was a very different environment to Belfast. Southern Catholic students' perceptions of Northern Protestants I found totally hilarious. They used to have this idea that I was Anglo-Irish and came from an estate with horses and servants! I tried to say 'no, no, I come from a wee street in East Belfast', but that just didn't have the same ring to it! The students were straight out of school of course, but I don't care what anybody says, the history that I was taught was much more objective than some of the Leaving Cert teaching. Northern students generally were viewed as exotic people because they had grants and could afford a flat of their own. Whatever way the punt rate worked I had a grant of about £75 a week which was great, but of course I was told that I wasn't Irish; after all look who was paying my grant! Still I was worth a tap for a pint. The Southern Anglo-Irish mob in Trinity sought me out very quickly too. It was interesting when I look back now and see the friendships that I made. I had a lot of friends who were Southern Protestants; they came out from nowhere. Trinity was their stomping ground.

Trinity had a strong students' union with left-wing civil libertarian politics, which was what I was looking for. I got involved in the Right to Information campaign around abortion information and various justice campaigns. It was beyond my comprehension that the state could censor information about abortion clinics in England or that a woman could not go to a counselling session where all her options were discussed, including the option of abortion. Of course, then I realised that there is an anomaly in the North around abortion too. What I liked about the South was that I felt it did have the ability to change. I liked the way you could go on a demonstration and walk to the seat of power and protest and shout. That was new for me, whereas here Stormont is a nice building up on a hill but all power has been removed. Where do you protest? Besides, protest here is frowned upon. If you protest here you are a Shinner or a Provo sympathiser. People's voices have been taken from them.

My father became ill and my mother needed help to look after him so I returned to Belfast and got a job researching women's needs in East Belfast. That was a real culture shock for me. I think coming back made it clear to me how much I had moved on in my thinking. It was like the women I was working with were no longer my people. I came from the same place yet I didn't think at all like them. I found it really hard to relate. What had once been a prosperous working class community was now feeling the effects of a hard hitting economic depression and even though they could see that everything was going horribly wrong, they still didn't feel that it was their place to protest about it. They still felt that they were better off than Catholics and that although they were poor, they still had the state behind them. I think that changed with the Stevens Enquiry; it shocked them that such raids could happen to the loyalist community. They always thought that the state was there to protect them.

I realised that my views about women's equality and women's participation were not really that relevant, that what was needed was very basic awareness raising. The level of women's development on the ground was invisible; the place was crying out for information and had a need to link in with the social providers. The women's lives had revolved around work and the family and they didn't see how they related in a collective sense to the rest of society. A few community workers had been trying to persuade them to go over and look at Ardoyne Women's Research Project to see what they had done and when that happened, the women did feel that they could achieve similar goals. So not only were we researching women's needs but we were also having to develop a project which was educational and informative and was putting some network in place.

I was always forthright about my political opinions, even though sectarian tension was at its height. Maybe I was naïvely stupid. At the start little things would happen. If I received a letter from the Republic literally everybody in the community centre knew about it. I felt the only way to deal with it was to be open. They asked me about going to university in the South. I told them I had been to Trinity and they all turned their noses up. I had to be bolshie and say: 'Do youse know nothing? Sure, that was a Protestant university.' I felt that I was on the counter attack and I always tried to sow another way of looking at issues.

Sectarian threats were made against me. It was an individual person but they used the weight of the paramilitaries to frighten me out of the place. I could never work out the reason, but I think it was because of the work that I was doing. It wasn't that it was cross-community work; that wasn't the focus of it, but it dared not to recognise barriers. We made no big deal out of going down to a Catholic women's group for a meeting or inviting their project into our space. We didn't cause a big fuss; we just did it. Others found that very, very dangerous and undermining. The sectarian card was a way of silencing me and silencing the project. I realised this later but at the time I was very pig headed. I felt that the people who were funding the project would have quite happily pulled me out of the centre and allowed me to finish the research elsewhere, write it up, put it inside a glossy cover and that would have been that. I said: 'No, I want to go back there. It's not fair; it's the women who are going to lose out. There's not going to be any development work if all the project is going to be is a dusty old report.' I brazened it out. It was a heavy time and I lost my dad during it all, but experiences like that make people stronger. Throughout my time at the project I kept on thinking this isn't sexy enough for me. When I look back now I can see that, although it wasn't sexy, it was very important work and I'm glad that I did it. People did rally round me and support me and so now when I go there I can say that these are my people and it is very important for me to remember that I share my Protestant identity with them.

By going to the South I had a stronger sense of my Protestant identity but I think that by working in East Belfast I came to have a more compassionate view of what it means to be a Protestant and of sharing the same identity with people who thought differently from me. Nowadays my work takes me into all the women's centres in Belfast and I think that, because of my work in East Belfast, I'm seen as a Protestant woman, a feminist but not a unionist. I think that whilst there are Protestant women airing their views and being seen to be politically active, there still isn't a voice for unionist women. Within the unionist parties they are not given their equal place and any politically motivated women who come from a Protestant background end up finding their voice through other channels – the trade unions, the students' unions, feminism, nationalism even, but not through unionism. The work that I do now is about breaking the silence and bringing women together to discuss contentious issues like the border, republicanism, loyalism, and also issues like lesbianism, abortion and women's work. I think the women's movement has become adept at getting the ear of civil servants and setting up centres but we haven't had an effect on changing social structures or seeing how we relate to the bigger political picture. The political situation has been closed off to us; we are not meant to ask questions about who holds power in the organs of government.

Whatever kind of political settlement that we have, if we ever get round to having a political settlement, I believe that there should be justice and equality for everyone. I would like to see a strong separation between the church and the state and I would be happy to see everything organised on an all-Ireland basis. I wouldn't like to see an Ireland where unionist people were in the minority and treated as second class citizens or more specifically, I wouldn't like to see loyalist working class people being discriminated against regardless of whatever evils have happened in the past. I do believe that cultural identity cannot ever be diluted, so we must find an accommodation which allows for strong identities to coexist. I like the idea of a federal system. Some people have said to me that is because I am still basically a Protestant and I can't get my head round being in a united Ireland, but I don't think that's true. I like the idea of decentralisation. I always think back to the United Irishmen and the reasons why they wanted a republic to take the power away from Dublin. In those days that was British power but in our own times I don't think there is any point in having a united Ireland if the disenfranchised and disaffected do not have control over their own lives, regardless of where the sovereign power lies.

Struggle for Labour

We participated in everything; we were not ashamed about campaigning and didn't care who saw us. People in Northern Ireland are so full of respectability; to me that is our greatest failure, respectability.

19

Jim Brown

Trade Unionist. Born 1924.

I'll tell you a story about the house that I lived in with my mother and sisters in Lisbellaw. We were very poor; my father pulled out at some stage of the journey and my mother worked as a scrubber night and day to make a couple of bob to rear us. The house was in a very bad condition; we didn't have the facilities like water or bins that people have now, but we still had to pay a poor rate. This remembrance has always stuck in my mind and made me detest the system and all it stood for. There was an old lady who lived up the stairs; she'd come back from America and she didn't believe in paying the poor rate. She never came down the stairs, nor would she open the door to anyone but my mother and myself. She would never open the door to old John West, the rate collector. Harry West, the Official Unionist politician was his nephew. One day he doubled back and as he was going up the stairs she opened the door at the top and hit him right between the two eyes with the contents of the bucket. You can imagine what was in the bucket because we didn't have toilets then. My mother took him into the old yard at the back and I remember her brushing him down with buckets of water and how the contents of the bucket had got caught in his goatee beard. He wasn't too happy and the old lady was summonsed and she was imprisoned for a month after that.

There was only one Catholic family living in Lisbellaw at that time; there are only two living in it now as a matter of fact; but anyway my mother used to make sure we went to Sunday school at the Church of Ireland. If you attended all year for the length of Sundays, you got going to Bundoran. Now I'd missed a couple of Sundays but the teacher gave me the ticket anyway. We were set down in a big shed in Bundoran to have our meal and on the table set in front of us were two Paris buns and a cup of tea. That wouldn't have cost more than one and a half pence in those days. The clergyman came round counting and he looked at me and he said: 'You didn't go to Sunday school for the qualified period' – which is true; I hadn't – 'You are not entitled to this', and he took the two Paris buns and the tea away from me. I had to starve for the rest of the day because I had no money. That finished me with the church. I'll tell you what age I was; I was 9, and that finished me.

I left school when I was 12; I could just about read and write, nothing more, and I went out to work for farmers. Then on January 1st 1940 I joined the army. I was only 15 and a half, but I was big for my age and I put my age on to 18. The next year I was fighting in the desert. I found this book in the slip trench in the desert, *The Ragged Trousered Philanthropist,* and I read through it and read through it; we had plenty of time when the fighting was slack, and I just thought, that's me! That book convinced me about the whole rotten capitalist system and I started reading books by Jack London and I read *The Communist Manifesto*. I'd joined the Enniskillen Fusiliers but I was transferred to the Highland Division and there was a fellow from Aberdeen, he was a communist, used to condemn Churchill for not opening a second front in 1942 and play *The Red Flag* on the piano in an old tent after the fighting was over. He convinced me too.

We came back for the landings on the Normandy beaches. Most were killed. I got a slight wound the night of the break through to the river Rhine and after that, I stopped for a couple of years in England. I got a job in Bristol and on Saturday afternoons I called up to the Communist Party offices to get copies of the *Daily Worker,* which later became the *Morning Star*, to sell; as a matter of fact I am still reading the *Morning Star* to this day. I used to sell the *Irish Democrat* as well. It was the paper for the Irish over there and I used to sell copies outside the chapel gates.

My mother wasn't in the best of form and my sisters had left, so I came home in 1948. In England I had joined the Transport and General Workers' Union and there was a vacancy here for branch secretary, so I took over and I have been branch secretary ever since. One of the first tasks I set myself to do was to organise the woollen factory in Lisbellaw. I thought that would be very difficult because the leaders of the Orange Order were discouraging the people from joining trade unions. I was in contact with a fellow inside the factory and we decided to get everyone's names and addresses and send them an application form with a return envelope addressed to me. There were 100 workers in the factory and do you know how many application forms I got back? 98! I couldn't believe it myself! I got 98 back.

The Labour government was in power then and it was much easier once you got the workers into the union, they couldn't be sacked at that time. Then we went after a pay increase. The workers hadn't had a pay increase during the whole war and we got a pay increase of 10 shillings a week at the first go and the next go we got a week's holiday for them. Well, I couldn't have done wrong after that! You see, at the back of their minds the workers knew they were being done and what wrong could I have done? I was in the army from 15 and a half, I'd been wounded, when I came back I'd tried to get them better wages; there was no point in having a go at me even if they didn't like my political views.

The only thing that ever happened me was when somebody wrote up on the gable of my neighbour's garage 'Jim Brown is a Communist bastard'. The boy who owns the garage was all embarrassed, saying to me that he had nothing to do with it. I knew he hadn't and I told him: 'They are right with the top one, but I couldn't tell you about the bottom one; you would have to ask my mother and she's dead.' It never annoyed me. I understand how the working class has been fobbed off by politicians and religion; sometimes you would have pity for them. What has happened here is that religion has been used as a political weapon and it's an awful state of affairs to see the working class attacking each other like dogs. When people say to me, 'the other side', I say: 'What other side are you talking about? We are all the one side; we are all workers.' I always looked at issues from a class point of view.

You see, the people were too respectful. The church had a lot to do with that. The people were taught to prostrate themselves to the clergyman and at school they were taught that they must respect their betters and that they must respect a gentleman and a clergyman at all costs. In the late 1940s there was a quango of big farmers here and I was asked to go on the committee to represent the farm labourers. John Brooke was the chairman of it; his father was the Prime Minister at the time, so you can imagine who was attending it. There was one old fellow from Derrylin who represented the small farmers and, you know, a man living on his own, he never was too hygienic about himself; his trousers used to be tied with a rope and he had a hole in his cap where it fell off the crook into the fire. There was a terrific smell off him especially going into the heat. The boys didn't like this old fellow but they could do nothing about it because the small farmers had elected him. I used to make it a point to go in with him to the meetings because I knew how it upset them all. We were trying to get the farm labourers an increase and this old fellow told me I would get nothing if I rocked the boat. I was out to tumble the boat if I could! The farm labourers in Fermanagh were the worst paid in the whole of Northern Ireland at that time and the committee agreed a rise of 2s 6d. They were all praising themselves and I got up to condemn it as a pittance. I said: 'John, can your father do nothing about this?' and one of them jumped up shouting: 'You are out of order, you are out of order, you can't speak to the chairman like that'. I asked: 'Why not? Is that not his name and is he not his father?' It didn't make any difference; they said I had insulted the chairman because I called him John and wanted to know was Sir Basil not his father.

The woollen factory in Lisbellaw closed in the 1970s and the workers were made redundant. The Marquis of Hamilton was the MP for Fermanagh and South Tyrone at the time so I got a couple of lads and three of the women to come with me to his surgery to see if another employer couldn't be moved in. We had a few drinks in the pub before we went in to see him. I wasn't too worried about him but the others were nervous because he was a Lord. I told him of the length of time everyone had been in work, their commitment to the factory and all the problems. When the people saw the way that I was talking to him, they started at him too. It was shortly after an election and I said: 'On top of that, every one of these people voted for you. The only one who didn't vote for you in here was me. I wouldn't vote for you; I'm a socialist.' Do you know what he said? He said: 'Mr Brown, you are a very honest man, I'll do what I possibly can for you.' He set up the sewing factory in Lisnaskea, which I thought was a terrific result from just one meeting.

The campaign for civil rights was one of the finest things that was ever set up here; it was wrecked by bringing in the gun. You know, if you wanted a house at that time you had to go to a councillor and beg for one. There was this Catholic family living in Lisbellaw; they went back four hundred years. The woman had a big family and she needed a larger house. She went to the Unionist councillor and he told her that he would put her name in the hat, that at council meetings all the names were put in a hat, and if her name came out, she would get a house, and she believed him! Of course her name didn't come out of the hat and I told her that it was all a tissue of lies; she didn't get the house because she was a Catholic. 'Oh, I don't think he would do that', she said! I knew the housing chairman and I thought I would try him out, ask him if there was any chance of me getting a house in Enniskillen. I wouldn't live in the town; I prefer where I am – it's quieter. He asked me if I was in the Orange Order and I said 'no' and there was no chance of me joining it either. 'You'll get no house', he said.

The Orange Order was always strong in Lisbellaw. I remember in the 1964 elections, I was in the Communist Party and the Northern Ireland Labour Party too at that time and we decided to put up a candidate. When it came to the day of the election, there was a boy at the gate, a real bigot, who asked the people as they were going in who they were going to vote for. I came out of the polling booth and saw this wee lassie crying. The fellow had asked her and she had said she was voting for Jim Brown's man. He'd told her she was a right fucking bastard and she wanted me to go tell the policeman who was standing further up the street. I knew there was no point telling the policeman, but I knew the form of the mother and I told her to go home and tell her mother what had happened. The mother was a real battler; she came up the street, her sleeves rolled up, saying: 'He'll call no daughter of mine a bastard' and boxed him in the mouth. I thought the policeman would arrest her but he didn't; he chased the man at the gate home. The population of Lisbellaw at that time would have been around 400 and the NILP candidate was given 100 votes. The Orangemen couldn't understand it. They had a post mortem up in the Orange hall and the conclusion they came to was that I had some influence. Not that the NILP candidate had a hope in hell of being elected; he was up against the Marquis of Hamilton. The way this place operates there are votes a donkey would get, no question about that. It doesn't matter who is standing, it's so polarised; people vote unionist or they vote nationalist. There was a time when a nationalist wasn't even allowed into a polling booth around here. I never used to vote, could see no point; I knew there were fiddles going on. Then I was told it didn't matter if I voted or not, I was voted for; so the next time I went up and destroyed the ballot paper.

The first American factory to be set up here was Taylor Woods; no question about it, the sectarianism that went on there was an outrage. It was the Protestants who were doing it and the tragedy is that it only takes a couple in the workplace to do the harm and set all the rest off. It was the first time that a decent wage had come into the county and the Protestants were jealous of their fellow Catholic workers getting well paid. Thankfully nobody was killed but the name calling and intimidation was shocking. Even the sergeant in the barracks was saying it was an awful carry on and could nothing be done to stop it. It was left to the trade union to sort out. Gradually it died down but that was the worst time. What I must say though is that sectarianism never entered into the work at branch meetings. We didn't allow it to; in fact the only people we had trouble with at branch meetings were the Militants. If you told the Militants that you were going to have the workers' revolution at 11 o'clock they would tell you you should have it at 10 o'clock!

I think that Protestants were always brain washed to believe that they were better than Catholics, that they were better living and really they had no better living. Strange, but I never felt that way and I never hid my political beliefs from anyone. There was one Twelfth of July celebration in Lisbellaw and all the houses in my area were bedecked with union jacks except mine. There was a strange policeman shipped in and he was overheard saying how he hadn't realised that there were Catholics living in Lisbellaw. The local policeman looked at him and then he said: 'The boy that lives in that house is worse than a Catholic!'

I've spent my whole life working within the trade union movement, served for 47 years on DHSS tribunals to get people their rights and what they are entitled to. In my opinion I think there might be some hope if the churches were separated from the state as their leaders are anti-union and dictatorial and I would like to see integrated education across the board.

I would have liked to have seen a socialist society here. I always believed that the North was a capitalist pigsty and so was the Republic and I believe in the emancipation and unification of the working class right across the country. I was always optimistic and never got downhearted, but unfortunately I don't think it will happen in my day.

20

Sadie Menzies

Retired Newsagent. Born 1914, died 1996.

I was born in Newtownards a month before the Great War started. We lived in a tied cottage on land which belonged to Dicksons, the rose growers. My father was their chauffeur and my mother was a millworker and would have brought some of the work home to do. My brother died in childhood of scarlet fever, so I was a very spoilt child and I never experienced poverty in so far as people would now. Clothes were always secondhand, but we were never short of food. Mine was a very happy childhood.

We weren't a very political family. My father was a unionist but he was also an atheist and none of the family were particularly religious. I think that is quite a good beginning, isn't it? My father wasn't a member of the Orange Order or anything like that, and during the Twelfth celebrations he would have taken me down to Strangford Lough to bathe or to gather cockles rather than going to the marches. I went to a school run by the Unitarian Church, a two-teacher school. I left at 14 to do a secretarial course and then went on to work for Anderson McAuley's department store. There were very few scholarships to grammar school in those days and one had to be good at all subjects to qualify. Although I was excellent at Maths, Algebra and Geometry and had good marks in English, I wasn't very good at Music or Art and so further education remained closed to me.

I worked in Anderson McAuley's general office and became friendly with another girl who invited me out to a dance. I had never been in a dance hall in my life and it was there that I met my future husband. He'd been a cricketer and footballer until he lost an eye in the shipyard and of course, after that he couldn't play those sports, so he had taken up semi-professional dancing. He saw me home that evening and a couple of weeks later asked me out again. He was very politically conscious and took me to political meetings with him. I remember going to a meeting place in somebody's outhouse off Bloomfield Avenue and desperately trying to understand dialectical materialism! I just became more and more interested in politics. I thought Lenin's works were wonderful – it saddens me that he has been so belittled – and James Connolly was way ahead of his time. The British got rid of all the good people, all those Easter Week people executed.

We had quite a lot of friends on the Shankill Road who were interested in politics and that's where I met Betty Sinclair during the 1930s Relief Workers' Strike. From that I went on to become one of the founding members of the Revolutionary Workers' Groups and later the Communist Party of Ireland.

In the early days the Communist Party in East Belfast had about 30 members, two of whom we lost in the Spanish Civil War. I had a great sympathy with Spain and worked really hard for the Spanish, raising money and opposing O'Duffy, who was campaigning in Ireland for the fascist opposition. I was also in the Russia Today Society, which later became the Friends of the Soviet Union. Various people would have been sent on delegations by the trade unions to the Soviet Union which the Russia Today Society organised. I went to the Soviet Union for a month once. At the time I didn't think it exceptional, but when I look back I can see how they made such preferences. We went from London via Helsinki and up into Leningrad and they wouldn't let anybody off the boat until we had disembarked, just because we were guests of the Communist Party. What has happened to Russia over the years is very, very sad. When we were preaching socialism and communism here I always remember people saying to us that you can't change human nature and sometimes you wonder, don't you?

The membership of the Communist Party grew and it became quite a big party before the Second World War. We opposed the war as an imperialist one and some of our members – Betty Sinclair, Billy McCullough and Val Murnahan – went to jail for writing an article in our paper. The paper was banned. When Germany attacked the Soviet Union, the war began to be seen in terms of a war against fascism and in defence of the Soviet Union, and so we worked hard as communists to increase war production for a second front and for a successful outcome of the war. The Party in the southern area of Ireland couldn't handle this change. The Irish Free State, as it was then, was neutral and our stance made them into outsiders. In the North it also made us very unpopular with Sinn Féin. The IRA came and lifted our printing press at gun point!

Local campaigns that we engaged in centred around unemployment. When my husband lost his eye in the shipyard he had received £250 compensation which he invested in a small newsagent's. In those days your best customer asked for two Woodbine and a match! We were close to the shipyard and always available and it was more like an unofficial advice centre than a shop. My husband took people to the bru [bureau or dole office], and fought their cases for them.

In 1944 we organised a huge campaign against the new Rent Act being passed at Stormont. It was going to mean a big increase in rents. The men came out of work and marched to Stormont. Dame Dehra Parker was the Minister of Housing and Terence O'Neill, her grandson, was her parliamentary secretary at the time. It was a most wonderful campaign. I've vivid memories of it. We argued that her government's own report had highlighted the many houses in Northern Ireland which were without toilets or basic amenities and were in a state of disrepair, and that tenants should not be expected to pay increases in rents until repairs had been carried out. A clause was inserted into the Act which meant that rent would not be increased provided the tenant applied for a certificate of disrepair. Until repairs were completed and signed for, the tenant would not be required to pay the rent increase. It was quite an achievement.

Then of course we had to organise a Tenants' Defence Federation because the people were not taking advantage of the Rent Act in so far as their repairs were concerned. Many Catholic people were frightened to hold the increase back. I asked them quite innocently why they didn't involve their priest; why didn't they tell him how they were being intimidated by the landlords? That was when I found out that the St Vincent de Paul owned most of the houses on the Falls Road!

I remember once having a wonderful experience up the Falls Road. Eddie Hanna, a joiner and secretary of the Tenants' Defence Federation, organised meetings on the Rent Act all over Northern Ireland. He organised a meeting outside Clonard and I, as Chair of the Tenants' Defence, got up and opened the meeting to great cheers. When Eddie got up to speak, pandemonium broke loose and we had to get police protection. The police bundled us into a police car and brought us out of the Falls Road. I didn't know why all this was happening until Eddie told me that he had once been a Catholic but had since renounced the Catholic religion.

I think the fortunes of the Communist Party ebbed and flowed in relation to the political climate internationally. We stood in the 1945 election and at that time the fight against fascism and the role the Red Army had played during the war meant that there was less anti-communist feeling. Our members polled well. Billy McCullough got 5,800 votes in Bloomfield, Betty Sinclair in Cromac got 2,500 and Silver Maitland in Banbridge got 2,500 votes. At that time we stood on an anti-fascist ticket, but when the war ended, we had to face up to the Irish national question again. Then the Cold War started and with it a rise in anti-communism. There were splits and divisions and the Party became much smaller.

Not that we ever suffered the same discrimination in the North as our members did in the South of Ireland. The communists down there couldn't even call themselves communists such was the antagonism. They called themselves the Irish Workers' Party; some were interned, others found it difficult to get jobs. I remember one of our friends was a teacher and he had a very tough time, ended up eventually with a job in a Jewish school teaching Latin. I think also that our members in the North had more roots in the working class and the trade union movement. Southern Irish communists tended to be intellectuals.

I think that these days campaigners are quite slithery and slow about getting anything going and there is more red tape about. I remember that we participated in everything; we were not ashamed about campaigning and didn't care who saw us. People in Northern Ireland are so full of respectability; to me that is our greatest failure, respectability.

As to the future, well, we couldn't wish for a more beautiful island, could we? I certainly would like to see both parts of the country united because I think our whole future lies economically and every way in the unity of the country. I feel we have so much to bring to the South and they have so much to bring to us. Our people, Catholic and Protestant, are the kindest and best in the world and they deserve the best.

21

Joe Law

Trade Unionist. Born 1946.

My first recollection of the difference between Protestants and Catholics was when I was about five years old and a Junior Orange Lodge was organised for the young boys in our street. There was quite a group of us and we thought it a great idea to get dressed up in a new suit – in fact our only suit – and parade at Easter and during July and August. We'd get to go on trips to exotic places like Portrush and Bangor, eat ice cream until we were sick and have a pocketful of change to play the slot machines. What really upset me was that two of my friends couldn't go with us because they were 'fenians'. That is my first recollection of difference and, in fact, of superiority.

My father came from Sandy Row and he used to tell me stories of when he lay on the Boyne Bridge watching the shoot-outs with the Black and Tans. He was for God, Queen and country, a member of the Orange Order, although in later years he fell out with them and never went back. He was talented, widely read and was able to write, so anyone who was going for a job or wanted something written would come to him for help. He worked for the linen lords, William Ewart, for 49 years and even in later years, after I became a trade unionist, he would maintain that working people had to accept the diktat of those who controlled society, those with money. He believed this even though, as he told me, he had been treated badly at work. His bosses would click their fingers at him to do their bidding. My mother, whose own father had been killed on the first day of the Somme, was the typical mother, always worrying about how to find the money to clothe and feed the family.

I went on to become the Worshipful Master, the top trick in the Junior Orange Lodge, although that was also the year that the Lodge collapsed! I can still rhyme off some of what I was taught. I would sit face to face with another boy and say,

'What is that colour you wear?'

'It is a bright orange.'

'Why do you wear a bright orange colour?'

'To commemorate the memory of the King.'

'What King?'

'King William III, Prince of Orange.'

'Why do you commemorate the memory of that King?' –

and I forget the rest of it!

The Order was full of rituals. I remember I had a wooden hammer, like an auctioneer's hammer, when I was Worshipful Master and we would sit around tables whilst the men conducted the meeting. Essentially, for me, it was a day out with friends. I joined other organisations too: the Life Boys, the Boys' Brigade, and went to Sunday School and church regularly, although for some reason which I can't articulate now and couldn't then, I refused to be confirmed into the church at 14 years of age, a decision which caused the Boys' Brigade master and the minister to come down to the house. No one could understand it, least of all myself, for the simplest thing would have been to go through with the ceremony, but I wouldn't and I didn't.

When I left school at 15 years old, a man across the street took me down to the Belfast Harbour Commissioners for my first job and I was given a choice of becoming a joiner or a fitter or an electrician. I was colour blind so I knew that I wasn't going to make it as an electrician! I became a chain boy before I started to serve my time from the age of 16, working on the construction of Richardson's Fertiliser wharf, carrying the engineer's theodolite for him and making his tea. I remember I had these water boots with the tops turned down where slogans like 'God Save the Queen' and 'Fuck the Pope' had been written. I had no concept of Catholics being in the workshops but I met a couple on site and became friendly with them, went to dances at the Fiesta or drinking in the Grand Bar in the Markets.

The Harbour Commissioners only paid a couple of pounds a week, so, after I started to serve my time, I applied for a job in Mackies where I could earn £7 or £8 a week on production bonus work. There could be hundreds starting and hundreds leaving at the same time, all because of the bad conditions. I was ushered into a green and brown cell of a room with a fellow sitting behind his desk writing something down. He said: 'Yes? What's your name? Where do you live? What school did you go to? Start on Monday.' He never looked up; he never looked at me. Start where on Monday? Do what?

I go the job because of my name, where I lived and what school I went to. Everyone knew that. When you went for your tea the union jack was wrapped around the machines of the Catholic lads. Nothing was structured; it was dog eat dog. I worked next to one of the Catholic lads and I was showing him a job; the jobs we used to get came off bigger machines that men worked. After I showed this fellow the job, I no longer got the good work.

I had my first experience of a strike in Mackies. All the boys walked out in protest at getting half the pay, plus it was a nice day and everyone was saying, 'Let's go!' It wasn't controlled in any way, just fuelled by enthusiasm and anger at all the old farts who didn't know what they were doing. My main ambition at this time was getting away. In those days you heard all these stories about different jobs to be had in England. So I teamed up with a friend from the Shankill and another from my street off the Old Lodge and off we went to Gloucestershire where there were a couple of factories we had heard about.

It was a change of cultures. We objected to being called Paddy of course and we were mad that the English didn't stand for 'the Queen' after the pictures. Back home we would have been the prods who always stood at the back of the pictures and made the taigs stand for 'the Queen'. We had this little ritual ourselves every Saturday night after we'd gone out for a drink. We used to go back to our digs and sing the National Anthem before we went to bed. People used to come and watch us; I don't think anyone could understand why we did this. I came back to Belfast after a few months. I remember that was the last summer I walked to the field on the Twelfth. I was still a loyalist but I was developing a strong anti-religious feeling, thinking that it was convenient and arrogant to believe that man could live forever. If you thought that, then you invented a God that accommodated that thought.

I still yearned for adventure and in 1966 I joined the Merchant Navy and boarded a ship bound for South Africa. I was 19 years of age and full of excitement at seeing the world. As soon as we docked in South Africa I was confronted with the apartheid system. All the black people came on board and the comments began about them being lazy bastards. They did the same jobs as the whites but they were only paid £3 a week compared to the £40 that the whites were paid. I remember thinking if I was only getting £3 a week I wouldn't be working too hard either! I looked after the food on ship and after the passengers and crew had eaten, the blacks would come on board with their tin cans. It was my charge to clean down and wipe up and they would help out and then I would give them the leftovers. The blacks mostly wanted meat and one day there wasn't much food left and I thought my black helper had done a good job so I tried to give him a rand (50 pence, ten shillings then) instead. His eyes opened up and he backed away from me. I went after him trying to explain that he had done all this work and there was very little for him but he ran away. I asked someone about this and he told me that my black helper thought I wanted his body.

We went ashore to explore. The towns were beautiful and the scenery unbelievable and in the midst of all this we would meet the Afrikaaners, enslavers in their mindset, who spoke down to anyone regardless. They thought it was their right, their country; they could do whatever the hell they wanted. The military beat me up for talking to a couple of black girls, called me an English bastard, and I remember shouting after them, 'I'm not English, I'm Irish!' It was the first time that I declared myself Irish, in the sense of claiming my nationality to be distinct from English. That was an eye opener. Later when I became more politically active, I joined the anti-apartheid movement.

For a few years I travelled, did some trips to New York on the Queen Mary; that was altogether different. Everybody loved to talk to you because you were Irish, asking after such and such a place in the west of Ireland. I got involved in picket duty during the seamen's strike of 1966, came ashore in 1968 and worked in Galway for an American-owned engineering company. Our Galway landlady used to call us bumble bees because of the orange stripe. Galway was a turning point. I began to read more, including some religious books published by the Catholic church. A priest came to see me at the digs; he knew that I was a Protestant, but he wanted to make sure I knew there was a Church of Ireland, a Presbyterian and a Methodist church in Galway, that there was a big Protestant community that I could be part of and he hoped I was still saying my prayers and going to church. He was a very kind gentleman. That was the first time I declared myself an atheist.

I ripped my hand open in Galway. There wasn't much different in wage levels between north and south, but the sick payments were very small and I decided to come home. It was the late 1960s and there wasn't much work about. My uncle spoke for me in Mackies and I went back to work there. It was always a fall back, a stepping stone to somewhere else. I worked on the night shift in Mackies during the early 'troubles'. Free Belfast was operational and there was a total breakdown in society, with bomb scares and bars closing early. I remember one night ending up with friends, most of them Protestants, in the Oak Bar which stayed open late on the Falls Road. We were young people wanting a night out. We would go anywhere without realising perhaps the dangers of where we were going.

My attitudes were changing. I'd moved away from religion and Orangeism but I didn't know where I was going and I was scared of breaking links. I was aware of the political disturbances starting to build: Paisley, Burntollet Bridge, the burning of Bombay Street, seeing shooting for the first time, pubs being burnt down, but not having any politics, I didn't understand it.

The first time I put myself out on a limb was after I went to work for Rolls Royce and was told the factory had to close for a loyalist funeral. The manager came down and said that I was the only prod left in the factory though the Catholics had all stayed in. I was told it was my decision but that the men were going to come round and beat people out. It was like I was 14 again and thinking: 'I am not going to get confirmed; I don't want to be involved with this.' I stayed and in the event no one came round with big sticks, although some people never spoke to me again.

One of the last times I went on to the Shankill for a few pints was in 1974 with a friend of mine who had done time for a Protestant paramilitary organisation. He asked me if I would fight for Ulster. I told him a story from our childhood about when we were all in the Orange Order, all queued up, waiting to march with the bands playing. Suddenly somebody shouted, 'Jimmy isn't here!'. So this wee lad said, 'I'll get him' and charged off, you know the way kids do, going 'dant-te-dant-te-dant' and making all these daft noises. He slipped and didn't so much as fall in dog shite but went through it and his clothes were ruined. He didn't have another pair of trousers or a jacket; none of us did. All the mothers went back into their houses saying, 'I've got a pair of trousers that will fit him' or 'What size fits him? I've a wee jacket; I've a pair of socks.' He was like a licorice all-sorts when he came back. That's your Ulster I said. I was trying to explain that if we were all going to fight for something, let's fight for something better. The UWC Strike had just ended and what did loyalist workers do? They gave everything back to the unionist politicians! I knew that I didn't want to end up like my father, 49 years being treated like a dog.

Anybody who is a Protestant from this society has to accept the fact that their economic well being is because they are a Protestant. It wasn't always my ability that got me the jobs, and, in the early days, most of the time it wasn't. I began to get more and more involved in trade union activities, began work for an American-owned company and became a shop steward. As my views changed from my contemporaries on the Shankill, I felt I couldn't argue with them anymore. I felt more alone, began to feel unsafe having a drink on the Shankill. More and more of my friends came from a Catholic background or were Protestants like myself wanting to discuss politics. Unfortunately that became almost impossible in the Protestant community and in my own area, which was a great sadness to me. Even today I would feel unsafe having a drink on the Shankill. My views were changing from everything that I had grown up with and had been taught to believe – like a metamorphosis.

I started to involve myself more and more in the trade union movement and in the early 1980s with the Belfast Trades Council. Belfast Trades Council is like a mini-TUC and you can imagine the debates around the political situation at that time. Although it was easier to argue politics in the trade union movement, like the rest of society the movement is divided into two sides. I really started to examine Irish politics during this time and discovered the United Irishmen and that period of richness in culture and Irishness within Protestantism. The United Irishmen were quite clearly Irish, quite clearly Protestant and indeed were the founders of the Irish republican movement.

Up until that time I was a republican in the sense of being an anti-monarchist. I did not believe that a family should be exalted into a position of authority and power in perpetuity but that society should be secular and democratic – more like the Americans or the French or the Germans. That is a difficulty for Protestants because of the link with the English aristocracy and English royalty. Reading about the United Irishmen and fraternity, equality and liberty made me realise where I fitted into Irish politics. I went on to read James Connolly's works. He is despised by the Protestant community because he fought in the 1916 Rising, but he was a socialist and a trade unionist and I found his brilliance at relating Marx to the common man astounding. I remember a startling comment of his that if Ireland was partitioned it would lead to a carnival of reaction. I think that since partition we have lived through that carnival of reaction and unfortunately still do.

In the 1980s I joined the Communist Party. It was a party where I saw that I could pursue some politics. I'm still a member, although not a very active one. My politics followed me in to Shorts and the first time I ran for shop steward's job a campaign was started against me. 'Don't vote for him; he's a republican; he's a fenian lover.' One of my work mates called me a traitor and he said: 'You also married a fenian.' My way of dealing with that at the time was to say: 'I'm sorry; I thought I had married a woman!' Another of my work mates came to me at the time to say that he had been told not to vote for me. I thanked him for telling me and said it was an issue he would have to decide for himself. Then he told me that he had spoken to his wife about it. She had been more circumspect, saying that if I was the best one for the job, the one who was going to look after his interests, then he should vote for me. The day of the vote, he didn't show up. He abstained. The shop steward's job was decided by a show of hands and I lost by a couple of votes. We never spoke about it again.

I was involved in supporting the miners' strike. In Shorts we tried to create a levy whereby the workers would pay £1 a week on the same principle as they would pay their union dues. A couple of miners came over from Britain and gave out leaflets at an anti-internment commemoration and a campaign started in Shorts. It was called 'No Levy for Traitors'. The campaign in Shorts was linked to British politics, that is Labour Party links to the trade union movement and their attitude to the question of partition and their policy of unification by consent. There was massive support from Dublin for the miners. Dubliners remembered the 1913 Lockout and how the British miners had supplied coal and food and clothing. At the end of the strike I went over to Scotland to present a plaque from the Belfast Trades Council and I was introduced to the chair of the Ayrshire Miners. He was an Orangeman and he asked me where all the money came from. He wouldn't believe that his loyalist brothers here would have dealt with him in such a way. Sadly they did! They orchestrated a campaign that the miners were traitors and supported by the IRA and all it was in reality was a couple of people from Nottinghamshire Trades Council handing out leaflets at a rally. If a couple of Orangemen had done the same on the Twelfth of July, I wonder if there would have been the same reaction from Catholics. I don't think so.

When you go against the grain, people mistrust you. The problem with our society is that you are either one or the other. There can't be any other way and the last 25 years of war has deepened those divisions. All unions, North and South, are affiliated to the Irish Congress of Trade Unions, an organisation only recognised by Stormont in the 1960s. ICTU does not take a position on the constitutional issue. We discuss wages and conditions, education, health and social conditions, but the issues and beliefs that divide us are very difficult to raise. Issues like flags and emblems, the hunger strike, the Ulster Workers' Strike do create huge difficulties for the movement. Workers have been shot and put out of work, and the work places are still dominated by one culture or the other. Arguing the issue of fair employment, which I supported, was difficult for me. Protestants saw it as a law which protected Catholic workers; they didn't see it in relation to themselves. There are problems with discrimination in this society, but the law itself embraces everyone, all workers regardless of their political and religious beliefs. That is a debate which is still continuing.

The trade union movement and the Belfast Trades Council have given me great insights, great debates and great friends and comrades – people trying to do the best they can in a divided society. I think we all have to understand that this is an unagreed state, an unagreed society. Taking positions outside one's tribe is difficult. People are judged on how they resolve situations and there can often be the accusation levelled that a

decision was made because people are fenian lovers or are sucking up to
the prods. For me it should be about republicans and unionists
disagreeing on a political ideal, not that they have to destroy each other
but should work towards finding an accommodation and a way to live
together. That can't happen until the military campaign is suspended,
but it does give me hope to see that within the last couple of years those
at the sharp end of the conflict, those who have been in prison, those
who have done terrible deeds, are the ones talking about an
accommodation and a way forward. I wish all those people good luck
and I continue to do my small bit towards developing political
accommodation and understanding. I think that the future holds many
difficulties but also many possibilities. The talk of peace and reconciliation
must be accompanied by an understanding of each other. The challenge
to our political representatives is to examine what is being said and to
ask themselves how they can contribute to moving forward in a
meaningful way.

I believe we have to build a pluralist society where all beliefs are
respected. The goal must be an Ireland that has the vision of Tone and
the United Irishmen, one where we can accommodate Catholic,
Protestant and dissenter.

The Socialist Tradition

For me the socialist tradition is an international tradition.
Socialism is inconceivable for me if it is to have borders
between peoples or eventually even separate national states.
I believe a socialist Ireland is our only hope for the future. I
also believe that in Northern Ireland socialism is a third,
sometimes obscured, tradition.

22

Digger

Wall Muralist, Born 1957.

My early childhood was spent in a small village outside Derry, the type of community, like so many rural areas, that categorised people in terms of their religion. One of the first comments that would be made about a person would be whether they were a Catholic or Protestant, and this religious label was as common a mode of description of an individual as saying that a person was tall or small, fat or thin. Thus comments such as, 'Oh, he's a decent fellow, but he's a Catholic', would be quite common. Of course, no one would admit that anything malicious was meant by such a description, but it had the effect of reinforcing the existing religious and social divisions that existed in the community. In a sense, a sort of 'apartheid' existed between Catholic and Protestant communities of the area, each living side by side yet rarely mixing. So it was that the absence of socialising or mixing with members of the other community did not seem unusual, and I don't remember ever really meeting an Irish Catholic until I was 18 and attending university.

Even within the Protestant community everyone seemed to know their place. My father was a Protestant clergyman and this immediately placed our family at the higher end of the social scale within the community, and placed certain expectations on me. Thus, it was always expected that I should attend grammar school and proceed to university and slot neatly into a respectable career. Nor unusually, there seemed to be an unstated assumption that I would draw my friends from families of a similar social standing to our own. Thus, mixing with the children of doctors, teachers or large farmers would be encouraged, at the expense of friendship with the children of farm labourers or council workers.

Ours was not a particularly strict religious household. Of course I regularly went to church, but in those days nearly all members of the community belonged to, and attended, church. I have always regarded my father as being fairly liberal and tolerant, something which had a particular resonance in the Derry area in the 1960s. However, I never remember politics being discussed in our house in those days and apart from a few incidents, the early years of the civil rights struggle largely passed me by.

Despite living in a fairly tight knit and closed community, one that seemed to turn its back on the outside world, it would be a mistake to think that it was possible to exclude all thought of the Catholic community. There seemed to always exist an uncomfortable presence threatening and looming over our lives. We were all hyper-sensitised to the existence and 'threat' of the Catholics. As a primary school boy, for example, I remember being admonished by my classmates for cheering when Glasgow Celtic won the European Cup in 1967. It took no more than that to remind me that Celtic were a Catholic team. I have a clear recollection of the B Specials mustering at the church gates, which were right beside our house, before setting off on patrol dressed in their black caps and capes. Neither I, nor my family, ever attended an Orange demonstration in my childhood (or indeed thereafter), although many of my classmates were, as much as anybody, caught up in the triumphalism that surrounds such events.

My first memory of the civil rights struggle occurred when I was attending grammar school in Derry. I remember one boy from the Claudy area, also, as it happens, the son of a clergyman, coming into school one morning bragging about how they 'had got stuck into the fenians' and how 'they had beaten the shite out of them'. This kind of talk excited everyone in the class and I suppose we all regretted that we had missed it. I have since worked out that this boy was referring to the bloody ambush of the civil rights marchers at Burntollet Bridge in 1969.

Events seemed to happen much more quickly after that. I remember watching agog as the first British troops entered Derry later that year and suddenly barricades sprouted up all over the city. I recall being shown around a huge barricade by its defenders which had been erected just off William Street, right beside the swimming baths. My guides were extremely proud of their barricade and eager to show it off, but what some might find surprising about the situation was that i was wearing the distinctive maroon blazer of the Protestant grammar school and I and my classmates were only in the area to attend swimming lessons. Whilst being aware of the rising tensions throughout the city, I must say that I never encountered any hostility or felt under threat from anyone, even though shortly after this our school advised us to stop wearing uniforms to school as it was felt that it too readily identified the community from which we came.

My family and I left the Derry area in the early 1970s when my father moved to a parish east of the Bann. My direct experience of the 'troubles' was consequently much less, although, like everybody, I was acutely aware of the deepening divisions within our society and of the escalating war going on in our midst. School life tried, and largely succeeded in ignoring what was happening. I studied Politics and History, but never do I remember any attempt to address or discuss the political situation in Ireland or to even examine its historical context or background. Politics was what happened in Britain between the Conservative and Labour parties – the events happening on our own doorstep could have been a thousand miles away. It was at school, however, that I first developed my passion for politics. I suppose I was instinctively attracted to left-wing radicalism, although it was to be some time and much agonizing before I had the nerve to apply these theories and ideologies to the Irish situation. As a schoolboy I was content with Che Guevara posters and Chairman Mao's little red book, but it wasn't until I enrolled at Queen's University that I felt I had the calling to right all the world's wrongs, and the time seemed right to apply all this political theory to practice. Yet Queen's was to prove a major disappointment to me. I was really looking forward to going there, expecting it to be a hotbed of political revolt. Images of the American student demonstrations and Paris 1968 fired my imagination and of course, I knew about the role played by students in the early Civil Rights movement in Ireland. Queen's, however, turned out to be a microcosm of society at large. Everybody stuck with their own kind; so there would be the rugby-playing crowd and the GAA crowd, with student politics mirroring the sectarian divisions in society at large. Instead of radicalism there was resignation; platitudes replaced protest.

Some time later I was introduced to a new circle of people, one that seemed to offer all that was absent from student life. They were a mixed bunch, comprising both Protestants and Catholics for whom one's religious and social background seemed to hold little interest. The one unifying factor was that all these people were very politicised. Some had links with Trotskyite organisations in Britain, others were very involved in feminist organisations; some had anarchist sympathies, whilst a few were members of the fledgling Independent Socialist Party. In this brew of ideas and opinions I felt, for a time, that I had found what I was looking for and before long, eleven of us had bought a communal house and attempted to put into practice vague ideas about communal living. Those were heady days, fuelled by an idealism and optimism that couldn't last and after a year, due to personal rather than political disagreements, the group broke up. Part of the problem was that the household and the surrounding social circle grew bigger and bigger as individual group members introduced their own friends and collaborators into the circle. Fragmentation and fracture was, in hindsight, inevitable as this exposed the naïvety and limitation of our project.

However, for me, I had been spirited into an exciting new world containing 'real' people whose background was not invariably middle class or based on university life. If anything, it taught me to be more critical of what was happening around me and the exposure to a multitude of ideas meant it was very difficult to offer loyalty to one faction, group or ideology. However there were some basic principles which seemed very evident, one of which was the impossibility of ignoring or sidelining the national question in Irish politics. The border was something that had to be faced up to, not closeted away in a pretence that somehow our political environment was similar to that of England, where the 'class struggle' seemed to amount to hawking the party rag around pubs and foisting it off on 'comrades' who were in such a state of inebriation that they probably couldn't tell the difference between *War Cry* and *Socialist Worker*.

I took the attitude then, and it is one that I largely retain today, that the British influence in Ireland is pernicious and that there can never really be a solution to the political problems of this country whilst they maintain a presence in it. Such a view naturally drew me to republicanism, or to be more accurate it was to the republican socialists that I gravitated. I began to go on rallies and marches organised by the Relatives' Action Committees, the prisoners' issue being one of the few outlets for street level political activity at that time. I remember going to some of the early meetings of the RACs and feeling very out of place. Very few men attended these meetings and, on one occasion, I recall being one of two men at a meeting which attracted twenty women. Interestingly that other man was Ronnie Bunting, also a Protestant.

Eventually I moved into another communal house adjacent to the New Lodge area of Belfast. In a sense this move seemed at the time to represent a break with my background as I left behind the security of the University area and entered a completely different community. Contacts with my old friends became more tenuous. One of my Protestant friends came to visit and when he saw the political posters on our walls, he was appalled. After that our friendship seemed to fade away. When the focus of your life changes it is somehow inevitable that so too your friends will change. It is sometimes hard to retain friendships from a life that you have passed through and left behind. My parents, of course, knew what I was doing and although this was clearly not the future that they hoped I would have, they never strongly voiced disapproval. I think they were more worried about my personal safety than anything. My brothers and sister were more opposed to what I was doing, but as I rarely saw them, this never became an issue.

For sometime I had been undertaking artwork for various groups and organisations. As political agitation and protest snowballed from 1979 onwards (particularly on the prisoners' issue), so too did the amount of work that I was being asked to undertake – so much so that it could have been full-time employment. I was producing artwork, cartoon strips and posters for Just Books, the IRSP's magazine *Saoirse*, People's Democracy, the Trade Union Campaign against Repression, and the Student Campaign against Repression. Just before the first hunger strike commenced in 1980 I was asked if I would paint murals in Ardoyne. I think I painted about six murals in this area alone in a fairly short period of time, before moving, as the hunger strike progressed, to areas such as Divis and Beechmount. By this stage street protest was becoming more and more organised, frequent and concerted and I became fully employed in the production of banners and posters. As time went by my work became increasingly ambitious as the sense of urgency, created by the imminent conclusion of the hunger strike, gelled previously fragmented communities into cogent political forces. I must say that, as I worked on street corners and gable walls throughout Belfast, I felt a strong sense of community approval. People often approached me and asked me to come and paint their house, as if having a mural on your gable end was a mark of privilege or distinction.

I never joined any one political grouping at this time or subsequently and I'm glad that I didn't, because to do so would have meant surrendering the political independence and mobility that I had. I suppose I felt an instinctive distrust of political parties and their necessary discipline and organisation. After the hunger strikes, for example, Sinn Féin recruited a lot of people who had become politically active over this traumatic yet tumultuous period. In many ways I saw this as a marriage of convenience. On one hand there was Sinn Féin, who suddenly woke up to the potential of street and community level political agitation in providing them with electoral success (which in turn gave them the greater political and social prominence and respectability which they craved). On the other hand were highly motivated, articulate and adept street level politicians for whom the end of the hunger strikes created a vacuum, in that all of a sudden there was no outlet through which they could channel their energies and creativity. Sinn Féin extended a welcome to these men and women. However, for those of us who declined to join Sinn Féin there was marginalisation and often exclusion from much political activity. Of course there were sporadic attempts by many to sustain their political involvement, but these frequently came to nought when faced with the juggernaut of Sinn Féin and the other major political parties. This is not to say that Sinn Féin didn't change, because of course it did. The hunger strike campaign had taught it a salutary lesson, one that its current politicking bears testimony to. However I never felt this change to be sufficiently attractive as to induce me to join the organisation. I have always regarded myself as a socialist and whilst I regard the removal of the border as being essential to the defeat of sectarianism and the withdrawal of the British presence as a necessary precursor to the building of a stable, secular and just state, I don't believe that Sinn Féin and the republican movement are capable of providing the unity or consent in order to bring this about, nor, indeed appear interested in widening their base of support sufficiently to seriously countenance such an effort. Consequently they will always be a minority political grouping with a limited electoral appeal, yet one that unfortunately monopolises the ground of the republican left – an area that might be colonised and shared by others.

All this might sound unduly pessimistic, yet I, and people like me, do not find it easy to find a political, never mind a real home in the current climate. Whilst personal security is always an issue and generally means that you have to live in a 'safe' area, this often has the effect of reinforcing the sense that political and often social acceptance is frequently dependent upon a very public kind of cultural assimilation and total identification with one community at the expense of the other (look at the number of Protestants who have started to learn the Irish language or play traditional Irish music). The sense of being an outsider and not quite belonging is a strong one and I don't think it ever totally deserts you. It is unfortunate then that perhaps things haven't really changed that much and even today, the political and social straitjackets which exist in Ireland still serve to categorise and confine us just as surely as they did when I was a boy growing up outside Derry in the late 1960s and early 70s. And as for me, well, I continue to attract the epithet of being called 'a good painter, but he's a Protestant you know!'

23

Robert Bell

Librarian. Born 1953.

At the time that our family moved out to Suffolk in 1955 it was just three streets of houses in a middle of a field beyond Andersonstown in West Belfast, but of course it grew into the housing estate that it is today. My memories are of it being a neat place with well-ordered gardens, not at all like the later suburban working class estates where the Housing Executive dumps families with social problems. Most people living on the estate were in employment. My father worked in the building trade and my mother worked part-time as a stripper in Gallaher's tobacco factory, a job description which always amused her. She stripped the tobacco leaves. Suffolk was an ideal place to grow up in, lots of families with young children for me to make friends with, fields, rivers, forests, the mountain, building sites to play on as new estates like Hillhead and Lenadoon were built beside us, a wonderful playground existence.

The changes began in the mid-sixties when I was about 13 years old. I'd started going to grammar school in nearby Lisburn. It was a predominantly Protestant middle class school and it was here that I met my best friend of those years. He was English and from an extremely liberal and educated family. For the first time my eyes were opened to the possibility that there were other ways of living and, coinciding with this, was a growing awareness that the neighbourhoods beside us were Catholic. We'd always played in the glen but that was becoming difficult as more and more houses were built for Catholics. Borderlines became an issue and we had to be ready to run at a moment's notice; occasionally it all ended in stone throwing. All of my friends were Protestants and although there were a couple of Catholic families on our estate, I wasn't friendly with them. I started to learn that Catholics were different from Protestants in a religious sense, that the Catholic priest was somebody who interceded between you and God and used your desire to speak to God, extract money and run your life, whereas Protestants were different, the basic Lutheran tenet being that every man was his own priest. Actually I think that from the point of view of an atheist, as I have since become, that's a progressive stance! In one step you can do away with God altogether; you don't have any priests to worry about! Nowadays I guess atheists would have therapists instead of priests.

When I was a child I was absolutely gung ho for Orangeism. I loved the Twelfth of July parades, but even better than that was the Eleventh night bonfire. My mate and I were the main instigators of the bonfire in our street. During the Easter school holiday break we would start collecting wood so that we would have the biggest bonfire. We went out cutting down trees. It was desperate really how many trees we destroyed in that neighbourhood just so we could have these huge bonfires, huge green bonfires! I loved loyalist songs, loved the drumming and the kick the pope bands, the rhythms and the dancing. I remember linking arms and dancing with a crowd down the streets singing: 'There's not a man like the Reverend Paisley, no not one', the first time I had heard the name, maybe 1965. I don't remember the song now; it was something like: 'Gerry Fitt knows all about our troubles; we will fight 'til the day is done'. Nowadays if I have people staying with me over the Twelfth I might take them down to the parades and of course, intellectually and politically, I see them for what they really are, but sometimes I still think it would be fabulous to switch off, let the body take over and go dancing down the street with them.

My parents were, in effect, atheists although they would never have described themselves as such and they didn't attend church. My mother did believe that the church should be supported and she paid money to a fund so that the Presbyterians could build a church beside the estate. I think my father was Moravian originally but he had no interest in it whatsoever. He was a nihilist really, hated institutions of any description. He'd joined the Orange Order for three months in his youth; he hated them – he was in the painters and decorators union – he hated them; he had an antipathy towards the ruling classes which was in no way thought out. He was what I would call a 'natural' socialist now.

Anyway, I was sent to the Presbyterian Sunday school and I also went to the Baptist church which used to drive a bus around the estate, round the kids up, steal them and bring them down for their Sunday school. I liked that. I liked the Bible and I liked the stories and I liked to win the prizes. Sunday schools were run by young local women who would have been friends of my big sisters. They were women I really liked. It was all very nice, very easy, not at all hell fire and damnation.

One thing though which set my family apart from other families in the estate was that we were a very bookish household. Everybody read all the time; we were just wild about books. That and a love of rock music broke me out of the mould. We had an excellent mobile library; incredible the books you could find there. I read *The Female Eunuch* at 17 and was just astounded, blown away by it, *Playpower* by Richard Neville, the Oz Trials, all the revolutionary student books. I think somebody must have been feeding these books into West Belfast! You can imagine how I rapidly began thinking about becoming a hippy.

I left school with 6 'O' levels. I knew it was nothing, but my parents were so proud of me. In those days what you did then was to try for the civil service, a job for life and indoors in the winter. That's what I did. It was 1969 and the British army was expanding and taking on civilian workers. I began work as a clerk doing audits of stores, which meant going out to all the barracks and counting everything from tanks to vests, checking books, ammunition. There were all sorts of shenanigans going on of course, but you had to count everything; every shot that was fired had to be accounted for and a piece of paper signed by an officer.

That's when I finally became a hippy. I was working in army headquarters with long hair and frayed jeans with bells, but it didn't matter; it was the civil service; once you were in they never sacked you, just kept on asking me if I wouldn't clean myself up. It was also the first time that I met Catholics of my own age from places like Cupar Street and Ballymurphy. I was working in the Imperial Civil Service, quite different from the ordinary civil service, and they had no time for discrimination. They took on two Protestants for every Catholic. Catholics got jobs and they got promotion. It was a strange time really; there were Catholics working there who would be on the barricades by night and working for the army by day and no one seemed to have a problem with it!

The first hint I had of what was happening politically in Northern Ireland was Burntollet. The *Daily Mirror* covered it on its front page, the second page, the third page and the centre spread had the most vivid photographs. It shocked me. The British army headquarters had a damned good library which I used a lot, partly for the books and partly because the librarian was gorgeous and I had fallen in love with her. I read the pamphlet *Burntollet* there, read other pamphlets and books and began to see the justice of the case being made by the Northern Ireland Civil Rights Association.

But although I started to understand it, I didn't get involved. I didn't seem to feel it was part of me. By then I had moved out of Suffolk, taken a flat in the University area of the city, was getting into drugs and pot power and all of those new ideas of the late sixties. To me, local politics seemed Neanderthal compared to the changes that were happening in the world. Nowadays when I look back, I can see that what was happening in the Catholic community and part of the Protestant intelligentsia was integral to what was happening in the world. I can also see that the same changes and ideas were not happening in the Protestant community.

After three years with the British army, I left Northern Ireland with a group of friends to live in a commune in Lancashire and rapidly became politicised with the ideas of the women's liberation movement, the gay political movement in Manchester and all of the non-aligned socialist/ anarchist groups like the Anti-Nazi League. This was class politics, something I could understand, something that I thought was important. In contrast, Northern Irish politics was a dinosaur.

That I became politicised in England is something that I have always thought relevant to this particular book that you are working on. During the time I worked for the army I often visited the Republic of Ireland. I had a great time there but I found it entirely different from the North of Ireland, whereas Lancashire was not and I had no problems fitting in. Like Belfast, it had been part of the Industrial Revolution, a culture which was within my blood and bones. I had no difficulty understanding the Peterloo Massacre or the Tolpuddle Martyrs, even though I wasn't taught their history at school, whereas Dublin was a colourful miasma of Irishness which wasn't something that I could understand. Perhaps if I had been brought up a Catholic then there would have been lots of ways through music and literature that I would be able to make connections with the rest of Ireland. I never had any of that and therefore, when it came to radical politics, what made the difference for me was the British link.

But that changed. After four years in Lancashire I found that I was gravitating towards Irish bars. I started to learn to play the bodhran. One day I turned round in a pub in Oldham and saw one of my childhood friends from Suffolk. He'd been living in Oldham for as long as I had but I hadn't realised. The last time I had known him he had been a militant loyalist and a member of the UVF. Now he was sitting in the corner listening to diddlidee music and talking to an old fella from Kerry. He too had gravitated to Irish bars for the same reason as I had. He was a paddy as far as the English were concerned. In some strange way, even given all that I said about the industrial revolution, he found it easier like me to be himself in an Irish bar even with people who were predominantly from the Republic – indeed from the West of Ireland; they didn't even have urban backgrounds; these were your country weirdos! I guess that is something that republicans here are relying on; sooner or later they hope that people will see and feel, not just that we are all commonly rejected by the English as being Irish, but that in fact we are Irish and that we have more in common than we have in difference.

I came back to Ireland and studied Irish History at Queen's University and began to work in a library. I can see now what has happened in Ireland, understand it and see my place in it. I ended up going back to live in Suffolk for two or three years around the time of the hunger strike. I managed to live in that community but I did find it stifling. The only bar to go for a drink was the British Legion where you would hear all the sectarian stuff; there wasn't any debate; if people had other ideas they kept them to themselves. It wasn't long before I was running across the road to Lenadoon, the Catholic estate, looking for discussions and having arguments which I couldn't have survived in my own community.

It seems to me that there is a situation where the Catholic community in Northern Ireland is catholic in the broadest sense of the word. It leaves room for different sorts of lifestyles and different ways of seeing the world. That's not to say that you can be a loyalist and live on the Falls Road, but there's room for the widest range and types of people; there's room for intellectuals, there's room for Protestants to live on the Falls

Road. In contrast the Protestant community is monolithic. It's also more individualistic, which can feed into the conservatism and right-wing ideology of loyalism. It does narrow down to that old saying that you are either with us or you are against us. It's arguably a very good political position to have and has worked well to date. Dig in, be defensive, don't negotiate. People don't question because once you begin to question, you are on the rocky road. If they do start to question they bail out, go to England, America, Australia, New Zealand. Protestants who begin to question the prevailing ideology break out of their community in a way which doesn't happen in the Catholic community.

I didn't want to live any more in a working class loyalist district which was a real problem for me because I had lived in working class districts for most of my life and that was where I felt comfortable. I didn't really want to live in a Catholic working district either, so I moved out to a village in the country, miles away from anywhere, although interestingly it was a Catholic village. I didn't consider living in a Protestant village.

I think for the unionist body politic to survive as a unit, certainly if it wants to have power, because it hasn't got any at the minute or very little, it has to be inward looking; it has to dig in; it has to be conservative. All of this makes up the whole. For Ireland to be a place in which the unionist community could exist would mean that it would have to become a secular state. That's an enormous change. Arguably the unionists could hold the dyke against a united Ireland for another couple of decades, but I think that, given the ceasefires, this is their best chance to get a settlement. For me the best ultimate future would be some sort of united Ireland, although I've no idea how we could actually construct one which would work. It would require radical transformation across every aspect of society.

People I know castigate me for having far too anthropological an attitude to what is happening here. I'm inclined to study what's happening rather than taking a position on it. I'm a fence sitter. Certainly I am not a unionist, but at the same time I am not a nationalist. I'm like a lot of people knocking around Belfast all doing interesting things. I'm disenfranchised, a non-aligned socialist and I haven't got any place to go with it.

24

Post Office Worker

Born 1959.

My father was working in England during the war when he met my mother. She was from a Welsh mining village, from that hard line Labour tradition and a confirmed atheist, and he was from the Shankill Road. When the war ended, they settled in Highfield, a working class estate in Protestant West Belfast, which was where I was born. My father would have described himself as a socialist, having been influenced by the general swing to the left in British society after the war ended. A Labour government was elected in a landslide victory and here at home, the Northern Ireland Labour Party were doing very well at the polls. He worked in the naval air yard in Belfast, overhauling and maintaining the naval jets. The naval air yard had its own Orange lodge which he was expected to join. I think it's one of those many contradictions within the Protestant working class that someone who describes themselves as a socialist nevertheless joins a sectarian organisation.

When I was three and a half we emigrated to South Africa and I have some stark memories of that time. We only stayed for three years because my parents were uncomfortable with the regime and were shocked by the racism that they found there. My mother was uncomfortable ordering black men and women around. She'd been a nanny in England and it was difficult for her when the roles were reversed. Then my father suffered a nasty industrial accident and part of his foot had to be amputated. There wasn't much of a welfare state in South Africa, even for white workers, so for a time we lived in poverty. When my older brother reached the age when he was to be drafted into military service, we left and came back to Belfast.

I was six when we returned home to live with my grandmother on the Shankill. It was a typical two-up, two-down house with an outside toilet and very overcrowded, with my grandmother, my uncle, my aunt and ourselves, a family of five living there. At that time the area was undergoing redevelopment and we were eventually rehoused on the outskirts of East Belfast in Tullycarnet. Nowadays Tullycarnet is a hard line estate, but at that time it was newly built, an unknown quantity. My father got his old job back at the naval air yard, probably through discrimination; I think he was aware of that. This time, though, he refused to join the Orange Order. South Africa had broadened his horizons and that was the end of his involvement with that sort of loyalism. He still voted unionist, still preferred the link with Britain, the welfare state, the health service, the education system. He had an inbred fear of the southern Irish state and was afraid of the Catholic church and of Catholic domination and really I think he had a point. I think it is dangerous and wrong to look at the history of Ireland or of this state of Northern Ireland in purely sectarian terms because I think that people have much more complex influences on them. There was a class consciousness there too. I can remember my father telling me about the men gathering on the street corners of the Shankill during the 1930s Outdoor Relief Movement to defend the Falls Road from the police. Like most people, my father was trapped by his background, but he knew he was trapped and that it wasn't a satisfactory situation.

Life on the Tullycarnet estate during my teens was dominated by loyalism. It was the time of the Tartan gangs with the UDA youth running down the street in uniforms interrogating people. They were playing games to some degree because Tullycarnet was on the outskirts of East Belfast, a huge Protestant bloc in itself, and so there was no threat from nationalists at all. There were band marches and UDA marches but I never involved myself in any of it. Once I suggested that I might join a band but my mother wouldn't allow it. To her the band members were thugs; it wasn't the sort of group which respectable working class people joined. Looking back, I think that at that time the loyalist paramilitaries attracted people as much for their radicalism as for their sectarianism. They were exciting, they were clashing with the police quite often, they were seen as these mysterious romantic figures who challenged the state and challenged authority. By comparison, organisations like the Orange

Order or the Unionist Party had little attraction for young people; they were organisations for old people, a joke really. A couple of kids would have been frogmarched to church, but in general the church had very little impact on the estate. I didn't attend myself.

Up until I was about 15 I would have mouthed sectarianism, but by then the ideas of loyalism were starting to ebb for me. I started mixing with Catholics from the Ards Peninsula when I went to the Technical College in Newtownards. By then I was beginning to question the sectarian divide. I think it was different for me. I wasn't living on the edge of a bubbling sectarian feud. Like I said, it was a massive Protestant bloc with no threat from Catholics. Years later, when I went canvassing in East Belfast, I noticed that difference. Even though it was a unionist area, there was not the same deep sectarian mistrust as there is, say, on the Shankill, because people have had a fairly quiet life and the brunt of the 'troubles' has escaped them.

I became an apprentice fitter in the shipyard. At that time I was involved in the same things that everyone else was involved in, getting drunk mostly. There was a group of us, Protestants and Catholics, who would go to the Pound Club where they had rock music, go down to Dublin or across to Scotland where I came into contact with left-wing ideas. I remember I bought Lenin badges and wore them into the shipyard. I got into rows with the older guys in the shipyard who thought this was all communist, republican nonsense. I remember one of them telling me not to push it too far or I could end up at the bottom of the dry dock, but on the whole I was generally tolerated. I had a real thirst for ideas and began reading books out of Tullycarnet Library; it's amazing what you can find in that library; and there was a bookshop in Newtownards where I got books on Irish history. A friend of mine, a Catholic from Portaferry, was a republican and I would discuss ideas with him. The Officials interested me because at that time they had called off their armed struggle and they seemed to me to be the only group who were socialists. I think if my friend had put me in touch with the Officials I might have joined them, but he was more sympathetic towards the Provisionals and I considered them to be sectarian. Not that I really had any objection to armed campaigns as such; I can remember from when I was 16 or 17 defending people's right to use violence to try and change society. At that time my ideas were very immature. Looking back, the Officials would have been a huge leap for a Protestant from an area like mine to join. I've since learnt that in the area where I am living now there was a Fianna branch which was 70 percent Catholic and 30 percent Protestant at that time, but then this area is a patchwork of Protestant and Catholic areas. The Officials were attracting Protestant youth, but not from where I lived.

I didn't get into any real trouble at the shipyard, but there were two incidents that distressed me. One was on 11th July when I was working in ship repair. On that day the flutes are out playing Orange songs, people are getting drunk and nobody works. There was one Catholic standing at the lathe working. Never mind the issues, never mind who is right and who is wrong, it was terrible the way he was so isolated. I would have liked to have said to him that not all Protestants thought the same way, but I wouldn't have known how to approach him; it was so out of my experience. The other time was when a brother of a friend of mine was killed in an industrial accident. The men were lifting a section of a ship into the dry dock and one of the welding lugs snapped. It swung and decapitated him. One of the shipyard workers asked who had died and when they told him he said. 'Fuck, that's only a fenian'. That shocked me, not just the sectarianism, but the utter barbarity that anybody could react to a workmate's death like that.

I packed in my apprenticeship and went off with a group of friends bumming around Europe and eventually ending up in Bristol. There were big riots there at the time and it was like a home from home; but in retrospect it was a waste of time for me, a reaction to not being able to find anything back home that reflected my ideas. I went to the political fringes, went to meetings of the Bristol anarchists, went on anti-nuclear demonstrations, legalise cannabis demonstrations. After a few years I decided to come home.

I arrived back in Tullycarnet and met up with my old friends. What was very noticeable was that those of my friends who were quite radical when I left, those who would have challenged authority and been rebellious, had all succumbed to the same pressures as my father had. They were more loyalist, more unionist in their outlook. I think it is very difficult to maintain ideas either in Catholic or Protestant areas that are different from the ideas that surround you. I think as well that when one is surrounded by the sectarian murder campaign and paramilitaries ruling the area then it is virtually impossible to speak out. I was talking to a social worker recently who had met women from loyalist areas and he said he felt they were showing signs of mental illness. When he got to talk to them he realised that they were not comfortable with the ideas dominating their area. They were isolated. They couldn't talk to people about how they felt. They were unable to express their views. He felt that they had started to demonstrate symptoms of mental illness because of it. Looking back, I think I was lucky to leave the North when I did.

I decided to have another look around to see if there was any way to express my politics. Funnily enough I went back to have a look at the Official Republican movement again. It's quite amusing in retrospect. A lot had changed by then, but I really didn't know how reformist they had become and how much they were into gangsterism. It was probably a stupid thing to do but I got a bus up the Falls Road, went into their party headquarters and told them that I was a Protestant from Tullycarnet and wanted to join. The next thing I knew I was taken upstairs to be interviewed by one of their most prominent members. That shocked me; why would he be interviewing some wee guy off the street? Maybe it was because I was a Protestant, maybe it was because who wants to join the Workers' Party anyway! He wasn't keen on me joining. I realised that from a distance they had appeared to me to be revolutionary; they were selling the literature of Marx and Lenin, but then when I talked to him, he was explaining how they were going to take power in Ireland through becoming the majority party in the Dáil. No harm to him, but it seemed a long way off to me. To give them credit, they were trying to build cross community links and it takes a brave person to go onto the Shankill and canvass for the Workers' Party. Anyway, when I said that I had thought they were a Marxist organisation and were out to change society, he told me that he thought I would be better joining a Trotskyist organisation. I stuck with it, said I wanted to join, and I was told I would have to go through six Saturdays of education classes. They said they would contact me and I gave them my name and address. They must not have had any education classes since because that was the last I heard from them.

I did finally find what I was looking for. I went along to a meeting in Belfast to hear Peter Taafe speak. He had just been expelled from the British Labour Party. On the platform were Belfast members of Militant and Nimrod Sejaki, a South African political exile who had been charged with treason with Mandela and jailed. He had helped to build the steel workers' union in South Africa. I had always had the impression that Militant sold papers on street corners but not a lot else, and the meeting lifted the organisation in my estimation. They took my name and address on the way out and contacted me a few days later. I joined within a few weeks. For me, I would still say that Militant is the only organisation which unites, although not in large numbers, Protestant and Catholic workers in a socialist organisation. There are plenty of other groups which unite Protestants and Catholics but not politically, not on the ideas of socialism.

I started to work in the East Belfast branch and began to meet the same sort of people that I had grown up with. It was a relief to me to meet painters and decorators and ex-shipyard workers who had been convinced by the argument for a socialist Ireland, people who were not put off by a united Ireland if it was attached to the ideas of socialism. The organisation is predominantly Catholic, but there is a sizable minority of Protestants. That's what convinced me that I had made the right choice.

After the signing of the Anglo-Irish Agreement it became more difficult for me to live in a Protestant area. There was a dramatic change in atmosphere, with people being forced out of their areas. By then I had married a girl from a Catholic background and was living in Wheatfield, a UDA-dominated area. There was one particular incident which convinced me to move out. In the flat below us lived a Protestant who was connected to the UVF. He was quite left-wing and a member of the Trades Council. Anyway he fell out of favour with the UDA and one night we were lying in bed when we heard a hammering. The UDA were slegehammering his door down and then we heard him squealing like a pig. They broke his hip, his legs, his arms, fractured his skull; it was a really terrible beating. I thought, if this is what they are doing to people connected to loyalist paramilitaries who are left-wing, then they are not going to take too kindly to someone who is married to an ex-Catholic, is involved in an organisation that has Catholic members and believes in a socialist Ireland. We moved out right away and have lived in a Catholic area ever since.

There is a distinct difference living in a Catholic area. There is not much overt sectarianism towards Protestants, although I challenge the idea that Catholics aren't sectarian. If you dig deep enough you'll find as much sectarianism, but nevertheless it is a more tolerant community. I have had no problems living and working in a Catholic area.

For a period Protestant areas were closed off to me. I still had family living there and my brother has been asked a few pointed questions about me in the past; not that I ever thought there was any danger of my family being affected. I can remember from my early youth up the Shankill a family who lived across the road from us. One of their sons joined the Provisional IRA and moved up to Ligoniel. They would have killed him if he had come into the area but the family weren't touched. In fact I remember his mother had a very nasty accident and the scandal of the time was that he had dared to come down, walk in and visit and walk out again. Fair play to him, I wouldn't have done that, but it never put his family under any threat. Loyalists can be extreme but they aren't that extreme.

I think changes are happening in Protestant areas. Since the ceasefire the overwhelming number of young people that have been drawn towards Militant have been Protestant youths. They are still a minority but there are people who are looking for alternatives to unionism. People still have to be careful about their safety. Loyalists can manipulate the ideas of socialism, equate them with republicanism and stamp them out. It's not so much that they necessarily believe that socialism equals republicanism themselves; it's just an open opportunity for them to stamp out any opposition in their area. Before the ceasefire it was difficult to hold people; we could attract them but we couldn't hold them; that's not the case now.

To me it is ridiculous to think that a socialist could be hostile to ordinary British people or ordinary people in the Republic of Ireland. I don't think it is possible to be a socialist unionist or a socialist nationalist. I think that for working class unionists here their identity is one of being British workers not just of British nationality. The empathy that many Protestant workers here would have for, say, the British miners or the loyalty to British based unions isn't a negative thing; those links should be strengthened as well as links, for example, through the Irish Congress of Trade Unions, with workers in the South.

For me the socialist tradition is an international tradition. Socialism is inconceivable for me if it is to have borders between peoples or eventually even separate national states. I believe a socialist Ireland is our only hope for the future. I also believe that in Northern Ireland socialism is a third, sometimes obscured, tradition.

25

Eleanor Rogers
Student. Born 1978.

I grew up surrounded by local sectarian Protestant groups in Belfast but I never fell into any of them. At school that was by choice, but at home it was accidental. The area that I have lived in all my life has changed over the years from being mixed to predominantly Catholic and so most of my friends in the street were Catholics. I think that when you are young, fighting over territory is like a game. I've seen Protestant kids play with Catholic kids in my street and then they would both organise attacks on Catholics who live on the other side of the bridge. As you grow older it becomes more than just a game.

I went to a state school which was situated on my mother's route to work. It's in an area where a lot of students live. The school's intake was mostly Protestant and a lot of the children came from liberal middle class backgrounds but there were a few Catholics from the local area. There was also a high percentage of children from single-parent families. I was in a crowd of about eight, and there was only two of us who had both parents living at home. More unusual, I think, was the policy of the Belfast Education and Library Board who sent non-English speakers to the school. There was always a child in my class who was from Africa or Asia and who couldn't speak English at all.

At the time I was there the local school for the Donegall Pass area, Porters, was closing down. It operated from P1 to P3 and then the kids arrived at our school in P4. Donegall Pass is a staunch loyalist area and the kids from Porters were real wee Protestant hoods, going around asking if you were a 'prod' or a 'taig', bullying everyone and generally being sectarian. Not all of them behaved that way of course, but the ones that did we classified as 'Porters kids'. A lot of the sectarianism was unknowing in the sense that they just thought Protestants beat up on Catholics.

By the time I was in my last year at primary school there weren't so many Catholics, so the fight was between the non-sectarians and the Protestant bigots. Not that we called ourselves non-sectarian or used words like bigots; we just didn't like the Porters kids and we fought back. We used to have big fights in the playground and for control of Botanic Gardens where the Porters kids beat up local Catholics.

Our teacher thought that education was all about how to read and write, be nice to people and not break windows. The last point was just as important as the first. She did all this through placing a great emphasis on religion, Protestant style. If you do something bad God will be cross with you, therefore you have to do good things. She was replaced by another teacher who wasn't religious and certainly didn't see social issues as part of his job profile. He was there to get as many children to pass the 11+ as possible. Consequently the school got much, much rougher.

There were exceptions which, looking back, I think are quite interesting. We had a girl from Dundalk in our class who had come up to live in Belfast. On her first day at school the teacher put a nice girl who wouldn't be sectarian and whose parents came from a middle class area in charge of her. Come break time the girl from Dundalk is cornered by the Porters kids wanting to know if she was a fenian. Of course she didn't know what one was. Was she a taig? She didn't know what that was either. She asked the nice girl what the words meant. When she found out they meant Catholic, well, there is nothing wrong with being a Catholic, so she said 'yes'. That should have signalled a campaign against her as a southern Catholic, but the catch was that one of the Porters kids fancied her so he defended her the whole way through primary school.

There was this phrase kids in my school used which my mother thought was very funny. It was 'half caste' which, I was told, comes from India. The kids in my school said you were a half caste if you were half Protestant, half Catholic. I have never actually heard the phrase out of primary school; perhaps it was because there were so many children there from different ethnic backgrounds. At the time I had two close friends, one was Catholic and one was a 'half caste'. My friend and I were jealous of the 'half caste' because she was both, though she always saw herself as a Catholic, politically though not in a religious sense. We didn't understand the political connotation of a lot of issues, but even as small children we slid into a point of view.

By the time I reached Methody my basic education as far as Catholics and Protestants was complete. Methody didn't influence my views half as much as my primary school did. Methody was full of liberal middle class Protestants who all got on with Catholics in as much as they had ever met them. Naturally they were non-sectarian; that's easy if you don't grow up in the front line, but they never did anything about it. All my friends were in the Christian Union, which drove me bananas. In primary school religion was taken for granted; people went to church; it didn't mean anything; it was part of people's social background. When I hit Methody, I discovered all these evangelicals for whom God was life. What frustrated me about the Christians was that they had great ideas about wanting the world to be a better place but then they went away and prayed about it. They never actually did anything! They attended this event called Manifest, which was when I realised that the Christian Union at Methody really was liberal in comparison to these other terribly repressive and right-wing Christian Unions from places like Bangor. None of them, and there were hundreds who attended Manifest, would ever accept that there were problems between Catholics and Protestants. Actually, once I went to a meeting when one of them got up and said he thought there was a problem and that everyone had to evangelise Catholics. I think most people realised that this wasn't on, but still they just couldn't bring themselves to do cross-community work.

The History course in Methody went like this. In first year it was the Kings and Queens of England from Henry VII to James I. Of course that included the abolition of the monasteries, which much amused me because I had just learnt the refrain 'Don't speak of the alien minister nor his church without meaning or faith; The foundation stone of his temple is the bollocks of Henry VIII' – and took great pleasure in reciting it to everybody. Second year was the Great Plague, the Fire of London and the Mayflower. That included a one-liner about Cromwell visiting Ireland. I was vaguely aware that Cromwell had done more than visit Ireland but I wasn't really sure until one of my best friends who was a Dublin Methodist and had studied Cromwell at primary school down South told me that he murdered Irish people. Of course we were doing what a great reformer Cromwell and how wonderful he was parliamentary-wise. Third year was the Wild West and the Industrial Revolution. If you did GCSE History you went on to an in-depth study of Germany during the wars, America in the twentieth century, and medicine through time. I went on to do A level, Great Powers in Europe in the twentieth century, and an in-depth study of the Ulster Crisis 1906-1920. So, if you stuck it right through to A level, you got to do local history.

I remember the 'A' level teacher asking the class what happened in 1690: everyone in class knew; then, what happened in 1798: one person knew; then what happened in 1916: three out of 24 knew. We started studying how Protestants reacted to the political events of 1892, 1910, 1912 and their siege mentality. A strange thing happened. No one could understand why the Protestants reacted in the way that they did. I was surrounded by Protestants who react that way now but couldn't understand why Protestants did it in an historical context; they couldn't understand why they all got so worked up about it!

The ideal Methody pupil is a liberal first and foremost. Now, it can be on the conservative side of liberal. That is the way the Methodists see themselves in the Protestant church; they're liberal, they're interested in social conditions. The ideal Methody voter should really vote Alliance, though in actual fact most of them would vote Official Unionist. The DUP is anathema and there is no room for nationalists, even though Catholics make up a fifth of the school population. This was epitomised for me when I attended the Upper School Senior Prize Day. It's a big event. Dignitaries come to it. We all learn songs to sing and then there is the school song sung in Latin – 'O Magnificent pile' – which is how the school is described in the translation. Suddenly the National Anthem was playing, which completely threw me. It didn't occur to me that we would have the National Anthem played at Senior Prize Day. My Catholic friends brushed it off saying they didn't care or it's a Protestant school, these things happen if you go to a Protestant school; but a number of us made complaints about it. The next year they didn't play it. They dropped it three months before Queen's University, possibly because of the complaints that were made.

Once a week we would take the school bus over to Ravenhill and play games. It wasn't far from where I lived so I used to walk home through the Ormeau Park. I'd meet the Catholic kids getting out at the same time; sometimes they didn't notice me and my school uniform, other times they would shout at me, though not necessarily in a sectarian way. A couple of times I was attacked. One time I kicked a wee fella so hard my shoe came off and landed about 5 metres away. He was smaller than me and he started to howl and throw stones and there was a whole gang of them attacking me. It always made me feel nervous, walking through the park. One day after the ceasefires were announced I was walking home and I saw three boys in their Catholic school uniforms. I knew I was going to hit the junction in the path at the same time as they did and I would have to dodge round them. The looked at me as I walked past but didn't say anything. Then I heard one of them yell and I turned round. He put his fingers up and said 'Peace, man'.

I was introduced to Militant through a friend I'd known from primary school. I had never heard about Militant Labour before. My family were all various shades of left. My father, who is English, was in the Communist Party in Britain in the thirties and forties but never affiliated to any political party when he came to Belfast. My brother had been in People's Democracy and Troops Out in London and my mother had joined the NILP in 1970 just before it collapsed and they were all arguing with each other. Her view was be a socialist but don't join anything. The only left-wing group which I knew existed was the British and Irish Communist Organisation because one of my father's drinking partners was in it. He was always arguing as well, so my impression of the left-wing was that it was a lot of people fighting with each other. Anyway, I went to a meeting. What surprised me was that everyone in Militant thinks it is an organisation for oldies; they don't have enough young people in it. Now most people in Militant are in their thirties and in my experience, I'd always thought anyone involved in politics was at least 50!

The first question I asked was what other left-wing groups are there in Belfast and do you get on with them. Then I wanted to know if you could be in the party and disagree; was there an ordinary level of democracy in it. I found out that there was. I'm not so sure that I believe in a revolution like so many in Militant do, but to me that's not important. It's hypothetical. I wanted to join them because of the work they are doing on social issues – saving the National Health Service and campaigning for the unemployed. I was asked what I thought of the border and I always try to be very honest about my feelings. Logically I feel that if

Ireland is unified the fighting will continue, but still I would like to live in a united Ireland. I'm more sympathetic to nationalism. Dublin is just a train journey away from Belfast; we have a lot in common, whereas I have been to England and the English are not like us at all. Even Northern Ireland Protestants don't like the English; in fact I've only ever met one who did!

I think everyone has a need to believe that our society can change for the better and that is what I have learnt through being in Militant. Society can and does change eventually.

26
Unemployed Youth

Born 1978.

My first impressions of Belfast when we moved here were of dull streets, kids hanging around or raking about, a place where I never fitted in and felt isolated because of my accent. I got a kicking because, when asked my religion, I said I was Anglican Catholic. We were always called that in the Church of England. My mum, who is from Belfast, explained to me that I had to say I was a Protestant; so I said I was a Protestant, became accepted and made friends. Gradually I learned that the way to mix was by joining organisations. First of all I joined an Orange flute band where I played the cymbals and I later went on to join the Junior Orange Lodge. All you did was walk. I carried a big Union Jack all around Bangor, which was exhausting for an eight year old. Then I joined the Boys' Brigade; it was more marching around the hall, it was rubbish. After that I joined various youth clubs more orientated around sport and then, when I was 12, I became an army cadet with the Royal Irish Regiment. My father was a British soldier, but when my mum decided to live in Belfast they split up and I didn't see him anymore. I joined the army cadets as a boy soldier; it was a way to look up to my father even though he wasn't there.

I went to the Free Presbyterian Church because everyone else did. They used to come round on a bus and ring a bell and everyone would jump on the bus and go over to Paisley's church. I went for the bags of sweets they used to give out. If you did something good or if you quoted from the Bible, they would give you sweets and prizes and colouring books, or if you said, 'I've hurt my thumb', then they would say, 'Oh, he's hurt his thumb; God will heal it; here is a bag of sweets'. As I got older I didn't like colouring-in books anymore so I stopped going.

School was cool. The primary school I went to was mixed. That was when I first made my Catholic friends and invited them home. Secondary school was cool too. I was the best fighter in the school and we had wee gangs to beat up first years. It was a Protestant school; there were a few bigots but most of the pupils were broad-minded.

My mother believed that Catholics were the same as us and that they lived the same type of life that we did, but my friends in the area where we lived were all into this religious divide stuff so she couldn't expect me not to get involved with it all. I joined the Young Citizens Volunteers, the youth wing of the UVF. There were loads of youth around and the UVF were into young people getting into fights, stuff like that, stealing even. We'd go up to the Mournes now and again and the men would come down with the guns and we would do a bit of shooting practice, bit of night shooting, clean the guns before they took them back to Belfast. They have the crappiest weapons ever, I tell you. Some of them were home-made and they would fall apart in my hands. In the army cadets we had the big L98s, high-powered rifles with sights which are single fire, like the SA80s the soldiers carry. In the Young Citizens Volunteers we would be presented with these old rusty things and you would go, 'Where's the trigger?', you know, 'What button do you pull?' If anyone saw you practising in the Mourne Mountains you just ran, but then the mountains are a very big place; there are a lot of isolated areas where nobody goes; chances are that you would never be found.

The UVF made us feel very patriotic. They told us that we were British, that we wanted to stay British and that we were fighting for our country. They said that the IRA were attacking Protestants and attacking our people on the British mainland. They told us that when we were 18 they would put us straight into the UVF, into the ranks and not with the foot soldiers. They would give us money and you know, £30 once in a while is a lot to someone who is still at school or can't get the dole; it helps the message to sink in. We would go to a pub in Bangor with about six of them and six of us, £300 would be put on the table and everybody would sit and get drunk and smoke cigarettes and you didn't have to pay for a thing. They spoiled us to keep us. I could go anywhere I wanted, any Protestant area in Northern Ireland, and just by mentioning their name nobody would touch me; if anything they would take me out and get me hammered, get me drunk. It was like an unofficial army cadet force. We had rank and meetings and paid duties. I found that it also gave me a position of power in the hierarchy of the community. People would come to me if they had problems and expect me to go and tell my superiors.

I left the Youth Citizens Volunteers because I got a Catholic girlfriend. I got a beating for that and I just thought to myself that's that, it's over. Nobody ever touted on me and I had a clean record with the police. I always managed to get away, broke my ankle once but I got away. I got a few broken teeth from the beating but that was all. I've friends outside the area now and I'm glad to be out of it.

I had my own personal views on politics but I couldn't really articulate them. It was more a belief that Catholics were the same as us. When I started to go out to pubs and met more people, talked to them and got drunk with them, I'd think that they lived just around the corner and I was shocked sometimes to learn they were from the Falls Road. I didn't start thinking politically, just started to think about people and how Catholics really weren't that different. I was against sectarianism because of what I had seen. I didn't agree with beating the hell out of Catholics and I was against the racism I had seen which was directed towards the Chinese and Asian communities. In 1994 I went to a gig organised by an anti-sectarian youth group. They had invited a heavy metal band to play and I was into that, so I went along. I went with the flow, joined the group and paid my £1.00 membership.

Then I promptly went off and joined Her Majesty's forces. That wasn't much fun. I left about three months later; it was just too hard. I guess the boy soldier didn't grow up to be a real soldier. It was unbelievable getting up at 5.30 in the morning and running about, so regimented, so disciplined; I just couldn't hack it. I was still only 16 and I missed my home comforts. Of course I got called a paddy but I used to say, 'I'm not a paddy; I was born in England; my father lives up the road', so they called me the English Paddy.

I missed Belfast, missed the Belfast life, missed knowing where to walk and where not to walk. It was too nice in England. I missed the feeling in the air, like when you go down to Dublin and the tension just goes and then as soon as you get back over the border you can just feel it, you know you are home. I missed that.

I went to an international youth camp and there were a couple of seminars on socialism. I got talking to a few of the organisers and I couldn't really disagree with anything they said. I thought maybe this was what I was trying to articulate for the last couple of years, that when I was thinking that Catholics were just the same as us, what I meant was that we were all working class people and that we should not be separated. It was just that I didn't realise it at the time.

I love reading but I had never read any Marx until I joined a socialist group. I was more into factual books, books about the SAS and Celtic mythology, which is interesting even if it is only mythology. The UDA use Cuchulain, because he guarded Ulster and they think of themselves as the new Cuchulain, the new guards who will defend Ulster from the rest of the Irish. At school we did a bit of Irish History but there was never any detail; we studied more about Nazi Germany and the American Wild West. Even after I joined the group I didn't read any Marx for a while because I wanted to learn more about 'the speak' [the language], before I started to read the books. I'd heard about Lenin and Trotsky, knew them just as names but didn't know who they were. I do now.

Sectarianism is the issue here. The British have divided and ruled and the politicians know that if there are divisions they will always come up trumps. The only way the people of Ireland can live together is if the working class, who are the biggest force, come together. I think identity is up to people themselves. When I was going with my girlfriend I tried to learn a bit of the Irish language. My friends in Dublin couldn't understand it because they hated having to learn the language but when I was at school I never got the chance; it was French or German not Irish. It was the same with sports. We played rugby, football and basketball; we didn't have the chance to play Gaelic football. I love Gaelic football; it's new to me. I think that if you say you are British, especially when you are abroad, people think you are English, but I realise that you can't coerce one side into a state that they don't want to be part of. If Catholics don't want to be part of the United Kingdom they have the right not to be but by the same token you can't force Protestants to be part of a united Ireland.

I would like to see a socialist workers' united Ireland, a workers' democracy with more grass roots democracy, not a state based on £100,000 a year politicians plus expenses. To me socialism is the only answer to the problems of Northern Ireland. Capitalism has given us war, loads of people in jail, loads of people dead; it didn't work. If you are a socialist you are an internationalist, a socialist for the whole world not just for one country, although your own country is a good place to start. I don't believe you can be a socialist and a unionist or a socialist and a nationalist. It's true that in the group we have more comrades from Catholic than Protestant backgrounds. The Catholics are easy listeners. You do find Protestants in areas who are broad-minded but then you find their friends are hard liners and they are afraid to speak out or be different. That's too general, of course, but in my experience that would be so.

I still live in a Protestant area and people think that because I am a socialist I am a Sinn Féiner but to me Sinn Féin are socialists when it suits them. They are very good with language, but they are concerned about just one section of the working class and to me that is sectarian; it carries on the division in our society. They painted a mural on the Falls Road just after the ceasefire. It was a pyramid of bricks with words painted on each brick. What was the one word which was missed out? Socialism! They want a united Ireland to try to get themselves into power, so what is the difference between them and Fianna Fáil and Fine Gael? They are still a capitalist party.

I was one of those people who liked to experiment and I have done a lot of experimenting in my 18 years, but I have stayed with socialism because it is something I believe in. Socialism and Liverpool Football Club that is! Socialism has broadened my horizons and through it, I started to understand the society I was living in. I think politically now, I think as a socialist.

The Republican Tradition

Within Sinn Féin no one has ever joked or commented on the fact that I am from a Protestant background. It's just not an issue within the movement; you're accepted because of your commitment to republicanism, not because of your religious background.

27

Sinn Féin Advice Worker

Born 1943.

I wasn't invited to the party in our street celebrating the coronation of Queen Elizabeth because my parents were members of the Northern Ireland Labour Party. I was ten years old and very annoyed about it at the time, although my parents made up for it by organising a special day for me. That was my first experience of difference, although generally in terms of growing up I did what everybody else did. All my mates were Protestants; they were loyalists; many of them later went on to join the British army. Perhaps I didn't take the Twelfth as seriously as my friends but I celebrated it; it was a great excuse for getting drunk! We all tried to join the junior Orange Lodge once, went off down the Newtownards Road to the Orange Hall. I just remember this huge wooden door and that it was locked and we were knocking to get in. Then a little hatch slid open. This man looked at us and asked us what the password was. We just fell about laughing. The only time we had ever seen a hatch open and someone ask for a password was in the movies, you know, when people were trying to get into a speakeasy.

My home life was different from my friends in the sense that it was not a loyalist or orange household. My father was always in the company of communists and trade unionists. He had made his own personal voyage which is perhaps a more interesting story than my own. He was born into a staunch unionist family and when he was 14, he went off to fight in World War One. The family managed to drag him back before he got on the boat but the army had already trained him, so he joined the UVF. I know that his duties included guarding big houses on the Lisburn Road in Belfast. After the War he became a sergeant in the A specials and was responsible for a team of Black and Tans. He used to tell us stories of how he had to maintain control by smashing them in the face with a rifle butt. He said that was the sort of language they understood. He was a driller in the shipyard and during the second World War he was posted to England where he got involved in labour politics and trade unionism. My mother had worked in the Poor House when she was young and had witnessed scenes of appalling poverty. That experience affected her deeply and throughout her life she felt the need to help the poor and contribute to the community.

Going to England at 17 to find work was a huge learning experience for me. Up until then I had been a typical only child. I was naïve. My parents had been very protective of me in the sense that I don't believe I knew how to boil an egg, let alone to look after myself. In those days in England looking for a flat took on a whole new meaning. It was very, very common to see notices saying, 'No Irish, No coloureds'. Whilst it took me a while to suss out what 'No Coloureds' meant, I was in no doubt that 'No Irish' referred to me. However I was very lucky to be employed in a large bookshop which was owned by Italians. It was there that I met an amazing variety of people – Greek, British Guyanese, Jewish, Australian, Irish, one of whom was a spoilt priest – I had never met a priest in my life before never mind a spoilt priest – and I began to read avidly, everything I could get my hands on, from poetry to politics. I got involved with CND and the anti-apartheid movement, went on demonstrations outside South Africa House, and I also met Francie McPeake, the folk singer, and started to knock about the folk scene, helping out organising concerts and small tours.

It's hard to look back and feel what you felt then but I do remember feeling very homesick. I came back and lived with my parents in East Belfast, got a job in a large printing works, but found myself socialising more and more at folk and traditional music sessions on the Falls Road. I think I drifted into things rather than made conscious decisions. I was mixing with students and civil rights campaigners who were very left-wing and when People's Democracy was founded it felt quite natural for me to join. I'd seen the appalling conditions that people lived with in the nationalist ghettos, both in Belfast and Derry. They were obviously being put down and I didn't see any difference between their calls for civil rights and those of blacks in America.

Although I joined People's Democracy I wasn't open about my politics. I was still working back in East Belfast. My mate and I used to joke that we were the only two genuine workers in People's Democracy, but joking aside, I always hung back at demonstrations. If anyone appeared with a camera I would have ducked so that my photo wasn't taken; God knows what trouble that would have created for me back in East Belfast. My parents were worried sick about me getting into trouble. They always thought that I was getting led astray whereas I always thought I was the one who would be leading people astray. Sometimes I'd talk to people at work. Obviously Catholics were supportive, but talking to your ordinary Prod is bloody hard. You'd get some who would agree with civil rights but they would be too afraid to speak out. They had quite an awful fear. One hears media commentators saying that people are afraid to speak out on both sides of the divide but I think there is more fear on the Protestant side because retribution tends to be violent and swift. They believe in the wrath of God, but we shouldn't forget that they believe in their own wrath as well.

A letter was hand delivered to me one Saturday morning. It had a bullet in it and a note to the effect that the next bullet was 'for you, you bastard'. It gave me a bit of a jolt at first and then I suppose I just couldn't believe that somebody was going to shoot me. I rationalised that if they were going to put the bullet in an envelope through the door then they weren't going to shoot me and I half suspected it was someone whom I had grown up with and had had a row with. Of course, I could have been totally wrong!

People were very frightened after internment and they erected barricades on the roads leading into the Falls. I remember I had a friend, a Catholic, who was very into music and offered his services as a disc jockey for Radio Free Belfast which was operating out of the Long Bar in Leeson Street. We met up one night in a pub and he invited me to join him. It was after midnight and we drove up the Grosvenor Road, parked the car and my mate shouted over to get into the Falls through the barricade. These barricades were over 20 feet high but there was a little door at the side for pedestrian access. The voice at the other side said

'Who are you?', and my mate gave his full name and explained he was going to do a show for Radio Free Belfast. The fella answered that he didn't know him and he wasn't getting in and then as an afterthought he asked, 'Who's that with you?' Now I have an awful Prod name, it's an obvious Prod name and I thought, 'This is going to be funny; we are definitely not going to get in here.' Anyway I gave my name and the voice at the other side said, 'Is that you, son?'. The door opened and I looked down and there was Francie McPeake who I had met in England; he's dead now. He told me I was lucky that he knew me and made a few threatening gestures with this thing he had in his hand. It was very dark and at first I wasn't too sure what it was. I looked at it and I just couldn't believe it. He had the shaft of a brush and attached to it with copper wire was a sword, a real sword. It was just like something from the French Revolution! I found that incredibly funny. Of course my mate was scundered; he was the well known disc jockey who couldn't get through the barricades and I was the Prod from East Belfast who was waved in.

The early seventies were heavy years and I felt there was an inevitability about the way events unfolded. On a personal level I had to be so careful about my movements. Travelling from West Belfast to East Belfast necessitated getting taxis, one from Catholic West Belfast to the university area which was mixed and where a friend lived, and then another from the university area to Protestant East Belfast. During the black out when there were no taxis I walked roundabout routes home. There wasn't any solution to it all. If I'd moved to West Belfast I would have had to give up my job. Some of my work mates were prominent in loyalist paramilitaries so I couldn't have an address on the Falls Road and still work there. At night I was mixing with prominent republicans in social clubs and because so many of my friends had been lifted, I started to worry that I would be lifted too. It was all getting too dicey and I decided to leave Belfast in 1974 and go to Dublin.

I drifted about in Dublin and came back to Belfast in 1980. This time I settled on the Falls Road. The hunger strike was happening and there was such anger on the streets. It hardened people's attitudes; certainly it hardened mine. I'd always believed that there is such a thing as justice and people who fought for justice would eventually get it because their cause was right. It doesn't always follow, if it ever does follow. The hunger strike made me realise, as I think it did many people, that we were going to have to fight bloody hard for justice. People did start fighting; they just raised the profile of everything.

I joined Sinn Féin and worked in the advice centre. It was a full time commitment and an amazing experience. Just after the hunger strike Sinn Féin opened a number of advice centres and all of them were very successful. There were so many issues that had to be dealt with. The centre was just full of people coming in with problems, problems, problems, problems.

I was asked to write for *An Phoblacht/Republican News* and went down to Dublin to meet people and see what the work would entail. I was amazed when I met the editor. He was an Irishman but he had lived a long time in England, which had resulted in an English accent, and then I met the sub-editor who was an Englishman and naturally had an English accent. There was me, delighted to be out of Belfast and away from English accents which were not quite so friendly! I took the job with *Republican News*, worked there a long time. It was quite hard work. I spent half the week in Dublin and half the week in Belfast, which led to an awful lot of stress for my family, but the work was great. The people I worked with were younger than me, very enthusiastic and very committed. I ended up doing the back page, 'The Flying Column', which was fun. I can remember writing a spoof story on a Belfast councillor and his supposed involvement with loyalist paramilitaries. After it was printed I was sitting in a club on the Falls Road and the paper sellers came in. Everybody used to turn to the back page first and I was very pleased when I saw everyone laughing and pointing to this story.

Working on the paper strengthened my republicanism. I was meeting people from all round the country and got a good idea of what was going on. The only time I was ever worried was when there was a statement from one of the loyalist paramilitary groups which mentioned that people involved in publicity would come under their attention. Of course at that time the identities of people working on the paper were secretive, more so than they are now.

Becoming interested in Irish culture and history and the Irish language was more gradual. I'd never learnt anything about Irish geography at school never mind Irish history and the cultural wealth I found did amaze me. Such a cultural wealth just doesn't exist in the unionist tradition at all; they only have lambeg drums and orange sashes; even their songs have no depth to them. Once I started to discover the language, the more I wanted to know and I've sent my children to Irish speaking schools. It's great to see people who still live in Protestant areas come up the Falls Road to learn Irish and delight in it in the same way as I did and it's such an easy step to take.

I had a few contacts with the Department of Education as part of a delegation seeking funding for schools teaching through the medium of Irish. We would be welcomed and given coffee and biscuits; they were very, very polite to us but it was amazing to see their underlying bigotry. Every obstacle was put in our way and there was no logical reason for them to do that. You would think the Department of Education would be there to encourage children to be educated no matter what language they would be learning through; you would assume an education would be the most important rationale for funding, but what it came down to was, 'You fenian bastards, you are not getting our money'. It took five years before the Meánscoil was funded. That's just a reflection of the whole strata in the North; when you are in control, it is easy to discriminate, whether it be through education or employment, so easy to keep people down and never give them encouragement. My daughter is now going to a state college in Belfast and on the first day the teacher was unable to read her name because it was written in Irish. My daughter said her name but the teacher's attitude was not one of apology at being unable to pronounce it, or saying that his incapability to do so would be rectified as soon as possible. It was: 'I've never come across anything like this before'. My daughter thinks she might be the only nationalist in the class but maybe not; maybe it's not that bad!

I still live on the Falls Road. I feel very much a part of this community. I love my neighbours who made me so welcome and made it easy for me to fit in. People accepted me for who I am. You know how you find this attitude among Protestants about 'how can you live among Catholics' and their religion being superstitious and so on? Well, lately my health has not been too good and my neighbours have called at the house with miraculous medals, wee drips of holy water, and though I'm an atheist, I take it gratefully and appreciate it because of the intention behind it. If it was vice versa, a Catholic going to live on the Shankill Road, do you think they would be received so well? I don't! In fact I don't think a

Catholic would wander over to the Shankill Road; any Catholic wandering up the Shankill Road is a fool!

Within Sinn Féin no one has ever joked or commented on the fact that I am from a Protestant background. In fact a funny incident happened on the Dublin train one time. I met up with another Sinn Féin member, someone I'd been friendly enough with; we'd attended meetings together. Anyway, we decided to spend our last punts in the bar. We were talking away when the guy realised I didn't know he was from a Protestant background and what was even funnier was that he didn't know that I was too. No one had thought to mention it before. It's just not an issue within the movement; you're accepted because of your commitment to republicanism not because of your religious background.

It's hard to say if I hold out any hope for the community I came from. Over the years I've found that when I talk to nationalist friends they never ever seem to be aware of the depth of hate that the loyalists have for them. You have to be from a Protestant background like myself to understand that. I was party to conversations that you would never hear if you were a Catholic. The hate runs very, very deep and I don't see that changing much. Their attitude really is one of, 'We're up to our neck in fenian blood; surrender and we die.' I think that was illustrated at Drumcree this year and it gave the nationalist middle class a terrible shock, a well deserved shock. I think they believed the situation was improving and the British were neutral. They wouldn't believe that now. I can't describe loyalists' attitudes as anything other than fascist and I think that in any society it's hard to bring fascists on board; sometimes I wonder if it is even worthwhile trying. Not an inch, not a blade of grass: that is their war cry. They're right. Once they start giving, they will lose whatever identity they have; they will be defeated.

So, looking back, although not everything I did was a conscious decision, although I drifted through events and there were chance happenings, still and all, I would strongly recommend it.

28

Ex-Political Prisoner

Born 1948.

I was born and reared in North Belfast. I lived in a two-up, two-down small kitchen house in a loyalist area. My father was a lorry driver and my mother was a cleaner who worked from 6.00 am until 10.00 pm, six days a week. Her only break was to come home around 4.30 pm to make my father's tea, then go back to work at 6.00 pm. Neither of my parents drank, but it definitely wasn't a religious household. For some reason or other my father hated the church; any religious fanatics who came near the door were soon chased; even the local minister was given a reddener on the one and only occasion I can remember him coming to our house. My mother would never go to a Protestant church because the women were usually well dressed and wore hats. She was really embarrassed by this as she didn't have those type of clothes. She did go to chapel on a few occasions with Catholic friends. She was a very simple woman who had a really soft heart and got into more debt helping other people, who did take advantage of her.

There was nothing special about my growing up. In primary school I used to rake about, getting sent to the knitting class with all the wee girls as punishment. My sister, one of three, was in that class and she would always squeal to my ma and da about me. After school, me and my mates would either play soccer in the street or go down to the pithead to play. We had our wee gang of about ten from the street, played 'chase, catch, kiss' with the wee girls, hopped lorries, done all the dares we could think of to prove ourselves in the gang. Friday was the day, like most families I suppose, when I was sent to the pawn shop to get my da's suit out for the weekend; then it would go back on Monday morning again.

Friday night was also bath night – getting the bungalow [tin] bath out by the fire and taking our turns in the same water. Haircut, until I was about ten, was a bowl round the head.

Although my mother rarely attended church, her side of the family were very religious and most of them were in the Sally Ann [Salvation Army], so I was thrown into it. First it was for Sunday school, then later it was into the band. I had to go out into the streets in my wee red top with 'Blood and Fire' written on it. I was really embarrassed as all my mates would see me. I was eventually thrown out when I was 13 for carrying on. Thank you, Lord!

My family had no Orange connections; I can only remember going to the Twelfth on one occasion as a kid. I hadn't a clue what it was all about, just bands and men marching. School never taught us anything about Irish history. It was all based on England: the conquerors, mostly names of the kings and queens of England and the names and dates of battles. As to the word 'fenian' or 'taig', I just knew that they meant Catholics. We learned from some of the older ones things like, if you passed a chapel, you had to spit three times or it would bring you bad luck. Then there were the stories of the nuns and the priests kicking people's doors in to get money. My first sight of this was when I was working in the Short Strand. I was standing outside the store and saw two nuns coming down the street opposite. They had big hard black shoes on and were kicking, rather than rapping, the doors and I thought to myself, 'fuck, it must be true'. No one answered the doors.

I remember we hated the cops, hated the way they chased us when we were playing football in the streets. The older ones used to play cards and they would have us watching out for the like of the cops. I began to notice them more as I got older and started drinking in bars. They would hit a few bars, hassle people and get their free drinks and then go back to their barracks. That was their routine.

I had no real ambitions when I was younger except to play football. School to me was, you went, when not mitching, you did it and got out as quickly as possible to enjoy yourself on the streets. I left school on a Friday and my parents had a job lined up for me that Monday. A friend of my father's, a foreman heating engineer, started me along with his son. I thought I'd have gotten a trade out of it but by the time I was 16, the books, as they were called, were closed, so I left and for the next year worked on building sites and in timber yards. By this time some of my mates had joined the RAF, the Brits and the Navy and I followed suit. I went to the RAF and did the 'brain test' to see what I might be good at. I was offered a range of things and as this sergeant, who I later found out knew nothing, was going down the list he came to Radar Operator. I asked him was it a trade in civilian life; it was already militarised in fact, but he said 'yes' and explained what it was. Nothing like it of course, but I opted for that.

I did the usual seven weeks square bashing. Then I was posted to Scotland and sat in front of a radar screen watching dots move backward and forward. After about three months I was posted to Aden for a year. I was sent to a place called Mukeros, somewhere up in the mountains on the Yemen border, because I was in a bar fight and called the officer in command a cunt. We lived in tents in the mountains and an odd time the N.L.F. (the Arab IRA), would fire a few mortars at the camp. I must admit, the first time it happened I near shit myself. My job there was to get up around 5.30 am, start the generator and switch on all the radar, then contact Aden about 6.00 am. On one occasion, they [Aden] asked me for a weather report; I thought they were joking, but Brits don't joke about the weather. I went out looked up at the sky and saw one cloud and I said to myself: 'I'm 7,000 feet up in the mountains; do I add the 7,000 on or not?' As for the wind speed they were looking, I just wet my finger and stuck it in the air. That was the weather report I gave them.

In my two and a half years in the RAF I was in jail on a number of occasions. In the Aden jail which was run by the RAF, there was a Welsh guard who had kicked an Arab taxi driver to death. He was sentenced by the civilian court (even though he was in military custody), to hang but they flew him out back home that same day. I also knew of an RAF bloke on guard duty who shot an Arab in the back. He was arrested by the Arab police but later handed back to the military and sent straight home. One of my mates who was in the Royal Engineers told me of the time they were coming down through the mountains to Aden when the local Arabs opened up on them. Two of them were killed and they radioed to Aden for back up. The SAS were sent up. I don't know how many they killed but they took eight Arab prisoners back to Aden in choppers and when they reached Aden, only one Arab was left. The rest had been interrogated and thrown out over the mountains.

I met a lot of blokes from different parts of Ireland in the RAF and I got on really well with them; the Scottish and Welsh people I liked and some of the English, mostly northern ones. I was never a bigot, but when I left Belfast my view towards Catholics was not so much narrow minded as ignorant. In the RAF my Irishness became more of a focus. I was seen as being as much Irish as any of the other lads, no matter that I came from a Protestant background.

I was thrown out of the RAF for not being able to take orders. The exact wording was: 'Better suited to a less disciplined life'. So I came back to Belfast and started working on building sites again. The Civil Rights protests had started and Paisley was running around shouting about popeheads and a united Ireland, but I didn't take much interest. I didn't understand about one man one vote – I thought everybody had a vote – nor did I understand the arguments over housing because our houses were no better off than anybody else's. I remember watching Burntollet on the television and I thought it was wrong that the B Specials and RUC, backed up by loyalists, were attacking people who were only out marching looking for something they believed was their right. I didn't see the big deal but then when the Brits came, I was against that. I thought they had no right to be here because this was our country and our problem and we should sort it out ourselves.

Around this time I started going out with a Catholic girl from the Whiterock and then shortly afterwards I met my wife who is also a Catholic. She worked at Gallaher's and was a friend of my sisters. We got a lot of hassle and even some of my sisters who knocked about with her turned from us. I was standing at the street corner one night with my mates and a mini van pulled up and said there was trouble on the Shankill Road. Did we want to go up? We said, 'Aye, we'll go up'. I was the last one to get into the van and this fellow stopped me – he was UVF; he's dead now. He said: 'I hear you are going with a fenian from the Whiterock'. I said: 'You heard wrong'. He said: 'That's all right then'. I said: 'I'm going with one from Andytown now', and pushed him away. Although our area was seen as staunchly loyalist, there were people in mixed marriages living there dating from the fifties. They were all sending their children to Protestant schools, but a couple of them were getting their houses painted with red Xs on the doors. One of my mates married a Catholic and he wanted me to join the Territorial Army with him. I knew why. He wanted to get military experience and join the UDA to keep himself right, which is what he did. He also sent his wife and kids to church.

Anyway, we got married and lived off the Cliftonville Road. Then later we moved into another loyalist area. One Saturday afternoon I came up from the bookies and was messing about with a ball with a couple of mates when two men that I knew to be in the UVF came out of a local bar and called me over. They said that they'd heard that I went up to my wife's mothers and stayed every weekend. I said: 'No, we go up every other weekend to see my wife's family'. They also mentioned a couple of bars on the Falls Road that I'd drank in with the wife's parents, which I didn't deny. They said that I went to chapel every Wednesday and her father gets me a taxi home. I didn't understand this at all. The only time I had been in chapel was when my wife's sister got married and I'd walked out after five minutes to get a smoke. I later found out that Wednesday night was the night for converts, but I'd never turned simply because I didn't believe in religion. They told me that if I ever went to Andytown again not to bother coming back or I would get a bullet in the head. I asked them about my wife, as it was her family, and they said the same goes for her, if her family wanted to see her then they could come down to us. I asked them where they'd gotten their information from and they told me, if I wanted to know, to come to the upstairs part of the bar at 9.00 pm that night. I didn't go. When I told my wife, she burst into tears and I thought: 'To hell with it, that's it'. My feeling was that if I had given in to them, then the next thing would probably be a rap on the door to keep gear for them or possibly join them and I wasn't really into their line of thinking.

Funnily enough, I almost joined the UVF accidentally. An advertisement in one of the papers was asking for people to help Protestant families move out of Catholic areas if need be. My mate and I weren't working at the time and we thought we might as well do something, so we went to this place in Shaftesbury Square. We were given a form to fill in when we got there asking us name, address, phone number, if we were working, what hours we'd be available and finally someone to second us. Once I'd filled it in, another door inside the room was unlocked and this client came out and picked up my form and looked through it. He read out the name of the person I had down as a second and when I said 'yes', he told me that this person was in the IRA. I told him that was a load of crap; he told me the man had been interned in the 50s. I told him that the man done three months for rioting in the 50s. He mentioned two more names he said were from my area who were in the IRA. I'd never heard of them. I started to wonder what this was all about. When we left there was a large crowd waiting to go in. It was only afterwards that me and my mate thought it was a recruiting campaign for the UVF. I thought that the man who questioned me, who wasn't from my area, must have had some intelligence source to know right away the person I had put down on the form. They did get back to me. A woman came to the house and handed my father an envelope, but he thought it was for him. I saw it the next morning on the fireplace inviting me to a meeting the night before at Shaftesbury Square. I heard no more after that.

My wife and I moved out the morning after I was pulled by the UVF and we went to live with her mother for a while. Then we got a house in Lenadoon a week or two before the truce broke. It wasn't difficult to see that the attitude of the British army was totally different in nationalist areas. Before I moved into a nationalist area I had rioted both against the New Lodge and also against the Brits/RUC, and been lifted a few times, but usually it was the RUC, not the Brits. I remember I used to watch the New Lodge when they were rioting against the Brits. I felt sorry for one bloke when a snatch squad came out of a side street; he turned to run and went straight into a lamp post. He got battered stupid.

I don't think I was republican minded at that time. Being out in Aden had opened my eyes and I was very anti-Brit, but not anti-English, as people try to portray us. Since a child I'd never liked the RUC, but that was more a case of being anti-authority and in those days in the 1970s, I never saw the RUC on the streets of West Belfast; it was always Brit foot patrols, Saracens and jeeps. For me becoming sympathetic to Republicanism and the IRA and getting involved wasn't a reaction to what I saw happening on the streets. I was never one of those people who sang 'Say hello to the Provos' in the bar, putting their fingers up in the air. I never knew the songs anyway. It was more a mixture of having my eyes opened in Aden and gradually coming to understand the nature of the state in the six counties. I'd never hated the IRA; I'd never thought a lot about them even when vigilante groups were being organised in loyalist areas, those old men with tilly lamps, Dad's Army. I'd never thought there was that much of a problem about having a united Ireland.

I know that some people, including a couple of my old mates, had similar views. As long as they had a job they would have been happy living in Timbuktu, although the power and control of the Catholic church in the Free State would have put even people from Timbuktu off from living there.

The first time I was scooped by the Brits was in 1974 when I was going to play a soccer match. They held me in Springfield Road for four hours for a check out. Then in 1977 I was lifted after a lot of gear was found inside and outside the house. They questioned me for three days and I got a lot of hassle about being a prod. They said I had the cockiness of a prod and the arrogance of a taig. They dumped me in a cell and told me to get in there with all the fenian fleas as I was lower than they were, things like that. During the last interrogation there were about eight Branch/CID men in the room with me, English as well as Irish. One of them asked me what religion I was bringing my kids up. I said 'Catholic'. I also told him that I had turned, which wasn't true. They asked me why and I told them because I felt like it as it was nothing to me. I was just winding them up which worked, as they called me a dirty bastard and a fucking traitor. I beat that rap saying that I was forced to keep the gear. The following year I was lifted again after a cop had been shot dead. I expected to get a hard time in Castlereagh, but that didn't happen. I ended up charged with killing one cop, attempted killing of another and a bombing.

In my first week in court I met one of my old mates who was a screw. He came over and asked me what the fuck I was doing with these bastards (the IRA)? And I just said: 'Never mind me; what the fuck are you doing with those bastards (the screws)? Of the squad that I grew up with, one was killed in a car crash, one drowned when he was 13, two are in the RUC, one was in the British army, one was in the Navy, three are screws, two in the UVF, one joined the 'Sticks', but is dead now from alcohol abuse, and of course myself. After a visit, I was walking back into the wing past a team of loyalists who were going on legal visits. One of them shouted out the street where I used to live. When the screw let me into the cell, he asked me if I was a prod. I told him I was and he just said: 'And you're in the IRA; fuck I don't understand'. One of the loyalists told me that they'd almost got me during a soccer match in 1974. I wasn't there. During my time on remand my wife had been arrested for possession; believe it or not I was relieved when she got charged, knowing that she was out of Castlereagh. One man who had been questioned for the same thing I was in for had been found hung in one of the cells.

My family got a bit of hassle when I was lifted. Someone phoned up and said there was gear in my mother's house and she was raided. She asked one of the cops about it and he said: 'Ah missus, someone doing it out of spite'. Even some of her so-called friends of 50 years turned from her. By then I really wasn't having a lot of contact with my family anyway. One of my sisters married a screw and I had a run in with him when I was on the blanket, but my sister had no contact with me. I wouldn't have wanted to have contact anyway. Since then my mother has died, but I would still visit my father and one of my other sisters.

I put my name down for the hunger strike. It wasn't until afterwards that I learned that there were only a couple more people to go and then I would have been on it myself. We knew that Bobby Sands was going to die but it still came as a shock. The screws had a stinking attitude towards the hunger strikers; what they did to some of the bodies afterwards, burning them with fags, was terrible. After the hunger strike I think people outside thought that we had got everything that we were asking for, but we didn't. We still had to fight to improve conditions in the jail. We just carried on because at the end of the day it was for our benefit and for the benefit of the other ones coming behind us. Today it is like night and day in the jail. You are still imprisoned, you are not free, but the conditions are very different. I was involved in the 1983 escape, but I was shot and trailed and punched back by a couple of screws, one of them a Christian screw who hated me all the more. With screws it is all about money, control and power. Their remarks were full of bigotry and their talk was very crude. I remember once listening to two screws talking after another screw had been shot dead. One of them was saying how he was going to touch for the man's wife. He had only been buried that day.

Until I went to jail I knew nothing of Irish history and reading opened my eyes to different periods: the plantations, James Connolly, the partition of Ireland in 1921. I didn't even know that King Billy had been blessed by the Pope! I came to the conclusion that if Irish history was taught in schools, ordinary Protestants would have a different attitude to the Brits. I learnt some Irish too, not fluently, but I was able to teach the bun rang. I also began to teach jail history, the history of republicanism, to prisoners who were coming into the jail in the 1990s. They didn't know all the events that had happened: the protest at Crumlin Road Jail, the blanket protest, the hunger strikes, taking control of the wings in the jail and manipulating the huns out of the wings, trying to end workshops and then the escape and its aftermath, when the screws regained control of the jail, then trying to regain control of the jail all over again. I had lived through all that history.

I've settled in easy enough on the outside with my family, even though we do have our ups and downs. I came out with a republican line on political issues but I couldn't force my beliefs down my children's throats. They had all grown up and had their own opinions and I think that's a dangerous line that you can cross with your children. The republicanism that is inside me will never go away. The Protestant part of my background is out of the window now but I still feel Northern Irish and I'm not over-fussed by the attitudes of some Free Staters. Most, if not all governments down South have the same line of thought.

I'd like to see a united Ireland where discrimination is a thing of the past and eventually I think it will happen. As to a socialist republic: I think we used to believe that, once Ireland was united, we'd go for socialism, but that was a radical idea. I would call myself a socialist and not because I haven't any money! I believe in equality. For me now it's up to Sinn Féin as a political party to get the votes and to have some say in government, to fight for equality in all sorts of ways. There are people in our society who are living below the bread line; some people haven't a house to sleep in and are left to lie out on the streets; there are kids running about with brains to burn because they can't get a job; it shouldn't be like that. Social issues like divorce and abortion rights for women shouldn't be decided on by the churches; it should be up to people themselves to decide where they stand on these issues. Equality should be for everybody, whether they be Catholics, Protestants, women, homosexuals, Travellers, everybody. I think it will take a couple of generations to change people's attitudes; the sooner the better.

Looking back over my life, I would probably do it a wee bit differently, but I don't know where I would start to do it all over again. If I hadn't joined the RAF, what would have been my attitude towards the British or nationalists? If I'd gone to that meeting in Shaftesbury Square, would my life have taken a different path? It's impossible for me to speculate on what might have been. I've learnt enough from my experiences in life to be content, to know that what I believe in and my part in it is right.

29

Sinn Féin Member

Born 1955.

My family broke up when I was four and my sisters and I were put into a series of homes throughout our childhood. Eventually my father took me out of the home to live with him and my grandmother. I didn't have much of a relationship with him; I just remember that he was very strict. We lived at the bottom of the Crumlin Road which is a staunchly loyalist area. My father was a trade unionist and a member of the Northern Ireland Labour Party but he was a unionist for all that. I went to live with one of my older sisters when I was 14. It was the seventies and the times were grim with the barricades going up in Protestant areas. My sister had married a Catholic from Beechmount and I was threatened for living with 'taigs' which made me very wary. I didn't think my life was in danger until a Catholic living beside us was stabbed to death and left up an entry. Then I started to get paranoid, imagining that people jumping out of cars were out to get me. I left Belfast and went to live with my mother in England.

My mother lived in Sussex, which was so English and middle class, and I was really homesick. My sister had a friend in Birmingham who was from the Lower Falls Road and eventually I went up there to live with him. It was my first introduction to nationalists, families who had left Belfast years before. Everyone felt strongly about what was happening back home; they drank in Irish pubs, sang rebel songs, made collections and sold republican papers in the bars. I still pined to come home but never thought that it was going to be possible. I felt that I couldn't come back to live in a Protestant area and I was too afraid to live in a nationalist area; besides I had no base there. I'd become friendly with the family of my sister's friend in Birmingham and I returned once for a weekend to attend a wedding in the Lower Falls and although I was afraid of the soldiers on the streets, the community spirit that there is in Belfast outdid those fears.

It was during a phone conversation that my friend's mother told me that if I wanted to come home I could go and live with her in West Belfast. I talked about it for a while and everyone kept telling me that there was no problem; no one would bother me in West Belfast. I got the plane and came home. I remember when I arrived. She was rightly, putting her arms around me and treating me like I was her son coming home and then taking me over to the club to meet people.

I wasn't a practising Protestant. I'd gone to Bible classes and to church with my granny. She was an avid church-goer, one of those Presbyterians who believe in hard work and no television on a Sunday. I was a Protestant in the sense that I had looked forward to the bonfires and the Twelfth of July every year and loved to run after all the orange bands when they walked down the street. I wasn't allowed to join one of the bands. My father didn't believe in it. Our house was one of the few that didn't put a Union Jack out or didn't have a picture of the Queen or King Billy on the wall.

When I started drinking with republicans my being a Protestant was near a novel factor. It wasn't that I was harassed or that there was bad talk about me, more that people wanted to sit beside me and ask about where I came from and how I had ended up in West Belfast. I was perceived as crossing over the divide. I sometimes think when people say they don't have a problem with Catholics it is because they literally don't have a problem. It's like racism. Racism isn't a problem if there aren't any black people living beside you. It was the same with my family. We weren't affected until my sister married a Catholic and I went to live in the Lower Falls, but by that time I only bumped into them in the town sometimes and saw them at Christmas.

I dabbled with the idea of converting when I was about to get married. There was a stipulation then that you had to get permission from the bishop. I went to a few classes and had a few yarns with the priest, although we usually ended up talking politics rather than religion. He told me that the children would have to be brought up Catholic but that if I ever wished to convert I shouldn't do so lightly; I should think about it. I wasn't put under any pressure. Only four from my family attended the wedding so we had to pre-arrange that my wife's extended family would sit on my side of the church so it wouldn't look ridiculous!

The people I met outside of my wife's extended family were republicans, certainly all the fellas of my age that I went out drinking with. A lot of them had been interned when they were very young. I was only 19 and I found this fascinating. The republicans I met became friends initially but the politics came very quickly. It wasn't hard to come to conclusions in West Belfast in 1974. I saw at first hand what I used to see on television. There were three barracks in the area and the British soldiers were heavy on the ground. There were raids, beatings, a lot of shoot-outs and a lot of assassinations. The area was totally militarised. I was living among people who had been put down for so long, had got up and tried to do something about it and the only reason they couldn't was because they were being put down again by a massive military force. There was no other way I could have looked at the situation I was living in.

I was a newcomer. I hadn't been put down or interned or beaten up. The unionist community that I came from had always inflicted on them. It wasn't that I was guilt tripped by this but it was a while before I said 'we', 'look what they have done to us', in conversation. I was wary of that, of forcing it, that feeling of wanting to be accepted, although I knew that by then I already had been.

I got the same harassment from the Brits that any young man who wore a wrangler jacket, jeans and Doc Martens got. It was three or four years before I was singled out for particular attention. I was arrested one day with a republican after a shooting incident. They took my details and after that I became more than just a young 'taig' walking down the street. They saw me out selling *Republican News* or postering, got to know my name and gave me a hard time. I was up in court for an illegal march once and I remember the names being read out: Kevin Patrick, Sean Gerard, Patrick Aloysius, and then it was my turn. The judge interrupted, 'Say that name again.' He knew right away that my name didn't fit in.

None of the harassment I got from the British was anything like what was to come later with the RUC. The British couldn't care less that I was a Protestant; I was a republican or a nationalist to them. To the RUC I was a turncoat. The RUC didn't really start coming into West Belfast until after the first hunger strike in 1981. They knew me the first time they got out of their jeeps. Their language was unrepeatable; it was sexist, filthy language about my wife and about being a fenian. I remember telling the boys this. One of them was with me a week later when it happened again and he said they'd all thought I must have been exaggerating. He'd been to jail and back a couple of times and even he couldn't believe the dog's abuse that I was getting. I remember one elderly peeler, a country man, taking me to the side and asking how I could live with such filthy bastards, like he was trying to be a fatherly figure, saying seriously, 'How the fuck can you live with them?'

I was arrested and questioned about different things in Castlereagh four or five times. The RUC on the streets operate to a different agenda to the ones in the holding centres like Castlereagh. The third time they had me in they tried to get me to work for them. They let me know that they knew I was a Protestant but they didn't make the same references. I'm not saying that they didn't have the same hatred and venom but they operated to a more focused agenda.

There is a bitterness in loyalism which is frightening. Some nationalists would have it but it's nowhere near as pervasive in the nationalist community overall. I remember being told a story by an ex-prisoner from West Belfast. One day he saw this elderly man walking up and down outside his house. He'd thought he was lost and he went out to ask him where he was looking for. The man told him he was from Highfield and that he used to live in the ex-prisoner's house. He was brought into the house; both the man and his wife were in the IRA, and they made him tea and sandwiches, had a yarn and a few smokes and then left him down to the barracks to find his way home. I couldn't imagine a Catholic going up to a UVF man's house and the same thing happening. There simply isn't the same anti-Protestant feeling in nationalist areas as there is anti-Catholic feeling in unionist areas.

I always thought of myself as a republican but it was the hunger strikes which reinforced everything that I had believed in up until then. History was laid out in front of me, both past and present. It's hard to describe the atmosphere there was in West Belfast at that time. The nationalist republican community gelled together. There was a great community spirit. Lots of local Armagh/H Blocks committees were set up. We marched, we white line picketed, we had candle light vigils, we had a cell which we stayed up in all night. We listened to the stories coming out of the jail from blanket men saying it was both the hardest and the best time of their lives. They were bonding stories, stories of ingenuity to beat the system, stories of the Irish language to counter the oppression. When Bobby Sands died everything erupted; there was rioting, women saying the rosary, people on the streets everywhere. It was my strongest period of commitment. Everything in my life that I was worried about paled into insignificance.

I ended up being responsible for the elections for Sinn Féin in the area. It's a bit embarrassing now when I look back and see how we handled the first election. We didn't have much of a clue and I think that was proven by the first vote that we got in West Belfast. I liked elections, though perhaps not for all the reasons that Sinn Féiners like them. It was one of the few ways that active republicans could see a result for their activities. If you are in the IRA and you go out and do a job you can look round and see half the town away or half the jeep away and say there is the visible signs of my work. In Sinn Féin, though everyone is busy doing things, there's not a lot which can actually be quantified. A lot of people weren't totally convinced about elections, but I thought that electing Sinn Féin councillors or MPs or assemblymen was all part of the struggle.

Up until a year after the ceasefire I was fairly optimistic that there would be progress even though the Brits were really slow at the start. I would have to say that I'm very pessimistic now about what will happen. I think the opportunity has been lost and I don't think republicans can give anymore at this point. The ceasefire was a big leap of faith to produce and it wasn't acted on.

Some people would think it a bit grand when I say I'm not involved in republican politics for myself but for my children. I really don't have any great plans for my future in terms of getting a great job or buying a house. I'm resigned to my life now but I would love my children when they do go for their jobs to be able to do so on the same basis as everyone else, for them to be treated like anybody else who lives on this island, whatever their politics. I don't think it is possible to reform the state of Northern Ireland but I think I could live with this state in a transitional period for another 30 years if during that time Catholics have parity of esteem and there isn't any discrimination and if there is a police force which maybe I could even advise my son to go out and join if he wanted to. If all that was to happen I probably could live with it even as a republican. Not all republicans could but I would be prepared to compromise.

At the end of the day I would still like to see a united Ireland. I'd like us to work towards it. In taking away all the benefits that unionists have I think this society will change. If there are no benefits in being a unionist there will be less fear of a united Ireland. It's not just the benefits that unionists have when they go for a job; there's the discrimination once they are in the job too in terms of promotion. It leads to an inbuilt mind-set that unionists think they are better than nationalists. There's a lot going for unionists in having their own police force and that is going to have to change. I think that change has to come from the unionist leadership. A lot of people might not agree with me but I think there is a unionist monolith. Unionists mightn't agree with each other on lots of issues but on the union they are adamant.

I see myself as a republican, not so much a Protestant but a non-Catholic. I don't practise any religion. It's not that I am an atheist – more laziness if anything; if something happened to me in the morning I'd probably be glad to see the priest or the minister, whoever came first. If we were having a conversation about the United Irishmen and 1798 then in those terms I'd be happy to talk of myself as a Presbyterian and to acknowledge that Henry Joy went to the same church as I did. What worries me more is the distance that there is between this community and the greater Irish community rather than between my own origins and those of my Catholic neighbours. Sometimes when I am in Dublin I don't feel at home and I definitely don't feel at home in Belfast city centre. I don't feel that it is my city centre. That has perturbed me at times because everyone likes to feel at ease in their own city.

What would have happened to me if I hadn't gone to England, hadn't made friends with people from West Belfast? I'm nearly sure that the way I was carrying on when I was 14 and 15, running about after orange bands, having no stable family home, I'd have been one of those 18 year olds sent out with a gun to somebody's door. I think I would have been stupid enough to have done that. I probably would have been arrested and signed a statement in the first hour of the interview. Today I'd have been coming out of a life sentence. I'm delighted that I escaped that.

30

Teacher

Born 1960.

There was nothing remarkable about the first nine years of my life although, looking back, it was a quite isolated childhood living in the countryside of County Down. The things which marked my Protestant identity were the obvious ones. My father was a staunch member of the Orange Lodge and as a child I went to all the marches and held the strings and so on. It wasn't as exciting as Christmas, but it was like a carnival, more like something that one did, something that happened naturally in the community. I've no memories of anti-Catholic feelings, although I'm sure that they must have existed. I went to the Presbyterian church regularly; again it was an ordinary and automatic part of life, neither good, nor bad, nor indifferent. It was there, like the way you had your dinner or went to bed at night.

What I do remember forcefully was my father joining the British army when I was nine and the family moving over to England. I didn't know where England was, nor did I have any idea of national difference but when we arrived, I discovered very quickly that I was different from the other children living in my street. People called me 'Paddy' even though that was not my name and I knew that this was a culture which I didn't belong to and that the people in that culture didn't feel that I belonged to it either.

Being in the British forces meant that we moved around so much and it was impossible to get seven years of education in any one place. Anybody posted overseas can get a grant to send their children to boarding school and I was sent to boarding school in County Antrim, an old-fashioned, dour, Presbyterian place with strict rules, the sort of place where they belted you for wearing your shoes instead of your slippers and your slippers instead of your shoes at breakfast. The general ethos was to fit the boys for the professions; the better ones became doctors and lawyers, ranking on down the professions.

Religion was forced down my throat, but I lost my religious faith during my teenage years and by my late teens I was an atheist. I think in an odd way that Protestantism sows the seeds of its own demise. Faith isn't automatic; you have to construct it yourself and it is your own individual responsibility. We were encouraged to question and I just went on too far and questioned it out of existence. Arthur Blisset came to Northern Ireland when I was 13. He was an American evangelist who wandered around the world with a big cross on wheels. We were all allowed out of school to see him and at the end he did the Billy Graham thing – 'All come out; anybody who's saved, come out the back' – and all my peers went out the back. Being a chicken, I went along with them but try as I might, I couldn't get it to have an effect on me.

I remember those funny little American cartoon books that were rabidly evangelical and anti-Catholic being passed round at school but I think my religious upbringing was sophisticated enough to knock such fanciful conceptions on the head. I would certainly have thought Catholics were theologically wrong, but it would have been on the grounds of worshipping Mary, graven images and confession to priests rather than direct communication with God. Certainly I wouldn't have been as sophisticated as to discuss doctrinal matters like transubstantiation. That's the gruesome one: eating the God. I still find the doctrine pretty bizarre, mind you!

There were one or two middle class Catholics in the school and they were conspicuous. You knew they were different; in fact, you knew everybody in the school who was a Catholic. I can't remember any deliberate spite or discrimination against them but probably my eyes were closed. There was one kid whose father was in the British forces like mine. He had an English accent, had been brought up in England and had never lived in Ireland prior to boarding school. He even attended the Church of Ireland. Then it came out that he was a Catholic and it was very traumatic for him. I remember remarks to the effect that 'I wouldn't have trusted him anyway', the usual bigotry. Obviously there was more going on to have made a child like that so fearful that he wouldn't even identify with his religion.

I still went home to England for school holidays and the sense of difference began to crystallise more in my mind. It was a paradoxical and completely contradictory experience to be sitting in County Antrim in this staunch bastion where everybody was British and automatically thought of themselves as British, and then to go home for Christmas where I was perceived unproblematically by everyone around me as Irish. It's bizarre; you get on a plane and go from the island of Ireland where you are British to the island of Britain where you are Irish.

At first I attempted to deal with it by becoming more unionist than the unionists. I had a Red Hand flag and remember going to a Vanguard rally to listen to Bill Craig. I piled on the British identity as staunchly as I could and spouted the common unionist and anti-Catholic assumptions of that era: Catholics weren't discriminated against, they were just lazy, and they just like murdering people – the usual. I think that over time I began to realise that my over-zealous defence of my identity was to try to shore up the insecurity that people in England didn't think I was British. It's difficult to say how it all happened and I'm wary of reducing my political views simply to the biography of my adolescence, but it was a process. At some point I gained more confidence; I thought: well, if they don't think I am British, sod it; I don't have to try so hard to be British simply because these people don't think I am.

I think as well that there was this ideological hangover from the sixties, this rejection of bourgeois society. There were boys at school who were disaffected, who thought about issues and rejected the consumerist capitalist society. All of this was done in a non-specific fashion; it was personal politics. We steered away from engaging in anything about Ireland and I had no sense of being part of what was happening in the wider society. The boarding school was a self-contained unit. We were only allowed out on Friday and Saturday afternoons and to go to church. As well as that, the town was a backwater; there had been a bomb which killed six people, but really it was one of those places which the 'troubles' didn't touch. The nearest I ever got to the 'troubles' was when one of my school mates blew himself up on a UVF bombing mission. By the time I was in sixth form I had rejected unionism, but I wasn't sure of what to replace it with and besides, it wasn't as if I could discuss it with my peers unless I wanted to be a pariah.

I left boarding school and went to England where I enjoyed a hedonist lifestyle in Birmingham for about four years. I signed on the bru, took various substances and had a nice late adolescence. I also got involved in leftist British politics. There was punk, there was leathers and safety pins and spiky hair and various Trotskyist and neo-left groups. At that time the National Front were in their heyday in England and I became involved in the Anti-Nazi League. I went along to lots of meetings of all the revolutionary groups, but after seven years of Presbyterian authoritarianism, party lines didn't appeal that much to me and I got involved with a group of anarchists. It was a great culture in Birmingham. There wasn't just punk; along came ska. It was a cultural cauldron: music, anti-racism and leftist politics. I got involved in the campaign to save the Murrays, the anarchist solidarity campaign. They were sentenced to death by the Irish state for killing a policeman. I occupied various Irish banks and Aer Lingus offices. I went to Bloody Sunday commemoration marches, even got myself on the back of the *Guardian*, a photograph which was a combination of political activism and the drug culture. I was wearing a multi-coloured balaclava but unfortunately the *Guardian* was printed in black and white in those days so I just looked like a thug.

Having had my fill of hedonism, I thought I would do something useful in my life, so I applied to become a teacher. I was still involved with British left politics but I was also spending a lot of my time in the Irish community in Birmingham. I began to read a lot about Ireland, made friends with Paddy, his name really was Paddy, and started to read *An Phoblacht* regularly. Over time I got involved in British solidarity campaigns with Ireland. One of the things which began to irritate me was the indifference of the British left to what was going on in Ireland. There would be great solidarity with Cuba or with Palestine but there was a complete blind spot on Ireland and when they were pushed on this, they just said that Ireland was a secondary problem to the crisis of international capitalism and anyone who kept harping on about Ireland was a reactionary nationalist. I felt there was something bizarre about proclaimed socialist internationalists thinking of fellow comrades in racist terms. *New Left Review*, for example, didn't publish an article on the North in all the time between when British troops were deployed twenty five years ago until three months after the ceasefire. That is indicative of the attitude I am talking about.

I began to lead two parallel political lives and what I couldn't understand was why they weren't one. It was the Irish hunger strike which was the final catalyst that completed my alienation with English society. I felt like a stranger in a strange land. I thought what was happening in Ireland was so momentous and yet all these people around me were laughing their way through it. Whatever one thought of the political motivation of the hunger strikers, there was the very idea that somebody would starve themselves to death for their political convictions. I just couldn't understand why anyone could not at least give respect to the conviction if not to what the conviction was for. But there was none of this. There were Bobby Sands jokes, there was anti-Irish hysteria, the Irish were damned by association of being Irish and the British saw it as a few terrorists doing to themselves what should have been done to them anyway. I can remember getting shit for wearing a black arm band in lectures – this wasn't the sort of thing trainee teachers were supposed to be doing – and having posters on the wall of my college room which the cleaners objected to. It was a time when the Irish community huddled together from the callousness of the British and suffered the emotional trauma of it all. After that I could never see England quite the same again.

I became more and more distanced from my leftist comrades. Again it didn't happen overnight; it was a process which resulted in me becoming an Irish republican. I thought of the Ireland that I would like to live in, simply transposed general leftist tenets onto the Irish situation. I didn't want to live in a monarchy; I wanted to live in a socialist country, I wanted to live in a secular country and I wanted to live in a country where there was political control over those in power, a democratic country. I have no desire to live in an expanded version of the 26 counties. The Ireland I would like to live in is considerably different from the 26 counties, but I would like to live in an Ireland that is united.

There is one thing I would really like to say. The amount of disaffected Ulster Protestants that I met in England was phenomenal. I was astounded to meet police inspectors' sons and literally all sorts of people. The sadness, the emptiness, the feeling that they could no longer live in their community because they had rejected unionism and had no other option but to emigrate. They were not necessarily republicans but they did have non-standardised political and cultural viewpoints, leftist opinions which they couldn't express back home. It's a terrible tragedy that we have lost all these people who could have added to the political and cultural future of the North. It was another impetus to me to come home. I didn't want to end up a pining emigrant, crying into my pint, singing 'Carrickfergus'. During teacher training I met my partner. She is first generation Irish from County Waterford, and we both decided to come back and live in Belfast. As soon as we qualified, we were on the boat home.

I wanted to live in a nationalist area in Belfast. I wanted to express my political views and put my political views into political action. I went down to the Sinn Féin office and said that I was interested in joining and explained where I was coming from. It was a fairly nerve wracking experience, as you can imagine it would be. There was some inquiry – I suppose I shouldn't have been amazed at that – but for the most part people were very welcoming. There was no sectarianism towards me at all. I think republican views of Protestants are very sophisticated. They know where Protestants are coming from and what their fears are.

On one level it's not surprising that the republican movement is the number one hate target for Protestants because a lot of the people who were killed, although not for their Protestantism, were Protestants. I don't construct the IRA's killings of police as sectarian, but most Protestants do. On another level though, it is surprising because the other parties like Fianna Fáil and the SDLP are ideologically more dangerous to Protestants than Sinn Féin. They are still very much part of a Catholic culture. Of course most people in the republican movement are Catholics but there is a genuine secular, democratic ethos. The republican agenda does not threaten

Protestantism in terms of Catholic domination. Of course I know that Sinn Féin will never have a significant number of Protestant members. It's been demonised and hated for so long that it could never happen. That's a fact of life.

Republicanism does threaten their British identity, but my conception of unionism is that this idea of Britishness is a very vague and amorphous thing. Certainly with Protestant unionists there is little time for the British mechanisms of government and there is very little time for the British really. There is this symbol of the Crown and this adherence to the symbol of the crown. I'm not saying it's not strong, but it is cloudy. Most of unionist identity seems to be a negative construction; in other words most of what they seem to be is what they are not. They are defending themselves against Catholic Gaelic Ireland. There is no reason why there should be a homogenous Catholic Gaelic Ireland; there is no reason to think that people are actually wanting that any more. I don't think there are that many people who do want it. I would argue to any Protestant or unionist that as a republican I don't expect them to become Catholic or Gaelic but they do have to agree to a democratic political structure which allows everyone to have their say and where there is no discrimination. Within that structure they could maintain their culture as they wished to maintain it. In terms of the Protestant ideals of liberty and freedom of conscience, I personally don't believe, even though I am not a practising Protestant, that there is any contradiction between those ideals and republicanism. In fact, there are a lot of things about Protestantism which are very republican: the way, for example, the Presbyterian church elects its elders rather than has bishops appointed from on high.

It would be ideal if in Ireland there was a confident Protestant community positive about itself and living harmoniously and contributing to the culture on the island as part of the island. I'm very suspicious of political revisionism but I think the island is big enough. Traditions and culture are actually created, so I think if people want to create a positive culture for themselves, then let them. The Protestant community can create or invent whatever the hell they like to invent that they find positive. Let them do it and be confident about themselves!

I would still describe myself as an Ulster Protestant. I'm not a loyalist but I am ethnically a Protestant. I don't think you need to be a loyalist to belong to the Protestant cultural tradition because there are alternative political cultural traditions, most famously 1798. I do find that there are differences between me and my Catholic friends. Take atheism. I find the whole religious construct ridiculous. My Catholic neighbours are very moderate and tolerant and they're also polite enough not to say in my company that this is not an atheist speaking, this is a bloody Protestant speaking, or a Protestant atheist! I asked one of my Catholic friends what he thought of my views on religion once and he said I was just one of those horrible Victorian rationalists! It's not the holy water and pictures; that kind of symbolism doesn't worry me. I would support Max Weber's thesis that Protestantism had the effect of demystifying the world; it was one step towards atheism, towards demystification and people being rational and I think that is the case, but negatively that means that Catholicism is one step behind. At least I can discuss such issues in the pub in a nationalist area if I wanted to! It wouldn't be possible for a Catholic to discuss such an agenda in a Protestant area.

When I joined the republican movement I accepted that I was beyond the pale. It was that rubicon step; once you are over that you can't go back. I still visit close relatives who live in Belfast. My other relatives, although they always thought I was rebellious and odd, wouldn't know anything about my republicanism. I'm married to a Catholic; that's probably why they think I live in a Catholic area.

The irony of course is that as a Protestant living in a Catholic area my worry was of loyalists coming and slegehammering my door and shooting me in my bed. That's not exceptional; I have the same fears as anyone else living in this area; the only difference is that as a political activist I was far more aware of the dangers and the precautions to take than the poor sods who did get shot, those who think that because they don't belong to anything and don't care about politics that they are not a target.

Being a Protestant and a republican living in a Catholic nationalist area sounds like a recipe for anxiety but I've actually become very happy with my identity. I have no desire to give up the cultural tag and cultural baggage of being a Protestant. I want that to remain a part of me. I still feel different but it is no longer a problem; it's not like when I was in England and thought I was British and they called me a Paddy. I suppose you could say that mine is a happy ever after story!

Meeting Places

I believe we are at a crossroads in Northern Ireland. I know everybody is always saying that we are at a crossroads! Well I see crossroads as places where people meet rather than depart.

31

Robin Glendinning

Dramatist. Born 1938.

Politics were discussed at great lengths in our house and there was always a tolerance for different political outlooks on life. One side of my family were staunchly unionist; my grandfather was Sir John Johnston, a Unionist MP who ran a linen mill in Lurgan and one of my uncles was a Unionist senator. The other side of the family were Protestant Home Rulers, a forgotten group of people in Northern Ireland these days. My great-grandfather was elected as a Home Ruler to represent North Antrim in the 1906 Parliament. He won the seat by splitting the Presbyterian vote, beating the Unionist candidate quite handsomely in fact. My father was a mixture of all sorts of things. I suppose he was conventionally unionist at first, a conservative really; he saw politics in the British rather than the Irish context and he was a great admirer of Churchill. Later, when we moved to the countryside of County Armagh, he joined the Orange Order. He left it and later became President of the Ulster Liberal Party.

For me, though, I would say that I was much more under the influence of the unionist side of the family. Generally it would have been British politics rather than local politics which I found most interesting. In fact, I think that it wasn't until I was 25 and teaching in Omagh that I seriously began to become interested in local politics. I always had this sense that local politics were nasty, dirty, fixed in concrete and I suppose quite ludicrous because nothing ever changed. Even when it came to Irish history, it was not this century which fascinated me but the history of the 19th century, the struggle for independence, for freedom and the history of the working man. For me that was the exciting struggle.

I had a comfortable upbringing. The pain in it was my father's drinking and the shortage of money which ensued, but I escaped most of that because I was sent to Rockport, a boarding school, and later to Campbell College in Belfast. On Sunday walks we used to pass an ex-prisoner of war camp and I often thought how much like a prison camp our boarding school was. One of the extraordinary things about the school was that the headmaster was a radio communications freak. Every room in the school was wired with loudspeakers and he would communicate with us from the communications desk in his study. On wet days the radio would be turned on in the afternoon and one of my earliest memories is of listening to the results of a series of British elections towards the end of the 1940s and the beginning of the 1950s. The results came out much slower in those days and my friend and I would sit with a newspaper listing every constituency in the United Kingdom, ticking them off and endlessly asking the teachers why areas were all Labour controlled and why the Liberals had been virtually wiped out. We were horrible little Tories of course!

We would holiday near Groomsport and it was here that I met a man called Denis O'D Hanna who was one of the earliest influences on my life. His father was a Protestant nationalist and had been a supporter of Redmond. He was a wonderful raconteur and storyteller who would draw illustrations and relate the Irish legends of Deirdre and the Children of Lir, a bit like an early Rolf Harris, only much better. He was obsessed with the 1798 rebellion, told us all about General Munroe and would take us off on expeditions to find Betsy Gray's cottage or down to Ballynahinch to see the streets where the yeomanry had fired at the rebels. All of this was quite different of course from what I was being taught at school! My teachers at Campbell were mostly Englishmen and Irish history didn't figure too hugely on the curriculum, so the Hanna family were a source of this other world for me.

My family wouldn't have been averse to such literary and historical facts about Ireland being discovered and discussed. They were all extremely well read, were members of book clubs and would have been up to date on all the latest novels. However, my unionist aunts would have been deeply suspicious of it. When Sam Thompson, who wrote the play *Over the Bridge*, stood for the Labour Party at one Northern Irish election, I remember my maiden aunt, who was very dear to me, saying:

'That bloody man thinks he's Shakespeare', and then all the venom came out. There was a grave distrust for Thompson, not simply because he was standing for the Labour Party but because he dared to write about contemporary Belfast, about sectarianism, about the darker side of Ulster life. I have a feeling that amongst people like my aunt there was a sense that, in the field of letters certainly, nothing really could come out of Ulster. Anybody who tried to write plays was a poseur because the only decent plays, they suspected, although they never saw them, were in London. Of course I would have to say also that Denis O'D Hanna thought a lot of local work was banal and poor too, but that was just because it was banal and poor, not because it was local.

Actually, I became much more interested in Southern Irish politics. I found it exciting going down to Trinity to study. The politics down South were so alive! I was immensely impressed when De Valera ran for President and tried to get rid of proportional representation at the same time. The people gave him an overwhelming 'yes' for President, but turned down the referendum on P.R. For me that was the people demonstrating democracy in action, which was quite different from Northern politics, where everyone just voted on the border issue.

I joined the Fabian Society which at that time centred around meetings where we would educate ourselves. One of the members wanted to change this, have us do something more specific, and he drew up this plan to survey the housing conditions around the docks area of Dublin. The conditions were frightful, with high unemployment and ferocious emigration. I thought it was a wonderful idea and to this day I don't know how it happened that we didn't do the survey. There was a point in the meeting where the chairman, who was a communist, proposed that we vote either for the housing survey or on condemning De Gaulle's policy in Algeria. Somehow these two issues became mutually exclusive in the meeting. I nearly went bald headed saying the French empire is really going to quiver the moment it discovers that Trinity Fabian Society, which consisted of about 33 people, had voted to condemn De Gaulle. To my despair, that's what we did and the survey was shelved. That's when I gave up the Fabian Society. It did give me an insight into human nature though, and looking back now, it was a fascinating revelation to discover that politics is a game, or can be a game that people play, and that the game becomes more important than any end.

After Trinity I went to teach at a school in Omagh. My landlady was a Unionist councillor and it was during this time that I saw Northern politics from the inside and realised that they were not only ludicrous, they were malign. I remember once going on a school cruise with pupils from France and their teacher asked me to talk to her pupils about Northern Ireland. I began to describe my experiences and I couldn't believe my own descriptions. The picture I gave of the place, the appalling corruption, one party rule, local politics organised on the unionist side by the Orange Order, how the unionists stayed in power and how the Nationalist Party for their bit of the cake connived in this, discrimination, gerrymandering, a police which was an arm of the government – the French pupils didn't think that was so extraordinary actually! They didn't know what else police forces were supposed to be! I told them stories about my landlady and the letting of houses, how in local government my father had six votes because he had a vote as a rate payer where we lived and one as company director of a firm in Belfast; he had a vote in Belfast City Council; he owned a house somewhere else and he had a vote for that. My father thought this was ludicrous too and he didn't exercise any of these votes. I didn't have a vote because I was living in my landlady's house. It was a rate payer's franchise and I wasn't a rate payer.

In Omagh there were three wards. The nationalist ward elected nine nationalists. If you had a vote you voted nine times. The two unionist wards elected six unionist members in one ward and six in the other. So, if you had a vote you voted six times. The wards were divided in such a way that the majority of the town lived in the nationalist ward. Nominally there was a nationalist majority, but of course with gerrymandering this wasn't reflected on the council!

I do remember one election when the Labour Party put up candidates. They were all set to end this cosy arrangement whereby the town was divided up between green and orange and so they put up candidates in all of the three wards. We lived in the nationalist ward where the unionists didn't put up candidates and vice versa, nationalists didn't put up candidates in the Unionist ward. On this occasion my unionist landlady went out and voted for all nine nationalists against the Labour Party and nationalists were told in the other wards by their nationalist politicians to vote for the unionists! I was flabbergasted!

When the civil rights movement came along, I very nearly joined. Maybe it was cowardly of me that I didn't. I went to a meeting addressed by John Hume and various people rushed to get me to stand. I was the only Protestant at the meeting and I knew that I was only being asked because I was a Protestant. It wasn't as if I was from the town; I was only a blow in. Something inside of me said 'no' and later, when they tried to co-opt me onto the committee, I turned that down as well. Looking back at those days I can say that, until people started dying, I found them exciting. I knew the North was corrupt and that it had to be changed. Then everything came apart. That's when I felt I had to do something and I joined the New Ulster Movement.

I was propelled into politics. My History class at school asked me if I would go with them to a Young Unionist meeting and in those days, of course, it was assumed that, if you were a Protestant, then you were a unionist and you could attend the meetings. It was at the time when the whole of the North was going up in flames and I remember one of the girls asked a question about the Unionist Party's policies during this present crisis. The speaker's reply was to talk about the Unionist Party's roads programme. Well, I realised that this girl was being fobbed off, so I interrupted, saying that I thought she wanted to know about the reform programme which the British were imposing on the Unionist government. Someone in the hall complained about New Ulster Movement members being allowed in the hall and I was thrown out. So I went down to the bar followed by someone from the press who wanted a statement from me. The next thing, I was being interviewed by the BBC outside the school and there were write ups in the press. I remember the press printed a photograph of the Young Unionist who had been elected Chairman and under him it said 'elected' and under my photograph it said 'ejected'. From that moment on I became involved in politics, went on to become active in forming the Alliance Party, stood twice, once for the Assembly and then for Westminster and lost my deposit both times, and generally became fascinated with the game of politics as well as everything else.

What the politics also did for me was that they encouraged me to write. I had always wanted to be a writer. I thought I would write short stories. I'd read Chekhov and O'Connor and all those people until I was blue in the face and I recognised their wonderful economy of detail. I could see when they had achieved it, but I was damned if I knew how to do it myself! The politics started me writing for another purpose. I wrote speeches for people and in so doing discovered that I had some facility with dialogue.

I had particularly wanted to write a play where there was a ferocious loyalist who had a credible argument, someone with whom one could identify. It seemed to me that loyalists were always portrayed as buffoons in plays and I always thought they were much more dangerous than buffoons. I had seen Ian Paisley at close quarters and realised that the man had charisma. He was pleasant and he was human despite all the awful things that he said which seemed to prove otherwise. I think also that I had realised that there were areas of politics one couldn't explain except by writing about them through stories and plays.

We succeeded in coming out against internment without a split in the Alliance Party, although of course Protestants in general were not so appalled with the introduction of internment as Catholics were. It didn't affect Protestants; it was Catholics who were being interned. The reason the Party held together under this pressure was because we consisted of both Catholics and Protestants and in the early days we spent a lot of time and energy explaining ourselves to each other. I have really to thank the Party for that experience. I continued to be active in the Party and around the time of the Ulster Workers' Strike I became full-time Party Organiser. I was on that bloody march, the back to work march with 15 others. I remember marching up the road with everyone screaming at us; that was a unique experience. The Convention came after the Ulster Workers' Strike and when that broke up, I became terribly disillusioned. I felt that there was just no hope for this place. I had a lot of disagreements and arguments with people within the Party. At the time I was writing a play for television about the Alliance Party canvassing in West Belfast. There was a furious attack on it in the Alliance Party paper, saying that it was all a fiction. Of course it was! It was a play! I felt I had to get out of full-time politics and because I didn't feel I would be able to become just a card-carrying member of the Party, I resigned and got more involved in my writing.

In the area of County Down where I am living now I have the opportunity to hear a lot of traditional music, mostly played by Protestants because the area is mostly Protestant. I also go to set dances. When classes to learn the Irish language were offered in Newtownards Town Hall I decided to take up the challenge. Whilst reading Irish history at Trinity I had realised that there was this other language which was the main language in Ireland and a potent force right through the 18th century and indeed was still the language of the peasantry in the nineteenth century, but I had never taken the decision to learn it. As I went to classes I gradually became aware of the fact that the people teaching me had a real love of the language. For me the discovery of the ghost of the older language in English speech in Ulster, our idioms and phrases, was a delight. One day travelling up to West Belfast for an Irish class I stopped in Comber to buy a paper. On the car park wall it said 'Irish Bastards Out'. I drove up the Falls Road and there was 'Brits Out'. Sometimes you begin to wonder if you are a different species, an alien.

I would say that I have an ambivalent attitude to Orangemen and what has become known as the Orange tradition, although I think that term is a misnomer. There is an Irish tradition and the Orange tradition is part of the Irish tradition. I think that the Orangemen represent a bloc which won't budge. It's not that I want them to become nationalists; I want them to be reasonable. In general though, I think we have a very narrow definition of the celebration of our culture in Northern Ireland. For example, we don't celebrate our economic tradition. The only ship building tradition we celebrate is the Titanic, the one that sank! I think people do know about the invention of the pneumatic tyre by Dunlop but Harry Ferguson is not one of our icons and yet, here is a man who revolutionised world agriculture! He invented the hydraulic system, the Ferguson three point connection, that works on the back of tractors and lifts machinery. Until Harry Ferguson in the 1930s, tractors were merely machines which pulled things after them. Horses were still more efficient. He was a brilliant man and yet the Harry Ferguson museum is in Birmingham, where of course they built the tractors. Quite frankly, in terms of the rest of the world Harry Ferguson is a great deal more significant than the Orange Order and the tractor he invented is as culturally significant as a tin whistle or a set dance or a sash.

I believe we are at a cross roads in Northern Ireland; I know everybody is always saying that we are at a cross roads! Well I see crossroads as places where people meet rather than depart. I think people should recognise more the mixture of identities that we are, the Gaelic Irish influence, the Presbyterian lowland Scots influence, the Highlands and

Islands' Scots Gallic influence, the English influence. All of these I see as a tremendous cultural enrichment. I hate this notion that one has to be in one camp or another. I hate this Ulster-British idea that I know the boys in school would have clung to because they have been pushed and driven into denying their Irishness. There must come a time when we recognise the interconnections of these islands and not compartmentalise ourselves. Perhaps there is a possibility, an opportunity now, after 25 years of violence, for this to happen, a time when the political and cultural gauleiters will not be able to control significant numbers of people.

There is a character in a Friel play who says: 'Confusion is not an ignoble condition'. I was reminded of that phrase once when I was interviewed by a German film crew. The interviewer became perplexed when I said that sometimes I felt British and sometimes I felt Irish. I asked him how would Kafka have described himself. There was a long silence, and then he looked at me and said: 'I think he would have said, "I am from Prague".' I said: 'Well, I am from Belfast.'

32

Janice Kennedy

Community Artist and Lecturer. Born 1955.

Do you know the theory that some people have about Ulster English – that it is really close to the English that was spoken in Shakespeare's time? Well, I thought about that a couple of years ago when I discovered to my amusement that, although I've celebrated my birthday on March 31st all my life, I was actually born just after midnight. When the repercussions of this became clear, my father, who was a Shankill Road man, boomed in true Shakespearean fashion, 'I will not be delivered of a fool', and he made the midwife change my birth certificate.

My parents had one of those disastrous war-time marriages which evidenced to me the essential split within loyalism: the love for the crown but the dislike of the English. Throughout my childhood I never met any of my relations from the Shankill Road who apparently didn't approve of my mother because she was English, but neither did I meet my English relatives because to them she had married a Paddy. My mother always said that she never understood Northern Ireland – all these Protestants and Catholics; in England she had just known of the Church of England. I have noticed differences in Protestants which I assume have come from the emphasis which each church places on its values. Presbyterians can be very judgemental. I was brought up a Methodist and I recognise that one of their values was that of hard work. I think that I am one of those people who jump into the twelve foot end of life and laboriously pull themselves up to the surface by their own boot straps.

My father was in business during the 1960s' boom time. He was a plastering contractor but he also lived up to his name and got plastered a lot. That was the sadness of my childhood, made more painful for me because I was the archetypal little girl who loved her daddy until she realised that he had feet of clay. My abiding memory, I guess you could get the Penguin Freud out for this one, is of standing in the dark mahogany panelled hall of our house on the Ballysillan Road when I was four years old. Straight ahead of me I could see our wooden slatted clothes drier in the kitchen and beside it my mother sitting at the table, crying. There was no light coming from the living room but I knew my father was in there and that he had lost his temper and was really drunk. I didn't have words like 'tyrant' or 'oppressor' at that age of course but, if I had, I would have used them. My father's alcoholism filled my childhood with violence and insecurity. When I couldn't sleep, I would tiptoe onto the landing and listen to my parents arguing downstairs and once I heard my father shouting that I was the only one of the family with blonde hair and blue eyes. I realise now that he was accusing my mother of having an affair but then I just knew that something was horribly wrong. When I was younger I'd fall asleep remembering the time I had paddled in the sea. I fell under the water and suddenly my eyes opened and I saw this beautiful landscape of coral and coloured stones set against a peaceful blueness. One night years later I realised that I had forgotten when I had last gone to sleep swimming in all those beautiful colours and was saddened that it had been taken away from me.

The year that my father died I became more estranged from my mother. I was in my first year at grammar school and the feeling of being trapped by my home life was emphasised by the fact that I was travelling across town to school and socialising with people of my own age from all over the city. I started to go out with a young guy who was a Catholic and we would tramp the streets talking and talking and talking about the state of the world. I really wanted to change society; I wanted to believe that there could be something better in the same way that I think every generation comes up with that hope and that promise of a better world.

That summer a friend invited me to go away on a camp with her in Kilkeel. It was only when I arrived that I realised that it was a religious camp. Our church had been reasonably relaxed about religion but this was a different experience, with people giving testimonials and being saved and born again. I remember being taken into a room with two or three other girls by a woman who said that it was like this: all the people who are saved and are going to heaven are up on the table and everyone who is not saved is on the floor and that includes Catholics. I just blurted out: 'I'm going out with a Catholic.' It must have been outlandish to say that I had a boyfriend in those days; I was only 13. They told me that going out with a Catholic was really bad; in fact it was terrible, and from that point on I rejected Christianity.

Later in life I came to understand about the privileges I had growing up as a Protestant which I could not have guessed at the time. One story which broke my heart was told to me by a friend who had gone to the same grammar school as my brothers. His parents had been socially mobile Catholics who must have thought that sending their son to a Protestant grammar school would help him to further his ambitions in life. He was bullied every day and used to wear cardboard up his jumper as body armour. One day the other boys punctured a football and set it on his head; they draped a red velvet curtain around him and put a sign around his neck saying 'The Pope', and marched him around the playground. The staff condoned it; they just let it happen.

The 'troubles' broke out when I was 14. I remember one day walking up the Antrim Road early in the morning and seeing all these people going to work. It was like an awful dream. I looked at their faces and they were blank, the buildings around them were grey and I looked at Belfast and I hated it. There was an eaves in the dockland which I used to see on my way to school. Jane Cassidy made a song about it; she is the only other person I know who has seen it. It was a big eaves with the words 'Who would have thought it' printed on it. Who would have thought it? That was what I used to think looking at Belfast; who would have thought it? I am in this place; it's full of people being burnt out and shootings and helicopters. I had this horrible feeling that suddenly all the buses would stop. Everybody would get off the buses. Everybody I saw on the television news would stop talking and they would say to me: 'Janice, it's just a joke; we have been kidding you all this time. The world isn't like this.' I had this awful horror that they would all own up, tell me it was all a joke and the joke had been on me, but they never did, they never owned up; they just kept that world and I spent years trying to understand how I could live in it and be a part of it.

Even though what was happening in my country upset me, I still thought of it as the beat of the drum which somehow didn't relate to me. At that time in the late 1960s the drugs subculture was hitting Belfast and when I discovered it, I ran away into a world where there was music and fun and where it didn't matter what religion anyone was. I turned on, tuned in and dropped out, although like Bill Clinton, of course, I never inhaled! It's hard to imagine those days now, the sense of feeling part of a world revolution, the intense search for some kind of identity that all my friends had at that time, searching for meaning in life and wanting to own a culture that was ours and which was just and right and creative and imaginative. It felt like we were a tribe who were holding out, being besieged by all the madness that was around us. It's not that I am promoting drugs, I wouldn't do that, but I think it is important to recognise they belonged to that time and that the drugs subculture became a refuge for many young people in a society which was in uproar and confusion.

I was still living at home with my mother, still at school working madly to pass my 'O' levels, although in my desperate alternative lifestyle I hated the way my grammar school was grooming me for the middle classes. I knew I should have gone to family planning but I didn't. I was 16 and fell pregnant. My mother told me that I had better get married and I just thought of the 21 years she had been unhappily married to my father and now she wished marriage on me. 'What will the neighbours think?', she said, and I thought, 'We don't even speak to our neighbours!'

I got married and moved out of Belfast to breathe in Antrim, to coin a phrase which all the advertisements of the day were peddling. I felt like some wacky freak living there on a housing estate with a small child. The houses had windows that went down to the ground and everybody walked by to see what everybody else had in their living room. My husband began another relationship with a woman who practised free love; it's difficult to imagine now, but I subscribed to free love too although I never practised it. Looking back, it was just an excuse for this woman to have an affair with my husband, disguised as a belief system. It was never going to work out and within two years I had left my husband and moved back to Belfast with my son. I found a flat at the bottom of the Antrim Road behind the barracks. I was 18 with a two year old son. I had nobody; my mother wouldn't help me. I spent hours and hours in the dole office trying to find a way to survive. I coped by living in a fantasy world. One evening I remember pushing my son down the Antrim Road and a bullet ricocheted past. This thought came to me that the pavement would open up and Galadriel [a character in *Lord of the Rings*] would come from Lothlórien and take me and my son to a better world. No one would care what happened to me anyway. I wasn't even scared by the bullet.

After the sixties people went in two directions, either into radical mysticism or radical politics. I managed to bring up my son in that flat for a couple of years but I was still searching for somewhere to belong. Friends of mine who had come out of the sixties were looking for another evolution too. All the attraction of that world of the drugs subculture was redundant and they had discovered Guru Maharaji and the Divine Light Mission. I went to live in the community house beside the ashram and took knowledge, essentially the four techniques of meditation. Guru Maharaji wore yellow robes – he dresses in a suit these days — but we didn't wear robes ourselves; there were no outward signs that we belonged to Divine Light. We were premies until we had kissed the feet of Guru Maharaji. There were many rituals based around Indian mysticism and the company of truth where we would gather rather like the Quakers do. People would speak of their experiences of meditation whenever the motion took them. The company of truth was very down to earth and I liked that but again, I was looking for an answer and I didn't find it. I went to one of the festivals to see Guru Maharaji and hated it. I hated all the hype. I kissed his feet but I hated it. I thought it was ridiculous and couldn't understand why everyone was so devoted. I left soon afterwards but I maintained my friendship with the people of that time. Like them, I sent my son to the Rudolf Steiner school when it opened. My son was one of the founder pupils.

I do see myself as affected by the world revolution that happened in the sixties and I was always open to the ideas which came out of that time. The first time I encountered radical politics was when I met the anarchist collective who ran Just Books. Again it was alternative, concerned with mutual aid rather than mutual aggression. I loved the people there; they are part of my history and they opened up a world for me that was international in its politics. During my time there I worked with the anti-nuclear group against Carnsore Point and concerned myself with workers' issues, democratic rights and sectarianism. I don't like slogans much but I do remember one from that time which expresses my feelings — 'sectarianism is a gun with a worker at both ends'. I identified with the cooperative nature of anarchism and its emphasis on people taking responsibility for their own actions within a non-hierarchical structure. There were people in the collective who sympathised with republicanism but they never preached to me. I think a united Ireland is a pipe dream myself and I can't imagine the South wanting x number of loyalists living in their society.

I still had to support my son and I was selling secondhand clothes in St. George's Market and driving taxis to survive. I'd passed a couple of 'A' levels at night classes but it wasn't until I was 26 and did a course called 'New Opportunities for Women' that I realised I could go to university. I went to study theatre and it was the best thing that I did in my whole life. I remember one of the Sociology lecturers joking with me that it was a course for single mothers and social deviants! Well, I got a first in that course! When I saw the university library I just thought, there is so much knowledge in here, and I joined extra-mural classes for the pleasure of learning more.

After university I had to work of course and I began to freelance as a community artist in Belfast. If you were to ask me where I felt most at home working in community arts I'd say it was in nationalist areas. There is more awareness in that community of culture, language, music and dancing. It was a strange experience for me when I first went to work in West Belfast, like being a social anthropologist who finds herself on unknown territory and has to learn a new language. I knew to say priest instead of vicar, but I was continually being caught out. One time I was working with children in the Whiterock and I said the priest is standing on the pulpit and they just looked at me and said, 'You mean the altar?' 'Yes, yes, the altar!' What struck me forcibly about Catholicism was its openness. In contrast, the community I came from was insular; we never really talked to people. I think Protestantism is very much about me and my God, me and my conscience, me and my family, me and my insurance policy and me and my thrift. In West Belfast I discovered things that I never knew as a Protestant, like you could phone up the p.p. (I discovered that meant parish priest), and say: 'There is going to be a show in the Conway Mill, 50p in, free crisps', and they announced it at mass. Free advertising; I just couldn't believe it; you could never get that done in a Protestant church. To my Protestant rationalist materialist mind, the churches and mass cards and medals and medallions were astonishing, utterly different from the strait-laced brown and cream Protestant churches with hymn numbers which I had known as a child.

At the same time, I have worked happily in all parts of Belfast and beyond. I spent five years devising cross-community plays with young people, Protestant and Catholic. The thing they all discover in the end is how like each other they are – sharing the same tastes in music, fashion, enjoying themselves, understanding and coming to terms with the realities of the world. Young Protestants and Catholics share the same need to question boundaries which have been defined for them. I do feel that what holds so many young people back in Northern Ireland is not necessarily sectarianism, but social and economic lack of opportunity.

What was so important to me was that after years of being an outsider, I finally discovered a way in which I could put something back into the society that I was a part of. I love community arts; it's a working class movement with many creative people working in some of the most deprived areas of the city and they understand that, although there are less economic opportunities for people living in these areas, creative expression flows. It is a continuous progression and that has nothing to do with social class. I love the work that I am doing now with children and young people. They have that same hope and promise that I had when I was their age.

My son is now grown up and I am fortunate that we share a great friendship and communication. I did not send him to any church and he was educated at the Steiner School in Holywood. The school was inclusive at a time when no integrated education was available in Northern Ireland. I wanted to leave him free to choose his own cultural identity and beliefs. Sometimes he and I smile about the fact that there are times when he feels the need for a cultural identity that indeed springs from my roots as his mother.

I think we should have political control over our lives in Northern Ireland but I don't think we should live out of London's pocket anymore than I think we should live out of Dublin's pocket. I think that what might be possible is some form of regional government with links to Britain and Ireland, but within that there must be parity of esteem. To me the North is a confluence of different cultures and aspirations and it's not that I think everyone can live together; obviously over the last quarter century it has been shown that people can't. Division is endemic now and it is all the more important for us to encourage dialogue and work out ways in which we can all live together in a society which recognises that everyone has rights and different aspirations which should be given the space to grow.

Sometimes I think I have been living in a parallel universe but I have been touched by everything, sometimes desperately, sometimes unconsciously, sometimes consciously, and it surprises me that more people don't realise how they have been shaped by their experiences and the society they live in. It saddens me that people who have a limited vision can't give others the space to live the lives that they choose. Even though I found it difficult to find my space, I never gave up my belief that life has so much to give and it gives me hope when I see people being creative and visionary in whatever sphere they have chosen. Freedom, I think, comes from responsibility. I remember Phillippe Gaulier saying: 'freedom you get little by little, every day and in every way.' It's barely perceptible. So many people live lives of quiet desperation; they narrow their worlds and they miss it.

Surviving Religion

Women remained silent. We were not allowed to speak. Our heads had to covered in shame because women were responsible for sin. Of course we were not held personally responsible, but it was our fault just the same. We dressed up in an array of ridiculous suits and hats. Our only contribution was making the sandwiches.

33

Lesbian Ceramic Artist

Born 1963.

I was brought up in a tradition which, on reflection, was more Scottish than Irish. Family relatives from the time of my great grandfather played in flute bands and pipe bands and the Twelfth, which was the big day out after having worked hard all year on the farm. Country bands were respectable, with girls' accordion bands and pipe bands dressed in beautiful Scottish uniforms with those tall busbies. I remember the Twelfth as being quite different from the blood and thunder bands people associate with it today which is more about males flexing their macho muscles. Membership of the Orange Order had a long tradition in our family and the celebrated story was how my great-grandfather, who was Master of the Lodge and used to wear an orange cloak, met his death from pneumonia on one very wet Twelfth. Over the years that family tradition changed and my father has nothing to do with it now. He says there is no heart in it; what is the point going out proclaiming to fight for God and Ulster protected by a hundred policemen walking either side of the parade? I can still see how the adrenaline builds up on those parades with that stirring music; it's not difficult to understand how they were all wound up to go into battle in the past. The music my parents played at home was Scottish, horrendous sentimental stuff. My granny talks fondly of Scotland and my parents took us on holiday many times there. My father uses many words that would be closely linked with Scottish dialect.

I don't have pleasant memories of the church and the way it controlled my life. I was a lively child with a creative mind and the continual

248

restrictions on my life led to a lot of frustration. The Presbyterian church which we attended, a plain square building, its only ornamentation an alpha and omega sign symbolising the beginning and the end, was linked to Scotland and on the old registers were the names of ministers who travelled over from there. The congregation of our church always had problems with the enthusiasm of evangelical preachers. They wanted their faith to be straight to the Bible, not too lively or fundamentalist. In the early days there were fights in the church with ministers who came with new ideas. The congregation locked one minister in the church because they disagreed with his way of preaching the gospel. Now of course the church is split between those who have been born again and the more traditional Presbyterians, which my parents favoured.

My father was a hard-working dairy farmer just outside Coleraine. We were comfortably off, so it never occurred to me that we would starve, but we were brought up in that Protestant tradition of hard work and thrift. As a family we never splashed out on anything frivolous. I didn't receive expensive Christmas presents and my parents would have tut tutted in a self-righteous way about other parents who spent a lot of money on their children. In some ways I'm glad that I have known that way of thinking and there are certain values in it which have stayed with me. I am not a great consumer of material things and I value simplicity. I don't think that was an intentional outcome of my upbringing but I do think it is a valuable principle to hold.

My problem was knowing how to enjoy myself and it has taken me years coming to terms with the guilt I had about going out and having a good time. I think celebration is hard for a lot of people who have been brought up in a traditional Presbyterian background. Thankfully, because I didn't enjoy myself when I was younger, I have a healthy liver due to a lack of alcohol! I really couldn't let go of the control and reservedness of my upbringing: this idea that one doesn't be frivolous – a dour attitude associated with Calvinism. My parents would not take alcohol or go into pubs. Indulgence was dangerous. My first impressions of the world as a young girl made me want to play and find pleasure in the life that was all around me but this was curtailed by the control of the ten commandments. I was continually taught to be reserved, careful with other people, especially Catholics; it was all right to talk to them but not to get too close. All our neighbours were Protestant farmers. They also would have had this code of behaviour, a closed door policy; the boundaries had been set. I attribute this to the generations of siege mentality and insecurity. Catholics had a much more easygoing and relaxed manner and the entrepreneurial Catholic dealers mixed freely with the Protestant farmers in a lifetime of buying and selling their cattle.

My family were strict and would have kept to the commandment of not working on a Sunday, not playing games or making a noise, but they were not fanatical and we were allowed to watch television for a couple of hours on a Sunday evening. We had Brethren neighbours. They didn't have a television at all and their children sneaked round to watch certain television programmes at our house. They lived in a big house behind trees and had been kept closed away. Friends were always brought to their house to play but they rarely went outside of that and they were so curious about everything. I remember they would never see us on a Sunday unless we met them on the road going to their Meeting House. Hard work and prosperity seemed to thrive in this environment. Ulster Presbyterians – 'God's frozen people', a friend of mine jokes! That was the community that I was brought up in, devoid of cultural growth, clinging to a fading heritage, afraid of change, a vacuum. The film *December Bride* is one of the few films dealing with Protestant rural life. It was set about 100 years ago and I found many of the attitudes portrayed in it very familiar.

I did rebel from an early age. I did things differently from the way I was expected to. I think that when you take your own path in life, it is more difficult; you put yourself in an isolated position. I see this as the more creative side of me. I was lucky to live on a farm and I had a pony which I loved and rode every day and entered into gymkhanas, but that was as a child. In later teenage years my life crashed on me. I rebelled against the church when I was 15; the guilt about sex together with the questioning of my own sexuality was too much for me.

We have so much segregation in this country in our schools – separate sex, religion and class. I never had Catholic friends until I went to Coleraine Tech at 17 and I felt strange about my friendships with Catholics because I had been taught to be suspicious of them. I liked traditional music but that was wrong and I felt uneasy about that too. Coming to terms with my lesbianism was just part of the break from what I had been taught. I constantly denied it to myself and experts told me it was just my depression, a part of my condition. I was struggling to find my identity and it became a whirlpool which got narrower and narrower until it became a vacuum. I was angry; I thrashed out the anger and frustration. My parents didn't know what to do. Everything I had been conditioned to believe in crashed and I spent a short period in a mental hospital. I will never be back there again no matter what.

I started to work out my aggression in a creative way though working with clay ceramics and went on to Art College, although most of my time there was a struggle to sort out what I needed in my life. I was more or less alone in that but people did come into my life at the right time and helped me, guardian angels who guided me and empathised with what I was feeling. Living away from my home environment and the freedom of Art College introduced me to new ideas which helped me to enjoy life. Religion in general, Protestant or Catholic, emphasises control and neglects to emphasise the love and celebration that God represents. We are constantly changing as we see and understand truths about ourselves. I have found a more loving God in myself, with universal concepts which give me the space to grow. I want to celebrate this in my art work. It is like seeing the world with new eyes.

I lived in a succession of shared houses. I had a room in a house full of girls who had just got out of convent school and were students at Queen's. They were wild – drinking, trying out everything, escaping from their background too. They always called me a grey prod because I hadn't strong political views! Then I spent a few years living in a house with archaeologists who introduced me to Celtic history and I gradually became interested in Celtic art and mythology. I'd studied for CSE which, unlike 'O' levels, concentrated on Irish History and Geography, so I knew about the United Irishmen, the Famine, Presbyterian ministers learning Irish, all the standard history, though I'm not passionately interested in it all. It's art that interests me. The weirdest place I ended up was a house of Irish speaking republicans. I love Irish culture and music but I also saw a lot of failings. Strong republican ideology makes me feel uncomfortable at times. I knew where I came from as if it was stamped on my forehead. I was a Protestant from Coleraine and at times I tried to hide that but it is what I was born into. Our conditioning runs deep; we are not without prejudice. I had difficulties too and that was scary. I think it is brilliant to learn Irish and wish I had the patience to do likewise but it can be dangerous to be too nostalgic or sentimental about the culture of nationalism. Like loyalism, it can become brainwashing and dangerous.

I think we can only struggle to be aware of our prejudices and awareness is half the battle. Later in life I came to meet people from other countries living in Belfast who had learnt about Northern Ireland out of books and told me what it was like to be a Protestant. I resented that. I was born into my Protestant culture; I can smell it, I can feel it. I know what it is like to be automatically assessing other people, their name, their school, their lifestyle, finding out eventually their religion from these telltale signs. It is something you have to be born into to fully understand. If I went to live in another culture, I might try to live in their culture but I haven't been conditioned in the same way that they have. Half my life was spent being conditioned to be a Protestant. I can't lose it overnight. Living in another country would make it easier, but I don't need to apologise either; it was part of my life.

When I was coming to terms with my sexuality I felt alone. There wasn't even a Lesbianline in those days. In many ways it has become easier in the last ten years to find a gay community. There is a much more open door feel to gay venues and many straight people mingle there. Discrimination is certainly still there and people are closeted at work. Many younger lesbians don't realise or care that the freedom they have to club was fought for by lesbian feminists who are now in their thirties and forties. There is not that same feeling of solidarity with many lesbians. This sexual freedom is delicate in Northern Ireland. We need not be complacent. The fear of losing respect or discrimination at work is very real. As an artist I do feel I have a bit more freedom to express my identity.

My first contact with lesbians was through women's groups. I found it very liberating to meet people with similar attitudes about their sexuality and feminist issues such as sexual stereotypes, discrimination against women and lesbians. I encountered the aspects of Northern Irish feminism which confronts nationalist/loyalist politics. Feminism easily follows the path of the nationalist cause and has a long history of this from the turn of the century. The unionist struggle never had room for women or fighting for their rights. I feel that feminism has leaned too much to the cause of nationalist women in the past, and Protestant women, especially from poor areas, had no voice. Nowadays, women's groups in Protestant areas are exploring Protestant women's culture. Many elements of women's spirituality are bound up in their Celtic past, folklore, rituals, land, crafts, language. We have lost touch with so much of this through sectarian paranoia, through fear of losing Protestant identity. What identity? I find this whole area of Celtic spirituality and lore fascinating and inspiring. It fits with my holistic approach to life and feeds my work too. Protestant culture, by comparison, is very misogynist and limiting to my creativity.

I think our society is changing and sometimes we are not really aware of it. In the last 50 years attitudes towards gay people having children or heterosexuals having children out of marriage have changed. There are struggles within Europe about identity and through time we are getting a little paler and I hope that will see changes in sectarian attitudes. I think there is an island mentality as well as a siege mentality. We have bonds between people which I don't think would have had the chance to survive if we had been living in the middle of the European land mass. That island mentality has been weakened by being in Europe and I wonder about the dream of the ideal country that some nationalists are struggling for. Ireland is still a beautiful country but our reality is not the same as it was 200 or 100 years ago and perhaps we will never have the power to shape our own destinies now that we are a part of Europe. I hope it will not become too homogenised, losing that special Celtic flavour and maybe we should be more concerned about our environment and Irish wildlife.

I worked in two different Catholic schools; they were situated beside each other, one a secondary and the other a grammar. They taught Irish culture in similar ways but beyond that they were two different worlds. The girls in the secondary school were the ones whose families had borne the brunt of the 'troubles'; their fathers had been shot and their families had been imprisoned. The grammar school girls came from wealthy families across the city and talked about going on exotic holidays. I think more people should look at our deprived areas where the social and economic problems reside; that is where our solutions can come from, seeing that the struggles of people in Ballymun in Dublin are the same as those that are found on the Shankill and the Falls.

I think anybody who is gay has a difficult path; maybe it is not by choice, but that is the path they are travelling and it gives a certain edge to life. I also wanted to be an artist – that is difficult too – and I spent many years thrashing out the negative aspects of my Protestant culture and religion which disparaged creativity. It was a big black hole which I had to find a way out of but in the end I had the strength to break free. I want to make a contribution to the new wave of Protestants who are finding an alternative to 'No Surrender'. We need to stop being the silent minority.

34

Youth and Community Worker

Born 1965.

I was brought up Plymouth Brethren. Let me explain first of all what our church was like. There was this big room, the gospel hall. It was completely bare. There were no pictures. Above the stage area it said, 'Jesus Christ is Lord'. There was no music, no organ or any instrument to which we could keep time; that would have been too much like enjoying ourselves. We sang hymns really rather badly. There were long periods of silence because there was no preacher. Occasionally a man who felt inspired would get up and talk. Sometimes some of the men got whipped up into such frenzy and enthusiasm that the service which was normally one and a half hours on a Sunday morning would go on and on and on. Men literally foaming at the mouth, almost having fits, ranting and raving that we were all going to go to hell unless we became saved. Even now, when people talk to be about being bored, I think to myself that no one can know what boredom is unless they have sat through those services week after week. Women remained silent. We were not allowed to speak. Our heads had to be covered in shame because women were responsible for sin. Of course, we were not held personally responsible, but it was our fault just the same. We dressed up in an array of ridiculous suits and hats. Our only contribution was making the sandwiches.

After morning service I went to Sunday school in the afternoon and then to evening service, and after that to the Youth Fellowship meeting. Throughout the week I went to prayer meetings which were similar to the Sunday services, although sometimes guest speakers were invited.

These were missionaries returned from Africa who told blood curdling stories of how they had exorcised evil spirits from black people and who showed us slides of their endeavours. During the holidays I was sent off to camp for a solid week of prayers and Bible reading. I don't know how I can express to you the greyness, the boredom interspersed with hysteria, the stereotypes, the clichés, the pettiness.

The Plymouth Brethren was my mother's church. My father is from Wexford; he was Church of Ireland and he continued to go to his church because he found the Plymouth Brethren too hysterical. His sister married a Catholic and whenever we visited them my brother and I used to think that Catholics had a great religion. When they went to church they didn't actually have to go into church; they could stand at the doorway and that was enough. We thought: bliss, that would just be perfect! When my brother was about six, I remember him saying that he wanted to be a Catholic when he grew up.

We lived in Holywood and our branch of the Brethren was not as strict as some of the other branches. We didn't have to eat separately from non-believers and in school we could attend other Bible classes. Girls were allowed to wear trousers; in other branches that was considered to be cross-dressing. Even so, my childhood was an isolating experience. I had to keep myself apart from the world because, if I died, my soul would want to stay with worldly things and not go up to heaven. It's not that I remember my childhood as lonely, more a childhood where I spent a lot of time on my own. I couldn't really mix with other children except at school, so I developed an inner world, a fantasy world where I enjoyed making up stories to myself, pottering about in my own daydreams.

I was allowed to join the Girls' Brigade, which is not at all like the Girl Guides or the Brownies who did activities which seemed quite fun. We marched, we read the Bible, we did a lot of military style aerobics, we did displays. Of course we were always out on Remembrance Sunday, freezing in our red, black and white uniforms with short skirts and ankle socks. The brigades were more like regiments; badges were awarded on how well the unit was turned out and how well we knew our Bibles and our drill.

Our church didn't have baptisms or christenings like those in the Anglican or Catholic church. They were considered akin to Satanism, the representation of all evil, for how could a baby be aware of its sin? You were baptised whenever you were saved and born again. In theory being born again is quite straightforward. It means accepting Jesus into your heart and asking for forgiveness for all your sins and acknowledging him as the one true God. It's not straightforward if you don't believe in it. By the time I was twelve I was absolutely petrified of going to hell and I thought the only way out of such a fate was to become saved, to be born again. I remember asking advice as to whether it was all right to be saved, not because you loved Jesus but because you didn't want to go to hell, and they said 'yes, as long as you are saved it doesn't matter why'.

My other great fear was water. I couldn't swim. To be saved you had to be baptised. The carpets and the floor of the Gospel Hall would be peeled back to reveal a tank where people were immersed in water to cleanse them from their sins. I never could bring myself to be immersed in water and so I was never baptised. As a result of this I had to sit separately from the main congregation.

Why did I not embrace it all? I could never understand why a God who created us and apparently loved us would do the things to us that they told us he would do. I think, also, that because my grandfather, who had a high profile in the church, sexually abused me, I saw the hypocrisy even when I was too young to have the words to express it.

My first memory of the 'troubles' intruding into our lives was one summer when my parents told me that we wouldn't be going down to Wexford to see family. They said there was a bit of trouble and we would wait until it blew over. It was years later when they realised that it wasn't going to blow over and we returned to Wexford. My dad worked for the Imperial Civil Service, which is different from the Northern Ireland Civil Service, so I do remember him checking under the car for bombs before he took me to school and wondering about who would want to blow up my dad. Thankfully nobody did. My mum always told us that, if anyone asked, we were to say that my dad was just a civil servant. Her background was extremely loyalist; she had uncles and relations who walked, the Orangemen in bowler hats brigade. A lot of them were in the military and they treated their families like their own personal private regiments, snapped orders at them in a quite impersonal way.

My uncle and aunt took us to the Twelfth parades, but my mum didn't really attend because of all the drinking that went on; all that was seen as sinful. I haven't seen any Orange marches for years. The Orange tradition seems sad in a way to me: how it means so much to them, how they get terribly affronted when Catholics from the Lower Ormeau put up those signs, 'No Orangemen, End Sectarian Marches', and how they continue to expect to march where people don't want them. I don't see the point of marching where you are not wanted.

After primary school in Holywood I went to Strathearn, an all-girls school in Belfast. The headmistress at that time was very old-fashioned, mostly interested in elocution lessons, drama and dancing classes. The school had the view that girls should find a nice man and settle down. After she left we had a headmistress who was more forward thinking, who wanted us to have careers of our own. She banned events like the Miss Strathearn Beauty Contest and drove us into the twentieth century. As to being taught anything about Ireland, there was very little. I can remember a lesson on the famine and asking why, when the Irish people were starving, had all the food been exported. My History teacher replied that it was because Irish people only knew how to cook potatoes and if they left the wheat behind, they wouldn't know what to do with it. Rather than waste the food it was more sensible to sell it abroad. She also explained to us that Wolfe Tone was a coward because he tried to commit suicide rather than face a firing squad; suicide was a cowardly thing to do. I suppose that you have to take into account that our History teacher had been brought up in China, completely detached from the real world, with nannies and governesses. I don't know why she was teaching History, probably because she was so old the school thought she had been there when history was happening!

I had one or two friends in school, but outside of school hours there really wasn't much point. My mum didn't agree with discos and parties. When I was about thirteen my friend's mother phoned every night for about a week pleading with my mother to let me go to this Blue Lamp Disco, which was the RUC's disco. I don't know what my mother thought went on at the disco. Eventually my friend's mother broke my mum and she let me go for this one time. After that, I didn't go to anything like that again until I was about 16.

My mother did send me to deportment classes where I learnt to walk, sit down, stand up, fold my legs properly, and learnt how to get in and out of sports cars elegantly. I did elocution to have a more English accent. Elocution, I think, is a very Protestant thing to do. There were other things that I would have liked to have done; for example, we didn't go in for singing and dancing and when I was a child I thought ballet was amazing, but my mother wouldn't allow it because it was too Catholic. I wanted a poncho too, but that was too Catholic as well. I worked out eventually that saying something was Catholic was a word for something that she didn't like, I don't think it really meant that she thought Catholics did ballet and wore ponchos.

Looking back, I can see my childhood as a time which was full of fear. I'm sure my family were no more broken down and ridiculous than anyone else's, but it was not a happy family. We kept up appearances. We were always clean and sparkling. We looked the part, our house looked the part and if you looked the part, then nobody would be any the wiser. From the age of 12 I reasoned with myself that I had only six more years to go before I could leave home and I just stuck it out. Strathearn Girls' School were pushing us out of the country, telling us not to stay in Northern Ireland where there was no future for us, and I applied and was accepted at a college in London. Just before I was supposed to leave I thought about how I didn't know anything about Northern Ireland; I hardly knew anybody and I decided to take a year out. I never did leave, I'm still here.

When I left home I discovered punk. Suddenly I was no longer this lone freak; I'd found a group I could join where I could fit in and I would be accepted. No more high heels and pencil skirts; I could wear boots and dye my hair lots of silly colours. When I left home I had nothing to believe in. I couldn't see anything positive or good in my religion or in my unionist background. For me all of that was dead and gone. With punk I felt a sense of people being equal. I didn't have to be quiet and silent like in church. People maybe would listen to what I had to say when I spoke; maybe they would accept me as valid a member of this society as anyone else; maybe I didn't have to feel ashamed all the time, have to keep quiet and just make sandwiches and cups of tea.

I joined a punk band and sang for them, wrote a few songs, toured England and Ireland and released a record. That was nice because I had no obvious musical talent and punk was ideal for someone with no obvious musical talent. I became interested in global issues, vegetarianism, feminism, wanted to find out about what was happening in the world. I got involved with Giros, which is a collective of people running a centre in Belfast and I've been there for the last ten years. It's a co-operative run on non-hierarchical and anti-sectarian lines. We have clubs, a café, practice rooms for bands, a magazine, silkscreen, a darkroom and we hope to have a recording studio one day. It was set up for young people, but today there are people of all ages who use the facilities and organise events.

Do I still think of myself as a Protestant? I've been thinking about this since you asked me to. No. It doesn't have any relationship to my life whatsoever, but as an Ulsterwoman, yes, over the past few years I have discovered that I do strongly identify with the North of Ireland much more so than I ever thought. The Ireland I would like to live in? It's hard to explain without sounding really twee. I would like to see Ireland united, not so much under any form of government that they are going to hash up over the next few years, but one where everyone is free and equal, where women are appreciated, not beaten up, not anyone being beaten up. I'd like children to have rights, abortion on demand for women, free contraception, workers' co-operatives with people making their own decisions for themselves. It sounds like an old-fashioned anarchist society, doesn't it?

Nowadays I don't see life in terms of black and white and good and evil. There is no longer just me and God. I don't live in a world where there isn't any light at the end of the tunnel until you die and go to heaven. I have free will and I accept myself. I've also learnt to accept my mother and her religion. I know I don't have to be a part of it and I try to be honest with her. Unfortunately she can't be honest with me, but that's okay; it would be too painful for her. It took an awfully long time to shake off that dirty feeling which the religion perpetrated and the sexual abuse certainly did, but I survived the religion and I survived the abuse. I don't need to be cleansed in the blood of Christ. I am all right as I am.

35

Thirty-something Lone Parent

When you grow up in a home where your parents profess to love God first, before their spouse or before their children, then along the way you realise that this belief, which at the end of the day may or may not be true, is more important to your parents than you are. My needs were always secondary to the church and it took me a long time to come to terms with that. When I look at the childhood my son is having compared to the strict Presbyterian childhood that I had, I feel that I was deprived of a lot of pleasure and fun. Fun is something which Presbyterianism is definitely short on!

Our lives centred almost exclusively around the church, and I remember it as a lifestyle full of don'ts – very judgemental and sickeningly self-righteous. We weren't allowed to play out on a Sunday, had to go to church, had to go to Sunday school, weren't allowed to watch television on a Sunday; in fact we weren't allowed to watch many programmes on television during the week either. Christian Endeavour during mid-week kept our spirits up; we weren't allowed to go to the movies, had to read the Bible, had to say prayers every night, no dancing, no gymnastics, no card games; there was never any alcohol in the house, rarely any cigarettes ... it was a childhood full of extreme behaviour patterns.

We had no social life really, apart from the church. There were the congregational socials and the Friday night socials, Brownies and Girl Guides on Tuesday night, sponsored walks for Christian Aid every year and the Christmas party. Being saved is big time in the Presbyterian church and I was born again along the way too, although for me it wasn't a great show, just a short prayer saying, 'Come into my heart, come into my heart, Lord Jesus'. It was an extreme way to have been brought up and very cold as well. It wasn't as if, whenever we were at church, people were brimming over with joy. It was all very superficial, anally retentive and respectable. People went to church to wear their Sunday hat and their Sunday coat and, if Jesus had turned up for the service, I used to imagine how he would have been bucked out onto the street. One of the final straws for me was when my mother threw me out of the car one Sunday because I wasn't dressed right. She would rather I didn't go to church than have me go not properly dressed.

Occasionally we would have people round for tea and sandwiches. The house would be cleaned from top to bottom. The china cups and plates would be set out on the table together with the three-tiered cake stand. Two minutes before everyone was due to arrive I put my best frock on because, if I'd got it dirty, I was in mega trouble. Yet again, appearance was everything. Personal problems were never shared, feelings were never discussed – cold, middle class respectability was strictly adhered to at all times. After tea, the women would retire to the kitchen and the men would sit in the living room and talk politics. Afterwards there would be the inevitable post-mortem, my mother worrying about what the tea was like, comparing her sponge cake to others. The whole process would be repeated when we visited other people for tea. I used to love going to one uncle and aunt's house because they were really laid back and you got the sense there hadn't been an enormous spring clean before you came, so it didn't matter if you dropped a crumb on the floor. They were an exception; the other houses were spotless. I must say that, thankfully, I haven't inherited that tradition!

I was 18 before I finally gave it all up. I questioned the sham and hypocrisy over many years and came to the realisation that so many things didn't add up. Protestantism is full of contradictions. On the one hand you learn that it is easier for a camel to get through the eye of the needle than a rich man to get into heaven, but on the other hand the church is very materialistic. A lot of the prayers would run along the lines of: 'O Lord, please give us money for our new roof'. In the Protestant church money is tithed, which means that a tenth of family income is given to the Lord. Every week a collection is made and at the end of the year a book is published detailing how much everyone has given, which my parents would go through, remarking on the contributions. I realised also that once I had accepted the Lord Jesus into my heart as my saviour, then that was me. It didn't really matter what I did with the rest of my life because once you are saved, you are always saved. If what they said to me was true and only about 0.2% of the world's population was going to heaven, I reasoned that it would be *them* in heaven and I didn't really want to be there. It was liberating for me when I worked that one out! Nowadays I am very anti-church, anti-all churches, including the Catholic church, although that feels different; it doesn't hurt the same way as the Presbyterian church does.

We lived in suburbia. Now I know that we lived in a middle class area, but to me then it was just like an ordinary house; in fact, I used to think that we were poor. My father ran a Sunday school in a working class area and the children there all got colour televisions before we did and always seemed to have money to spend in the corner shop. I had a real sense that I was different from them and I used to be jealous of how they were allowed to play on the streets and called adults by their first names. With us it was always 'Mr' and 'Mrs', though I didn't realise this as a class difference at the time. The first area we lived in was Protestant at the outset, but it changed over the years and my father worried that if we were the only Protestant family, we might suffer intimidation. My mother is a genuinely non-sectarian person, which probably has to do with being from the South of Ireland, though I don't think that she would have liked to have lived in an area where she was the only Protestant, which I think is understandable. I think my father was quite sectarian. There was a Catholic family living at the end of our street which confirmed all the stereotypes that Protestants have of Catholics. They had seven children, so obviously their house was more run down than any of our Protestant houses with their one- or two-children families. Their furniture was never as nice, their clothes were never as nice, there seemed to be beds everywhere and they had a run down car. Once, when I was playing in their garden, I came across rosary beads. I thought I had found a necklace and I took it home. My father went spare telling me to get it out of the house. They were the devil's beads.

The Presbyterian church fed stories about the Catholic church all the time. They couldn't go to heaven for a start! Generally their antipathy would have centred around the role of the priest and worshipping graven images which was seen as breaking one of the commandments. When the 'troubles' started, the priest talked for the nationalist community and appeared to have more of a hold on Catholic people than the minister did on Protestant people and this reaffirmed the power of the priest. During the civil rights days Bernadette Devlin would have been seen as really extreme and people would poke fun at her rather like the way nationalists poke fun at Ian Paisley. I remember a fancy dress party in Brownies and one of the girls dressed up as Bernadette Devlin and brought her petrol bomb. Everyone thought that was really funny.

The big issue for my family, though, was religion rather than politics and I never remember being brought up to be a unionist. As a teenager I don't even know if I would have wanted to retain the link with Britain. A lot of unionism is based on negativity and is directed towards the South of Ireland, but we travelled over the border all the time to see relatives. I grew up seeing my Protestant family down south living a middle class lifestyle in a big house and sending their children to Protestant schools. I never saw them being forced to be Catholics. Though, having said that, I never had the sense that the nationalist community was made up people with differing opinions. I saw their community more akin to the pan-nationalist point of view that many Protestants have. They were just Catholics and that equalled the IRA, which meant riots and bombs and trouble. In my last year at school the hunger strike happened and everyone talked about what would happen when Bobby Sands died. Again the concern was more for the trouble that Catholics would cause; it wasn't that it mattered if he died. I watched the women out with the bin lids on the television after he died and I thought they were slightly mad, like Jane Eyre's woman in the attic. That summer I went down to Carnsore Point for the anti-nuclear demonstration with a group of friends. We were all Protestants. On the journey down we saw all the posters in support of the hunger strikers and met people from Greece and Portugal and Spain who supported them. We were absolutely gob smacked, astounded that the hunger strikers had support from all over the world.

After school I worked in a sweet shop in a Protestant area of East Belfast. That was when I realised what sectarianism was like for the first time. I used to get off the bus in the heart of Protestant East Belfast, but for some reason the local hoods got it into their heads that I was going to the Short Strand and that I was a Catholic. They used to come into the shop and torture the life out of me. It was sectarian harassment and very intimidating. After that I did some child minding, first with a French family in London, which made me realise how many people in the world hate the English, and then in Belfast for a lone parent who was a republican. That was a good experience for me, seeing her as a person with children and a job rather than thinking of her as a republican in that demonised manner that so often happens in our society.

When I went to university I mixed mainly with Catholics. Partly that had to do with the Social Sciences course that I was studying which attracted students who were more likely to be left-wing and nationalist, but it wasn't that I just happened to be in that milieu; I chose it. I joined the women's group and became involved in the Right to Information Campaign in the South of Ireland, around the time the family planning clinics were being sued. I also became friends with the Gaeilgeoir crowd and I started attending Irish classes.

I'd always wanted to learn Irish even as a child and it frustrated me that I couldn't learn Irish at school. I think Irish is a beautiful language. It's so lyrical; I love the sounds of the words. It's a much nicer language to think in than English which has so many words to do with ownership. 'I own this house, this house is mine, this house belongs to me, this is my possession.' In Irish you can't actually say that. Things are either 'at you', 'with you' or 'on you'. That's a different concept of ownership, greed and material wealth to have when things are temporarily with you in your life. Through Irish culture, its language, politics and music I discovered Ireland as my spiritual, emotional and political base. I wouldn't say that I am an atheist; I still recognise that there is a spiritual side to oneself, but nowadays I find that spirituality in my sense of belonging to Ireland, its mountains and sea and ancient history, more a gentle women's spirituality based around nature rather than the Christianity that I was brought up with which was based around buildings, rules, divisions.

For a long time I had a problem owning my Protestantism and it is only recently that I have come to say that 'Yes, I am a Protestant', and feel okay about saying it. I think that had to do with wanting to be accepted, not for my religious background, but as a feminist and socialist, which is how I see myself. I felt shame because of what the Protestant community had done over the years and I didn't want to be identified with the baggage of the James Molyneaux, Ian Paisley and David Trimble brigade. I've never joined a political party; I think it would be too restricting, like the religion I gave up, but the demands of Clar na mBan would be my ideal. A united socialist Irish republic where everyone including gays, women, Travellers, have equal rights and parity of esteem. I believe Protestant culture and identity would survive in a united Ireland. Northern Ireland is too small to exist on its own; partition has been a disaster and I think the only way forward for Ireland is reunification.

To those Protestants who don't agree with me I would ask them to think about why they want to be part of Britain. Is it economic reasons? Is it based on fear? Is it based on ignorance? I would say: spend some time down south, see how Protestants live. Do they all live in squalor and abject poverty? Do they have to go to mass every Sunday? Go down and see for yourself. I would say: look at the social security system, look at the welfare system, look at wage levels. Compare them to Britain. Look at the economics. Are we going to be any worse off if we reunite? Think long term; survey after survey shows that Britain doesn't want us; Ireland does want us. Go to the people who want you, not the people who don't want you.

Leaving Ireland

When you go away from your home you get a greater sense of your identity. I am Irish. I have grown up in Ireland.

36

Tom Bevan

Artist. Born 1946.

I don't know much about our family background – it was all rather vague – but my aunt used to tell lots of stories. She swears that part of our family came over with William of Orange and we were also supposed to be illegitimately connected with Brian Faulkner's family; Faulkner was my mother's family name. But all of this may just be fantasizing. The men on my mother's side were arrested at the beginning of World War One in a fit of frenzy because the British thought they were German spies. I have a book in the house, a pocket book of orders on how to salute superior officers, belonging to my grandfather. He was wounded during the war and it actually does have the bullet hole through it, complete with the stain of his blood. He became a shop owner in Dee Street in East Belfast, which was where I was born. My father was Welsh, conservative but not in any way loyalist; he thought that was all pretty stupid although he didn't talk much about it.

My mother's impulses were to better herself. She had designs to be modern and, as my father didn't smoke or drink, all the money went back into the house. My mother delighted in contemporary furniture, thin legged Scandinavian tables, geometric decorations and the flowery wallpaper of that time in the fifties. We were generally known as the neatest and cleanest house in the street. In that sort of upbringing it would have been considered too working class, too beneath ourselves, to be overtly loyalist and as far as being Protestant, I picked that up from the society around us. I was taken to see a film on Martin Luther whilst I was still at primary school. I can't remember much except that it was very dark, lots of black and dark red. And I remember the Twelfth bonfires;

I would have gone to those, and we did see the Twelfth parade, but never really took part to any great degree.

My particular struggle in life was not breaking away from loyalism but really breaking away from a very conservative family. My family wasn't particularly religious but it was very disciplinarian and I saw that reflected in the society which I was brought up in. Codes of behaviour and religious attitudes were extraordinarily disciplinarian, all to do with how you were failing, what you were not doing right and why you should be punished for it. I had so many rules to abide by that I couldn't cope with them and my road to being free of the Ulster Protestant trappings was quite simply that I saw them as an extension of my family's values which I certainly wasn't going to obey.

I think my mother confused me and my older brother with ornaments. She was very young and confused life with a tidy home. She wanted us to sit still and do nothing, completely Victorian; we were allowed to read but not play, so I became more intellectualised. The books I would have read would have been encyclopedias and books on history and other cultures. My mother also kept us away from the ordinary people; I can certainly remember being beaten because I was rolling in the gutter and playing with ordinary children. We were trained to be different and supposedly better and that has had repercussions on my life ever since.

I went to elocution; that was all part of bettering oneself. I don't think there would have been too many people in Dee Street who would have gone to elocution. My father was a singer which was seen as artistic and was much admired as an attribute which was different to the usual. As a child I became a very good opera singer but it meant that I was a bit of an outsider at school. I visited friends once who lived on a housing estate and the local people took a sort of frenzy for some reason and trapped me in a house for 2 to 3 hours while 100 people milled around the door. I had to stand on the balcony and sing songs before they would let me go. That was a bit strange. I sang for St. Anne's Cathedral choir and was picked for the English Opera Group to sing in the Aldeburgh Festival in the early 60s. I went there as a small Irish boy and I remember them saying that when I talked I had an Irish accent and when I sang I had no accent at all, together with remarks about whether I had pigs and chickens in the kitchen at home.

I knew the word taig for Catholics but I really had no idea of the lives other people were living. I remember one of those particular moments of childhood; I was about eight years old, and I was quite adventurous, tended to wander off. Anyway, I did walk up Seaforde Street to see what Catholics were like and I can remember looking into the windows and seeing small ornaments on tables and window ledges and thinking they were exactly the same as the ornaments I saw in Dee Street. At that early age something must have clicked in me. To be conscious that I was thinking these people are just the same meant that somewhere along the line I must have been receiving messages that they were different. We had a neighbour who had been a member of the old Royal Irish Constabulary and later on in my childhood he told me about his exploits, going out and abducting complete Catholic families, murdering them and throwing the bodies in the river. They did this, he said, to get rid of dead wood from the ship of state. That shocked me.

I left home when I was 16. My parents told me to leave because I was wearing this green army jacket; that was too much. It was a tactical move on their part; they assumed I couldn't survive by myself, so after they let me wallow in my misery for a couple of weeks, they said I could come home. I just said 'no thanks' and struggled on from there, found a job working in the spice store at Purity Irish sausages up the Cregagh Road and became Assistant Purchasing Manager at the age of 18. That didn't last so long. I spent a couple of years hanging around the alternative culture of the late sixties, bumped into people like Terri Hooley and the crowd who hung around the Linenhall steps. It was a very mixed group of people, very anti-establishment, though I was on the fringes of it all. I didn't play their music, saw their drugs but didn't take too many of them. I was more likely to be lying in a corner reading books. I remember we drank in a bar called the Pike on the Crumlin Road where they had Irish music. In my innocence I was under the illusion for a while that the Pike was to do with fish!

I had a generalised interest in art and when I started beginning to have an opinion, I found that I was actually very conservative. However I was able to learn quickly and to change. People often imagine that I am very intelligent. In fact I am not; what I am is not exactly a part of my culture and this has meant that I am freer to push forward a little more that others are, in art and other things. Not being limited by one viewpoint gives one the freedom to do that but it also means that I never really felt a part of anything.

When I am away from Ireland I don't miss it in the slightest. I like the landscape but I don't feel that it requires 1000 years of history behind every movement to walk across it. Yet I'm conscious that at the same time as my saying how non-Irish I am, in actuality I am Irish in ways that I cannot see. One of the hobbies I had as a child was gathering fossils and I have always been fascinated by the idea of defining societies by the objects which are discarded, rejected as not worthy anymore. In one of the Arab countries I visited on my travels I remember seeing buildings where the stones had been inscribed with Roman lettering. They meant something to me but the Arabs had a complete disregard for their original meaning and had used the stones in new ways which meant something in their culture. That resonated with me. I like the idea of something which has once been important treated with disrespect, a sort of uninterest; I like that a lot.

There is one incident from my assemblage *Nothing is Lost* which is taken from my childhood. The minister came into school and we all had to write an essay on what happens when we die. I wrote down two words and spent the rest of the period looking around. I was about 12 years old and I could see the minister watching me, wondering what I was up to. All the other children were writing away: if you were a good little girl or boy this and that would happen to you, whatever, whatever, whatever. At the end of the period it was time to read our essays and he came over to mine and picked up the page. The two words I had written were 'you rot'. He went crazy, dragged me around a bit and said, 'Will you die in this belief, boy?', and when he said 'boy', he spat all over me. I don't like religion in education; that should go for sure.

I always thought my work was not political. I have lots of arguments about how it is not political but in fact I suppose it must be. It is very socially orientated anyway. I wonder what there is in idealism that drives people to join the IRA or the UDA. I tend to be more anti-Protestant than I am anti-Catholic or anti-nationalist because I suppose I grew up in the Protestant tradition and I loathed it, whereas nationalism has an unknown quality for me which holds out the possibility of being something different. Some of my work has dealt in a small way with the weight of history. One piece is called *A Fall of Dust*. It's a sculpture, essentially a box with Orange masonic emblems falling down like dust falls down, or rather like the way the limestone of County Antrim was made. All those small animals falling down to the bottom and building up a huge layer. Another sculpture was *Orangemen with Fruit in Season* – old dour Orangemen connected with images of bright fruit, strongly coloured bananas and so on, showing their death, how deadly they are, how lacking in juices. I've drawn Orange men with pink socks, wondering what would Orangemen be like if they traditionally wore pink socks. Could they have the same attitudes of mind about 'no surrender' and 'not an inch'? Those phrases that they choose to mark out their attitudes on the world are very lacking in life to me.

I went to New York in 1993 with an arts residency and I stayed on. The apartment they gave me was in Sunnyside, which is an Irish area but really, I saw very few Irish people. I did go to Irish pubs but I found them very conservative and I didn't feel any deep connection. I've always been intrigued by the messages one receives as a Protestant about being careful of Catholics in Northern Ireland and in New York of course the messages one receives are about being careful of blacks. I think there are enormous parallels in how minority groups cope psychologically with the pressures that they are under. I think generally humans react very similarly to resentment and being defined by stereotypes that others have determined. I was refused a job only once for being Irish. That was in England. They said I would be drunk every Monday morning. Of course, when I went to America I was seen primarily as white, probably quite establishment; that interested me, the way one moves through categories.

I met black people after my studio closed at midnight. I would go out gathering material from big dumpsters for my art works and they would be there gathering materials to survive. Generally everyone was completely okay and I had lots of interesting discussions but they were rather wary at first. They thought that I looked Jewish but of course when I said I was Irish, it was of no advantage in understanding for them. The Irish and the blacks have had such a bad history anyway; that's the pity about minorities, that they have not been able to learn from their own experience of being the underdog in their dealings with other minorities.

I had an exhibition in Manhattan called 'Imaginary Categories'. I used both real and unreal categories. I made up ridiculous categories but then, even the real categories are ridiculous. I showed lots of faces of Asian people, merely defining them as people who can't distinguish L from R sounds. It really is a category but it shouldn't be the most important category of how they are defined. I made up a category from photographs of schoolgirls from the *Down Recorder* and defined them in terms of how strongly they aspirated the letter H. I did find it fascinating how black people have such a problem escaping being categorised. If a black man is rough and violent it is because he is black, but then if he tries to be a businessman or live a modern American life he is Uncle Tomming and that is also because he is black. A black person cannot escape being black just as in the same way in Northern Ireland Catholics cannot escape their being Catholic. Once a person is defined, their every movement is interpreted in terms of that definition. Again I wonder about internalised sense of shame and alienation. The anger one sees in black people in America is very much to do with the hundreds of years of humiliation that they have received. It made me think of Catholic people here. Why should they take part in this culture that they don't feel a part of?

In America people often feel that life has no meaning, whereas in Northern Ireland I think that people feel that their lives do have meaning – not just in religious terms, that they think God is weighing up everything, though that is certainly a part of it, more this cultural habit of feeling that their lives are being considered. That means one considers one's life has some meaning. Maybe you lose that when you become very secular, although of course in America consumer fetishism takes the place of religion; people buy more objects to fill the void. My mother would have been quite at home there.

I don't have deep emotional connections with society which clearly other people here have. I know that we really can't forget the past but we can consider it of no account and I'd like the opportunity to step afresh onto this land and not be trenched by history. I can't feel a deep-seated need to hold the line. As far as I can see we are only trying to find a way to live. Let's talk about it, what's the problem, particularly now when we can't escape into fantasies about the people in the South of Ireland being so poor that they have to travel North to grab our shipbuilding. Many people do feel that Ireland is one nation; maybe the weight of history means a united Ireland will be the answer, but for me it is only one of many possible answers. In any event, I doubt whether anyone will come to seek my opinion when they are about to make that decision.

37

Christine Bell

Lawyer. Born 1967.

I've tried to think recently about attitudes to Catholics during my education given that my school was in a staunch loyalist area. I have to say I can't ever remember anything sectarian being said. The first time I heard about Catholics and Protestants was when a minister came to preach at our church in the 1970s and I remember having to ask my mother whether I was Catholic or Protestant. I knew I was Presbyterian but I was unclear as to which that was. I think we accepted our lives the way they were and Catholics didn't really exist for us. Later, when Bishop Tutu visited our church, he was asked a question about white Christians and he said that a lot of the time they didn't know what was happening in the townships; all they saw was black people coming into their areas to work and then going home. It struck me that I lived with that sort of apartheid. Apartheid can be a very loaded term but I just mean apartheid in the sense of separation. I had secular friendships at school but socially my life revolved around the church and my family; that really was my life. People talked politics but even then those politics were not particularly about Catholics and Protestants.

I think the divisions that plagued me in my life were similar to the debates over Catholics and Protestants. They centred around whether people were proper Christians or not. The key factor we were taught in becoming a Christian was praying to Jesus and asking him to come into our lives so that we could be saved. So for me the fundamental division between people was whether they were Christians or not Christians in that personal faith context. Certainly anybody could take that commitment and that included Catholics; it was always very clear that the Gospel message was for everybody.

The church that I went to, and still go to, is regarded as one of the most liberal, but I always feel that liberal is used in a strange context. The church is politically liberal but it stands full square evangelical. This is where I think one can cut across the divisions normally associated with religion and Protestantism and where I would see a radical potential for the church. For me, Evangelicalism, if taken seriously, means a commitment against bigotry. The reason our church is considered liberal is because it is ecumenical. I could never understand Paisley or anyone who is evangelical not including Catholics within the context of the second commandment, to 'love your neighbour as yourself'. It seems to me that the Good Samaritan story, which is the illustration of that commandment, could have been written for Northern Ireland. The story is about a religious group, the Samaritans, who came from the same roots as the Jews but were considered heretical. That is an analogy one cannot escape. Catholics are preeminently the first people for Protestants to be neighbourly to.

I did question the influence of the church as I was growing up. It gave me a very conservative life and as a child and a teenager I hated that I was the odd one out. It is often assumed these days that Christians were in the mainstream, but in fact at school we were very much a minority, a handful of people at odds with the rest of the class. I'd say that if you asked people I knew at school about me they would say I was all right but I was a bit weird or I was a bit religious. I never really wanted to be a stuffy Christian and tried to do all the things that teenagers do as well as drawing the line because of my faith. A really big conflict in later teens was alcohol. It's changed now, but at that time one couldn't really be a Christian and drink. That meant not ever going to a pub either. I made a decision that I wouldn't drink but I would go to pubs, but winning that concession from my parents was a battle in itself. Discos and boyfriends were another problem area. All boyfriends are people one might potentially marry and one can't marry people who aren't Christians. Darkness and light don't go together.

Now I sit in church and feel very angry at its teachings on sexuality. Not having sex before marriage is a fundamental definition of whether you are a Christian or not. There are lots of other things you can disobey and still be a part of the body of the church but that one puts you outside. People will really deny what I am about to say but I think it is a burden which is put on women more than men. Whether they will be able to get married is a real concern for teenage girls within the church. I know a lot of strong single women in our church and a number of them are openly unhappy about not being in a relationship. I sometimes think that's why there is a harshness towards lesbian and gay people which condemns them to a life of celibacy. There are a lot of people in the church taking that on themselves anyway and they don't see themselves as having a choice.

I also think that it is unforgivable to refuse to teach sex education and contraception. People don't decide not to sleep with each other simply because they don't know how to use condoms. Yet that seems to be the rationale for not telling them. What would the moral value in that be? I think in situations where a woman has an unwanted pregnancy, abortion is often an easier option than facing everyone as a single mother. That is seen as having committed a huge sin, not to mention all the other strains of single motherhood, like poor job prospects and lack of adequate childcare provision.

Presbyterianism doesn't dictate any political viewpoint. It's possible to be a republican just as much as it is possible to be a loyalist. Certainly I don't feel Presbyterianism means 'For God and Ulster'; in fact it is the Presbyterian Church of Ireland. My grandfather was a Presbyterian minister and after he retired from the church in Belfast, he worked week ends and holidays in Carndonagh and Malin in Donegal where the congregation hadn't had a minister for years. Realising that unionists refused to address this very vibrant religious Protestant Irish community only 20 miles north of the border was a formative experience for me and an illustration that a person could be Protestant and not unionist. Although there were still Catholic and Protestant divisions in that community, especially around the issue of mixed marriages, there were no unionist and nationalist divisions. Everyone was proud to be Irish.

The other big influence on my life was music and particularly attending the School of Music on Saturdays. I was the only girl from my school to go there, so for the first few weeks I didn't have any friends. I remember standing at break time, wanting to play with one group of girls who used to play the most interesting games and thinking what lovely names they had. I realise now that they were Catholic names – Áine, Orlaith, Bernadette – but they were names that I had never heard before. There were greater opportunities to socialise at the School of Music when it came to my teenage years. We would have classes in the evenings and sit and talk to each other. Most of my social life still took place through the church but my secular social life began to revolve around the School of Music rather than through my friends at school. I found myself much more comfortable with that. The way to be cool in the School of Music was to be good at what you played and being a Christian was less of a problem than it was at school because people were coming from different backgrounds anyway and I didn't stand out as different in the same way. We did talk about religion. A lot of my Catholic friends were very religious and much more Christian than my Protestant friends. I genuinely made friends irrespective of whether they were Catholic or Protestant and those friendships have lasted to the present day.

If I hadn't joined the School of Music I wouldn't have met Catholics until I went to university and even then I think it would have been possible for me to go through university without making any Catholic friends. In the event I didn't stay in Northern Ireland but opted for Cambridge. It wasn't that I was trying to escape Northern Ireland, more that I wanted to be involved, but I could never really find the way to be involved. I did go to lots of peace initiatives and was very attracted to non-violence and radical approaches to Christianity like those espoused by Martin Luther King. The degree course at Cambridge was a year shorter than at Queen's and I reasoned that a Cambridge degree would give me better opportunities.

Looking back, it isn't an experience I would want to repeat. I am so biased against living in England that people keep saying to me it is not all like Cambridge. It was the worst combination of many things with students living up to some pretentious Cambridge stereotype and most of them came from wealthy backgrounds. That was a shock to my system. Class took on a new meaning and I did feel like the poor relative even though back home, with both of my parents being teachers, we would have considered ourselves to be comfortably middle class. I think going to England is a shock to your system as a Protestant anyway. I was regarded as Irish – there wasn't a choice about that – and it made me really unionist. I became interested in the Equal Citizenship Campaign, I think as a way of trying to address the racism, this idea of being treated as unequal and lesser because I was Irish. I wrote a diatribe which was published in a magazine against the Anglo-Irish Agreement, looking up international law and arguing whether it had impinged sovereignty. Now I think, why did I do that? Back home I argued that the Anglo-Irish Agreement was a good thing. I did think that it was insulting for the British and Irish governments to deliberately go against the wishes of the Protestant community but in terms of the content of the Agreement, I agreed with much of it.

I found politics in England more primitive than here. I felt people squandered their political liberties and didn't exercise their political views with any degree of respect for other people. In Northern Ireland the opposite is true. The strain of being nice to people is terrible and a lot of political issues like abortion, for instance, are not discussed because it might reveal people's views on other issues and that would be impolite. I felt people in England didn't appreciate the worth of their political freedom. It wasn't that I was sitting feeling vastly superior but definitely feeling that growing up in Northern Ireland had given me insights into the fundamental issues of life, what makes people tick and how to accommodate people who are different from yourself, in the same way, I think, that women often think about power and conformity whereas men, as a rule do not, because they haven't had to live the same experiences.

I returned home after Cambridge and spent a horrible year at Queen's. I was looking forward to the course which was about the bar and law and I thought I would be with quite a political group of people. I was amazed that they didn't want to discuss Northern Irish politics or indeed didn't want to discuss politics elsewhere in the world. They simply weren't interested. I was told that when it had been discussed previously there had been some bigotry and no one wanted to raise issues which might give rise to that.

I really did want to get away then and I applied for a scholarship to Harvard to study civil rights and law. Harvard was my political birth much more than Cambridge. I was on an international programme with people from 52 countries and it was definitely the best year of my life. We talked about politics and country situations all the time; there were meetings on human rights, the wall was coming down in Berlin and for the first time I met people from countries in Latin America which had recently emerged from dictatorship. Those students had been active in pro-democracy and pro-human rights campaigns in difficult situations.

I did relate issues back to Northern Ireland but the more you look into countries and attempt comparative analysis, the more you realise that issues are specific to local experience. Northern Irish Catholics can't be equated with African Americans, there are just so many different factors affecting each group; but where there are parallels is in concepts of democracy and civil liberties and how absence of power reinforces itself. Even though America has a Bill of Rights, the apartheid and racism one sees there is shocking. A lot of white Americans make excuses by saying that black people are more into crime or they have a drugs problem and that made me think about the excuses Protestants make about Catholic disadvantage. It made me realise that what was necessary was a need for concrete policies to prevent job discrimination and unequal opportunities in life. I would see some of those same dynamics at work in Northern Ireland.

In terms of remedies and political debate and what constitutes discrimination I think that the Protestant community hasn't really grasped that discrimination isn't about sitting across the table from somebody and saying, 'I won't give you a job because you are x, y or z', but that it is about the choices that society makes as to what structures to set up which address the legacies of the past. I think Protestants hate the discrimination debate because they see it as pointing the finger at them, saying they are still bigots. In effect the discrimination debate has moved on from that. Many of the issues people are discussing, like targeting social need, stand to advantage Protestants. Fair treatment is about fair treatment. These are principles which should guide policy decisions.

North Americans are always very optimistic in thinking that every problem has a solution whereas I think my natural instincts, and it is a Northern Irish cultural perspective too, is that every problem generates ten more problems and is insoluble. I was always really irritated by the North American approach but also quite surprised how many times approaching problems in that way can work. Nowadays I would be less concerned with unionism and nationalism and some way of splitting the difference between them either geographically or in terms of joint authority and more interested in establishing an equal and fair society. I think a variety of institutional and political structures can deliver that. When people say they want union with Britain or union with Ireland, that is really a summary of what they want in life and and a statement that those solutions will best deliver it. Lurking in there I would have my own sense of identity – Irish, although some days it is different from others! I don't believe in absolutes; I don't believe that the solution has to be either an internal one or a united Ireland; I don't believe in those notions of sovereignty. I think they are out of date and often don't reflect the political realities of who holds power.

I'm more interested in identifying people's different interests as opposed to the different positions that they adopt. Some can be accommodated, some can't. An interest to dominate can't be accommodated but an interest in religious freedom and a way to express political identity is relatively easy to accommodate. I think the big shift is not in finding new solutions but finding a way to shift the language of negotiation away from the 'what I win you lose, what you lose I win' scenario. One of the ways of shifting that is to sit down and work out fundamental rights and freedoms as set out in lots of international instruments and seeing how those can be used to underpin negotiation.

I work with many different groups and I do lose hope sometimes when I see how views of history are so contingent on people's identity and how their concept of justice and fairness is totally different because they are coming from different places. It always seem silly for talks to address this because it is not directly related to the end outcome, but I do think people should try to come to general principles of agreement on the nature of the problem here. Everyone agrees that we have a democratic deficit, that the status quo is unsatisfactory and that there is a need for change but people may believe this for vastly different reasons.

Whilst some of what I have said may sound community relations orientated I actually think this idea of bringing people together in the hope that somehow they will all love each other is rather like the Christian approach that, until everyone unites under God, there is no hope. I don't subscribe to that and although I don't like saying community relations of this sort is a waste of time, for me it just misses the mark. There is bigotry. We all know that when people go off on holiday they get along fine; the question is why they cannot maintain those relationships when they get home. The problem is not so much that they are bigots or may suffer recrimination from their neighbours. The problem is society's failed structures.

I think people need to embrace new ideas of what compromise involves. It doesn't necessarily involve giving up on a bit that you really want; sometimes it involves trying to create a way of getting what you want which also gives somebody else what they want too. There is a negotiation story which I really like which seems to me quite appropriate here. It's about two chefs fighting over an orange they want to use in their baking. They cut it in half and then they discover that one of them actually wanted the flesh of the orange to flavour a cake and the other wanted the peel for marmalade. If they had talked and explored their interests in having the orange they would have realised that cutting the orange in half was a hopeless compromise. A lot of the solutions put forward for Northern Ireland seem to me to be different ways to cut the orange in half instead of looking at how we can have structures which protect people. Although it is all much easier if people do love each other I don't think people have to get on or trust each other to have solutions. The key issue is: do they have institutions, like law, government, a criminal justice system, which people feel they own, a police service which serves all members of the community equally, ways where people can all be equally heard and have an equal chance to influence decisions? Once the decision is made, does the state endorse it or not? Can one side undo it? Can people have a sense that sometimes they get their way, sometimes they don't and sometimes they find joint solutions? It's not that the constitutional issue becomes a non-issue but it does become less loaded if you are trying to address equality on a whole range of issues. I suppose that is a big shift from when I was a teenager and would have been on lots of peace initiatives which had a 'let's bring people together' approach. Now I would see myself as more pragmatic.

I'm comfortable with my Presbyterianism. As a persecuted people who fled to America I think Presbyterians can feel proud that they helped to formulate the notion of religious freedom which underpins the United States constitution and indeed in many other countries too, including Ireland. I like the title dissenter; I do think I am a dissenter and on issues where I believe Presbyterianism has solidified and not moved on I am happy to dissent. Sometimes I think it's funny that the church that I have belonged to all my life is the one I would choose to join today but then

I also do feel that in a small way I made that church what it is. The church has heard people like me talking and it will change; it will also do things which I disagree with but that has always been the case. In the New Testament there is the conservative church primarily being about religious leaders caught up in their own rules – the Pharisees after all were the only group which Jesus condemned – but there has always been the prophetic voice of the church bringing it back to addressing poverty and social issues, trying to remove oppression. I feel I can attack the church without actually being in conflict with the tenets of the faith. It seems to me that that is a vital part of what the church is.

38

Worker for the Homeless

Born 1952.

My mother came to Belfast when she was five months pregnant with me and stayed in a homeless hostel run by the Legion of Mary. She had lived with my father for a short while in Dublin but he wouldn't marry her and she decided to come back home. It must have been pretty horrendous in the hostel, lots of women on national assistance living in shared rooms with tiny babies. Housing in Belfast in those days was so desperate and maybe because my mother was from a Catholic background, she never thought to register with the Belfast Corporation. Eventually she managed to find a rented room owned by a rag and bone man somewhere off Denmark Street. It was appallingly invested with bugs and we had to go to some Social Services place to get cleaned up. After that we lived in a whole series of rented rooms.

When I was three and a half my mother became very ill with TB and went to hospital. It seemed like an eternity before my mother came back; I suppose in those days the treatment would have taken 4 to 6 months. I was left with another woman and her three children. Basically she neglected us. She didn't feed us. I remember we used to creep down the stairs in the middle of the night and steal sugar and bread. During the day she would lock us out in the yard. Once, she actually put us on the roof of the return, got us to climb onto the bins and then she pulled the bin away. We had to stay on the roof until she came back. Interesting childminding arrangements!

When my mother found out what had happened to me, how the woman had been drinking the money she was being given to look after me with, we moved out of the house pretty sharpish. That's when we moved to Agnes Street off the Shankill. Again it was a rooming house, a typical terrace with a communal living room and shared scullery with jawbox and cooker and an outside toilet. There was no electricity. The landlady shared the first floor big room with her daughter; a mother and her six children lived in the wee room beside her; a middle aged woman lived in the front parlour and then the floor that we were on, the attic rooms; the smaller room was for my mother and I and the larger attic room was given over to a husband and wife and baby. It was a mixed household, Catholic and Protestant.

Overall I think I was happy when we lived there. I certainly thought of myself as very privileged in that I compared myself to the girl who was living in the room with her five brothers and sisters and her mother, all of whom had to sleep in the one bed. My mum got various wee jobs which she had to give up because of lack of childcare arrangements for me, but she always made sure that I was well dressed; she made beautiful dresses and matching bows for me and knitted lovely cardigans. She had lots of friends who would call to see her in the evening and I would lie in the bed listening as they sat talking about all sorts of things beside the fire. There would be things said in hushed terms that I would try to work out, but I reckon a lot of it had to do with violent husbands and women being pregnant and not knowing how to cope with it.

The landlady was a Methodist and one day the Methodist minister called and got talking to my mother. He invited her to go to the church on Sunday. When he was leaving he walked me up to the corner shop and bought me a bag of buns and gave me ten shillings to give to my mother. So lo and behold, that Sunday we got kitted out. We had no hats but my mum had two berets, so we wore these berets going to church. I think my mum must have made a calculated decision. The Legion of Mary had called a few times to see her with holy cards and medals but they never brought any money like the Methodist minister had. So anyway we started going to the Methodist church in Agnes Street and that was that.

I went to a Presbyterian Church school. I learnt to accept the repressive conditions of really big classes. The school was actually a large hall which was divided into different classes. I had to be very quiet most of the time. If you got into trouble you were put out into the yard and left for hours in the cold. There was assembly every morning where we would sing songs like 'All things bright and beautiful, All creatures great and small', images of the countryside which I had never seen. The only holiday of my childhood was after I had developed double pneumonia and was in hospital for a long time. My mother and I were given a holiday which the Social Services paid for. We went to Donaghadee where we shared a room in a guest house with another girl who had been given a special holiday too. My mother looked after her as well me during the holiday. I remember the beach and the amusement arcades, and the machines with movie stars; the lights would flash and you picked a movie star, people like Greta Garbo, Rita Hayward and Gregory Peck. My mum and I made all this money on Gregory Peck. He always came up trumps.

We continued to attend the Methodist church. When the adults were having the sermon, all the children went down to the Sunshine Corner to colour in pictures of Jesus and be told Bible stories. I used to love the Bible stories, especially the Old Testament ones and loved singing songs like 'Build on the rock, the rock that ever stands, build on the rock and not upon the sands'. All these songs had actions like any good playgroup leader would do nowadays. You made signs so that the religion sank in, waving your hands about and building rocks. It was good fun. I went to the Girls' Life Brigade as well although I could never keep in step with everybody else. In all the displays I would be the one who upset the geometrically co-ordinated synchronisation. The Methodist minister gave my mum bits of work to do: mending coats, making curtains. We looked after his bedridden mother one summer. She lived in a mansion of a house. Whenever the minister's sister came down to visit she always insisted that we ate somewhere different from where she ate.

One of my mum's friends worked as a housekeeper for an old man up in North Belfast but she was giving up the job to get married. My mum went to see him and got the job so we moved in with him. I was about eight at the time. I remember going up with my mum to meet him. His house was furnished with Victorian furniture, all very dark and heavy. I remember when I was leaving he insisted on kissing me on the lips. It was all wet and slobbery and horrible. But the house had a garden front and back and a bathroom and inside toilet. I was quite excited to be moving in there. It seemed like a hundred miles away from Agnes Street.

He was just a dirty old man. From the moment we moved in there he kept trying to touch me and telling me not to say anything to my mum.

It blighted all the nice things, like not living in an overcrowded house anymore and being quite comfortable and warm. He was seen by the community as a respectable Orangeman, in his seventies, in the Black Preceptory and the Freemasons. He worked in a moneylenders off the Shankill. I threatened to tell my mum but in the end I got big enough and strong enough to tell him to go away and leave me alone. My mum married him and it stopped. He was pretty old and frail by this time.

When the abuse started I went through a total fascination with being born again. I was born again in different evangelical mission halls and really liked the whole feeling of being saved. It was having a weird psychological function. I was feeling cleansed. If we need to have a cultural idea of a father figure, there was me coming from this single parent family, having this dirty old man as the first man I had lived with and then I got this Protestant God as a father figure, pretty stern, preaching hell fire and brimstone. I suppose I was a prime target for that all embracing black and white religion.

Friends of ours from when we had lived in Agnes Street became Mormons and they invited my mother and I along to one of the services. My mum wasn't impressed but I thought it was great. I was 11 and I found these Americans fascinating, with their different accents and way of looking at the world. I'd seen movies about America and these were real people from California and Arizona and Utah with totally different experiences to me. It certainly was an indoctrination process and there wasn't one question they didn't have an answer for. They had quite literal beliefs. We were all the children of God and God had lots of wives up in heaven. I questioned how could this be. There had just been Adam and Eve and Cain and Abel, which implies that we are all descended from brothers and sisters getting married, but, they would refute this. They believed that the descendants of Cain were black. That's why they couldn't hold the priesthood. From when I was about 13 to when I was 16 I was in the Mormons.

There was a Mormon mission on the Shankill and the elder in charge there thought I was something special. I was chosen. I was trained to be Junior Sunday School Co-ordinator for Northern Ireland. Hands were laid on my head; I was filled with the Holy Spirit. Can you imagine the attention? It was just wonderful. I would be picked up every Sunday at 9 am and I would go everywhere in Northern Ireland, pontificating to qualified teachers who were running a Sunday School, telling them how to do it because I was inspired and chosen by God to do this. I would give talks at the big Mormon church out by Sydenham where they packed hundreds of people in. I fasted for 24 hours every month. I watched people bear witness. Sometimes odd things would happen. Women would get up and say things; they would be so vulnerable and break down and cry and really be needing so much support and help. I began to think there was something not quite right, that the religion was just a crutch, it was so inappropriate. In school we were studying evolution in Science and that set triggers off in my head. In History we were studying civil rights in America. I began to question their doctrines about women being fallen and not allowed to hold the priesthood, black people having the mark of Cain. Perhaps also because when I was 16 my stepfather died, maybe I didn't need a black and white religion anymore because he was no longer a part of my life. I decided that I didn't like the Mormons any more.

It was nasty when my stepfather died. This was 1969. My mum received threatening letters, possibly because we had Catholic friends. I came home one lunch time from school to find that my mother had phoned the police after she received a horrible letter that said, 'Get out you Fenian turncoat or you will get burnt out'. A Catholic family lived next door to us and the army was constantly coming round and digging up their garden because someone had phoned to say that they were burying guns. Their attic was wrecked as well. Eventually they emigrated to Canada but we decided to stay on.

Even though I passed my 11+ I didn't go to grammar school. My mum told me that I had been refused and I believed that for years but in fact that wasn't true. She simply couldn't finance additional things that would have been needed: uniforms, sports outfits, and there would have been additional fees to pay. I met Catholics whilst I was in sixth form at secondary school through a peace conference that had been organised. We decided to form this group called CONTACT which would continue to meet and do community gestures. I missed one of the meetings where it was decided to deliver hampers to the poor for Christmas. Comes Christmas and there was this knock at our door. I opened up the door to see these two from Methodist College who I had met, delivering a hamper to me as a poor family! It was so awful!

Our headmistress was not at all happy when it came to the school dance and we wanted to invite the boys from the Catholic school. She made it plain that she would not be happy about one of her girls going out with a Catholic, not for any prejudiced reasons but it would be very dangerous for young people to be travelling in and out of different areas. She wouldn't feel easy about it being on her conscience. CONTACT folded when the Treasurer, who was a boy from a Catholic grammar school in West Belfast, ran off with the money. A bit like the Peace People really!

I repeated my 'A' levels at the College of Business Studies. That was a brilliant year. I was studying with people from all sorts of backgrounds, working class, middle class, upper class, Catholic and Protestant. It was 1971 and there were a lot of people who were into being revolutionaries! It was the first time that I came up against people who had a republican outlook, a socialist outlook; the debating society was fascinating: the intensity and enthusiasm with which people took up positions and argued. There were fierce debates about the violence and whether it was okay to have violence to make things change. There was a bomb at the BBC and one Catholic would say, 'That's real dedication and such courage of your convictions' and another would say, 'Yes, sure it takes guts to carry a bomb which could explode and kill you but it's guts without imagination'. If I had just stayed in a Protestant area I would have thought that all Catholics believed in the violence.

We had all gone to different schools and the arguments, the way we had been taught, the way we viewed the world, it became so apparent that it was different – even the way I had been taught English at school. I hadn't been taught a world view; I hadn't been taught that it was not just about studying a Shakespearean text but about placing it within an Elizabethan world view. When someone is from a working class background you can't assume that these things are gently dropped on them just by breathing in the atmosphere of books at home. It has to be filled in, you have to be directed towards it. It was a challenging time.

I was mixing with Catholics, going for a drink, meeting people who were in People's Democracy and yet I realised that I didn't have the same strong feeling on nationalist issues. I agreed it was wrong that there was discrimination but it didn't seem like it was affecting me. The conditions that my friends told me about on the Falls Road reminded me of how we lived in Agnes Street but I didn't feel connected to it. I felt rootless. Anyone who starts to question things and doesn't just accept what is handed down begins to feel rootless. I no longer accepted the Protestant ideology but I certainly would never have seen myself as a nationalist.

I left Belfast and went to university in London. Suddenly I became the soft spoken lilting Irishwoman, the one who was asked to read the poems in English class because they just loved the way I talked. 'Say "now" again, say that again!' It was really bizarre in the History seminar, me doing a potted answer to the Irish question and the History lecturer saying, 'Well, that's a nice middle class Catholic interpretation of Irish history'. I thought, 'I'm not. I'm just trying to be objective.'

I was living in London when the Birmingham bombing happened. We had a local pub where we used to go. Of course we would always be called paddy but they had always welcomed us. I remember after the Birmingham bombing they told us to get out, we weren't welcome there. They would have spat at you and the same in the shops if they realised you had a Northern Irish accent. There was great hostility. Thankfully, quite often they thought I was Scottish. The violence in Northern Ireland permeated a lot of people's thinking. When I was interviewed for an education course to complete my teaching qualification, one of the questions the professor asked me was, 'Do you think all the Irish believe in bombing to achieve their ends?'. I couldn't believe the question and said, 'If they did there wouldn't be much of London left; come to think of it there wouldn't be any roads in London either.' I was quite surprised when I got offered a place on his course.

I came home to see my mum in 1973 for Halloween. By this time the area where I had lived and where my mum was still living was a heavy Protestant area. By the end of that week, people came with guns to the house, knocked my mother over, looking for me. Luckily I had stayed out with friends overnight. Who knows what they were thinking? I had Catholic friends. I was a student in London. I was drinking in Kelly's Cellars. Maybe they thought I was involved in People's Democracy or the Official IRA; maybe they thought I was a fellow traveller, although I wasn't even that. The police finally found out where I was and phoned me to explain what had happened and to advise me to get out of Belfast. From the moment I got that phone call it was the most frightening night of my life. Every car that pulled up outside the house I was staying in terrified me. I remember we even put statues up against the window with umbrellas that looked like guns so that anyone coming would think there was a gun trained on them. It was the time of the Romper Room incidents, women torturing women and killing and mutilating them, Protestant women doing this, all those awful murders of Catholics in the Cliftonville, the Shankill Butchers. My teeth chattered most of the night in fear.

After university I came back to Belfast. I was too scared to live in the north of the city again. There wasn't a great deal of choice; life had become very entrenched into Catholic and Protestant communities. I didn't want to live in a Catholic area and settled around the university. I joined the Belfast Women's Collective, a socialist feminist group and got involved in campaigns for the improvement of maternity services, having somebody with you during childbirth, your partner, your mother or a chosen person. In those days that was not allowed. Only the medics were really encouraged to be there. I became involved in other women's issues too: nurseries, abortion; all these years later and we still don't have any state-funded nurseries in Northern Ireland.

When you go away from your home you get a greater sense of your identity. I am Irish. I grew up Protestant in the North of Ireland. I am European. I don't think there is still an Ulster Protestant mentality within me but I suppose it would take an outsider to be able to see the ways in which I do think like an Irish person or have Protestant strains of thinking that have been diluted by education. I would still have a feeling of alienation, of being an outsider. This feeling is kept in perspective as in my work I meet people who really are dispossessed in every sense. As someone who benefited from the welfare state, I worry that changes in social policy have resulted in a fragmented provision, where ability to pay rather than need determines the quality of service.

I'm nervous of anybody who sounds fanatical. After my flirtation as a teenager with black and white philosophies I have always maintained a fairly healthy scepticism about people thinking there is only one way to do things. I think we have to recognise that there are different interest groups within society and find ways of accommodating each other. We have to make sure everybody is listened to. I'm very lucky to work in a place where there are Catholics and Protestants and that's how you do learn that you can get on with people who have grown up in a different community. You see all the ordinary things, the joy, the grief. What is so bad about our society is that people are kept separate; it's like apartheid in South Africa. In the inner city, whether you are Catholic or Protestant, the chances are that you are going to be unemployed and the unemployment keeps you stuck in your own community and it's the not mixing that is the problem. The violence hasn't solved any of the problems. We desperately need peace.

A future Ireland? I quite liked the idea of a federal Ireland made up of four city states based on the old provinces and linked into a federal United States of Europe – Britain included. I long for real participative local democracy where the issues of poverty and unemployment – social inclusion, to use the jargon – would be given priority. I believe there should be equality of opportunity for everybody. I suppose my greatest worry would be that I would be overwhelmed by puritanical views, rigid views in a united Ireland, although I accept that such views exist in Northern Ireland too.

39
Anthropologist
Born 1959.

My father's politics were one of the most significant influences on my political outlook. He was of that generation which went through World War II when the Soviet Union were allies, communism was respectable and Joe Stalin was regarded as a hero. I'm not sure if my father's admiration of Joe Stalin has survived the collapse of communism but the politics of the labour tradition marked him for life. Sadly, that tradition has all but been obliterated after 20 years of the 'troubles'. People criticise it with hindsight – perhaps they are right; nevertheless, I think it is remarkable that it had a sustained and continuous existence over 60 years.

One of my earliest political memories was at the time of the Burntollet march. My father was very angry at loyalists attacking the march and I unthinkingly repeated what he had said to my friends at primary school. That provoked a very bad reaction and it was my first realisation of difference. I think another significant divide was when I went on to grammar school. That fractured my friendships in the working class area where I was brought up. I remember I left the Boys' Brigade at that time and joined the Boy Scouts which was seen as a less proletarian and more respectable organisation. Respectability had a capital R in my mother's eyes. She was against any wishes that I might have had to walk on the Twelfth and considered a whole range of party songs unacceptable. I remember 'On the green grassy slopes of the Boyne' was respectable, whereas 'The Sash' was not! There was one Catholic family living in our street and their father was a policeman and in my mother's mind this classification of tunes which were acceptable and unacceptable was linked to not causing offence to that family.

We lived beside a very loyalist estate and I remember the kids there calling me and my friends fenian lovers. I'm not at all sure why; perhaps it was a class thing in that we lived in a nicer street. When they called us fenian lovers I think I felt the most guilty! I do remember a boy in the Boys' Brigade hall throwing a free state shilling away in a bravado of display because it was fenian money and me being quite happy to spend it. I was stopped a few times and as I grew older was quite fearful of the roaming tartan gangs. One instance I recall happened in the centre of town. From the age of nine or ten, my parents allowed me to come into Belfast on my own to visit the children's library and the gymnasium at the Co-op. The Co-op on York Street was a significant institution for my mother and her friends who participated in it in a real way. Anyway, one day I was stopped by a gang of kids demanding to know if I was a prod and an Orangeman; I remember I was wearing a Manchester City football badge on my jacket. I ran and was caught in the doorway of Robbs department store. I'm quite serious when I say they were hitting me with a large yellow-handled screwdriver! I escaped into the store quite helpless and out of it and slumped over the counter. As one of the boys was going through my pockets the woman behind the counter said to me, 'Excuse me, are you with these boys?' It's interesting that this probably happened before the 'troubles' started. Another time which was quite scary was having a knife pulled against me in the grounds of Belfast Castle and being asked what religion I was. The guy had UVF tattooed on his arm so it wasn't too hard to guess the right answer!

I wasn't at all happy at school and my only clear ambition was to get out of Northern Ireland. I was 18 when I did get away to college in London and I thought I would never come back. I wanted to study Anthropology, which my teachers and my mother thought was an unwise choice. The most obvious subject for me to study would have been Engineering, but I was reaching towards the political sciences. My elder sister was influential in that she was passionately into youth culture and introduced me to music. Somewhere in all of this was the idea of the bright lights of London.

At that time Marxism was big in the social sciences and certainly in Anthropology. So was feminism. My head exploded with new ideas; it was magnificent. Through Anthropology, a subject which is tied up with issues of colonialism, I became interested in Irish history and gradually became politicised. Having left Belfast thinking I would never return, the reverse happened. I was turned on to the place I was from and although I don't think I understood it fully at the time because it was wrapped up in a political rhetoric, with hindsight I realise that I had a desire to suss out my place in the society that I came from and to make sense of it.

I came back ardent in my Marxist rhetoric, off the wall in terms of my friends, with a comprehensive knowledge on all the different political lines on Ireland. I can remember sitting in a serious bar in a loyalist area, with my friends, mouthing off about James Connolly. They weren't offended or angered by my politics. I think they indulged my eccentricity. During the summers I had worked as a bin man and after I left college, I got a full-time pensionable job on the bins working in a Protestant yard. A couple of Catholics also worked there and they were tolerated because they lay down. One was an elderly man who embraced his elderliness and the young man presented himself as traumatised and indeed had been traumatised by receiving serious attention from the security forces in the area that he lived. They existed as Catholics in the yard by trying not to be noticed. I can't remember them being baited in a systematic way but in the hut where we drank our tea things were routinely said which must have been offensive and they didn't respond or interject. That's a grim but fascinating area of human relationships. I do remember making awkward approaches to broach subjects, more so when I moved on to a mixed yard and became shop steward for a while. I meant well but I wasn't particularly sensible or sophisticated in my approach. Nowadays the conventional orthodoxy is to attempt to open up issues of sectarianism and face them head on but I found getting through the politeness barrier and the situations which can arise out of such an approach difficult.

I still had an unresolved set of ideas about socialism. I'd never joined a political party but I read a copy of the *Belfast Bulletin*, a publication which researched Irish issues, and had the ubiquitous advert saying: 'if you want to help out, contact us'. To their credit, they took me on and that was wonderful of them. I guess it was a substitute for not joining a political party and I suspect I got more out of it than they did from my endeavours. I edited a few pieces, became interested in abortion law reform and researched a file of information on a mysterious spate of murders of gay men in Belfast, but overall my contribution was more in the distribution of the publication.

During the hunger strikes the contradictions that I felt between my Protestant background and my politics were fierce. The day that Bobby Sands died I was in London and I went down to Downing Street. There were not many people there and I stood, as spits and spots of rain fell, my hand shaking as I tried to roll a cigarette. An old man's hand wrote a phone number on the back of my hand and I asked what it was for. He said 'solicitor's number' and I wondered what I would need a solicitor's number for. As the people in their cars left London for the week end they shouted abuse at the demonstration. Members of a British socialist organisation began cranking it up to raise the tension. I felt this need to be there but at the same time, being there did not sit easily on me. I was there on my own but after a while a friend of mine came down, which was good. I stayed another wee while and really I left when I did because the contradictions were freaking me out. I felt the same when I attended a hunger strike march in West Belfast; it was like I was half in, half out of the march and the heavy security presence was scary.

Marxism for a certain generation of Protestant young people who wanted to reach beyond their backgrounds was beautiful. It provided a way of being turned on and progressive without necessarily having to embrace nationalism or republicanism. I'm not sure what would serve the same purpose for young people from that background today. I was never able to embrace violence for political ends but neither was it the biggest issue in my head. In a sense, growing up in Belfast and at that stage living in Rathcoole, the realities of life on a loyalist housing estate had inured me to violence, disliking it but at the same time recognising it as a commonplace reality. I was the victim of a very ugly attack in Rathcoole, not political, more a case of being in the wrong place at the wrong time. In the aftermath I was very angry at the five people who attacked me and my family and it was put to me that the perpetrators could be sorted out. I deliberately did not pursue the invitation but I was aware at the same time of why some people might in those circumstances. When you are subject to ugly attacks of violence it puts punishment shootings into a new context. I think what also helped me at that time was knowing that there were people living in Rathcoole who were very progressive, particularly the Rathcoole Self-Help Group, which was trying out novel ideas and providing a much needed space for young people. It had its own dynamic which was great fun and innovative and perhaps I wouldn't have stayed if they had not been there. I think generally there are some unsung heroes in Belfast who have organised and run events for young people and contributed to the vibrancy of youth culture over the years. Sectarianism is a contextual thing and people can mix freely in one context and yet behave in a sectarian manner in another; so it would be a mistake to exaggerate the significance of non-sectarian youth subcultures. Nevertheless, the existence of non-sectarian space for young people is terribly important.

My politics, though, became a bit of a millstone. The research I was interested in doing was in trying to understand the relationship between sectarianism and trade unionism. I began interviewing people about their lives and why they had done the things that they had. Having a head full of structural Marxism, I expected to hear certain answers, but of course people talk in very personal terms about their father or their mother, humdrum ordinary things. That confused me a lot at the time and I thrashed about trying to work it all out. The ideological certainties that I had were subverted as I realised the importance of the personal in people's political and public lives.

Gradually I became less interested in politics and more concerned with exploring issues of identity, albeit more obliquely. I became aware that there are more aspects to identity than national identity and wanted to understand the role that emotions and the personal play in public life and political identity. I think it is interesting to look at the way in which the politics of reproduction have entered into constructions of different identities in Ireland. Women have contributed to the growing secularisation in the South of Ireland by campaigning around the issues of abortion, contraception and divorce and that has fed back into the debates and, indeed, has informed the dilemmas that my father and his generation would have had in accepting a united Ireland given the power of the Catholic church over social legislation in the South.

I also came to understand that the community from whence I came couldn't be understood as being simply a place where bigotry resides. Reading Irish history, I realised that Protestants do not have the monopoly on sectarianism and the Protestant community is not irredeemably bad. Even to utter such a statement is difficult. People who voice such an opinion get howled down for doing so and I'm struck by the fact that I'm using the double negative, 'not irredeemably bad', rather than being more positive. Unionism is a rational ideology even though its expression has often been in a sectarian form; similarly I believe Irish nationalism and republicanism to be a totally reasonable and legitimate ideology but tainted at the margins by sectarianism. When you asked me to do this interview one of the thoughts which occurred to me was that in some ways it is easier to be a dodgy prod than a dodgy Catholic. Someone like Conor Cruise O'Brien, not that I invest hugely in his views, is vilified for deserting Irish nationalism. I'd like to see more freedom of expression in Ireland, people being able to articulate their positions and explore political ideas without being maligned – not that I am optimistic that this will happen.

In personal terms, when I was a Marxist, I think somewhere in the back of my head there was a part of me that wanted to smooth out cultural differences between Catholics and Protestants and it is only in the last few years that I have realised that the depth of cultural differences in Ireland are profound. It is very easy to miss how profound they are because we have all absorbed the politeness barrier and we don't talk easily to each other. The profundity of difference is amorphous and intangible. The best way I can describe it is to say that I worked in Glasgow for a couple of years and I now live and work in Dublin. Culturally Glasgow was strangely familiar; I felt very comfortable there. Dublin, by comparison is strangely unfamiliar. Having said that, I think it is important to say that I was given opportunities in Dublin which I didn't get in Belfast.

I do love living in Ireland but in formal political terms I'm pessimistic about the future. Whatever political arrangements are worked out, the divisions, the sadness and bitterness and tensions will remain. Even after all these years, I still find it difficult to resist the temptation to over-compensate for the fact of being Protestant by being politically correct in how I present myself. It saddens me that Protestants who do get into intellectual work of some description often feel the need to distance themselves from the community from whence they came. It's the case of 'the sash I never wore'; that community is left bereft of people who might be heading in a progressive direction. Where then can progressive politics come from?

40

Robbie McVeigh

Community Research Worker. Born 1962.

I grew up on a 'Big House' estate in Tyrone. On the one hand it was an idyllic place to live; on the other it was a survival of feudalism. The estate involved a working relationship which implied ownership, one that most people in employment situations do not have with their employer. Looking back, I can see that a lot of my politics actually come out of my experiences of childhood.

My parents were fairly progressive and never anti-Catholic, but my extended family was sometimes unproblematically unionist and sectarian. Later in life my father became a mature student and his views changed as he came into contact with the student radicalism of the late sixties, but that sense of unionism being right, implicit rather than explicit, was present all the time. Sectarianism, for my family, was largely of a political nature rather than being informed by religious beliefs about Catholicism. I think we were like the majority of Protestants; we believed that the Church of Ireland or the Presbyterian religion was somehow better than Catholicism but we were not a particularly religious family and certainly not evangelical.

I was inculcated into a loyalist identity in small but continuous ways. My family didn't fly a flag during the Twelfth but my grandparents were activists in the Unionist Party and I do remember the thrill of putting the flag up at their house. We always had Catholic neighbours and Catholic friends so I didn't connect the pleasure of hanging out a Union Jack with the pleasure of putting down Catholics. I didn't see the implication between the two which I would do now. Loyalist identity does have an appeal if one abstracts it from its sectarianism; I think almost every young Protestant wants to be the young boy who marches at the front of the parade with the stick. The problem is that one spends so much time trying to unpack the bits of the culture that in other contexts would be fine from the triumphalist reality of it all.

I know a lot of people say that their education sectarianised them and had an inability to engage with Irishness but my own experience of a rural Protestant education wasn't particularly sectarian. Perhaps it was an accident of particular teachers, but Irish History was taught from first year in secondary school and the whole course was centred around it. I think the problem was more a structural one. The teachers weren't educating Protestant boys and girls to be sectarian but if you segregate children in education inevitably there's an informal culture in the school which reproduces sectarianism. In primary school we all learnt Orange songs, not in the classroom but in the school yard. Similarly at secondary school there was a hidden curriculum where an identity based around sectarianism and the Orange Order was learnt outside the formal parameters of the classroom. The only organisation I joined in my adolescence was the Young Farmers. It was formally non-sectarian but the oath to the Queen was one of the informal mechanisms which reproduced Protestant separateness and identity. Apart from the oath there was nothing excluding Catholics from the Young Farmers but, as far as I recollect, it was an exclusively Protestant organisation.

I went to Sunday school out of obligation. Attendance had more to do with being seen to be respectable within the community rather than any pretext of religious faith. At primary school we were taught religious education every week, though it was more like a quiz. We were divided into teams and asked questions about the Bible but the first round centred around points for going to church. I got points for having attended church but I also got points if my parents had attended: two points if they had attended and one point if they had a good excuse for not going. Every week I would rack my brains to find a good excuse for why my father had not gone to church rather than just accept the fact that he was an atheist. The sinister aspect of it all was that it was encouraging young children to lie in a completely unproductive way!

In terms of Protestant identity I see the absolute division in Northern Ireland as not between Protestant and Catholic broadly defined, but between people whose religious interpretation of the world informs what they do and everybody else. Within the Protestant community I think that division is profound. Religious fundamentalism makes it possible for Protestants to demonise Catholics and this is compounded by a lack of contact between Protestants and Catholics in daily life. Although life for my family in Tyrone was completely stratified in that crazy way where you have Catholic and Protestant shops selling exactly the same products and you supported your own kind, nevertheless we always lived in areas which were roughly 50/50 Protestant/Catholic. Everybody had social relationships with each other.

I was saved by music as punk rock began to filter through to Ireland in 1976. I was at school in Omagh then and everyone I knew seemed to be in a band. The music became a catalyst for this peculiar meeting of middle class Protestants and working class Catholics who were attracted to punk and its anti-sectarian stand. Before then I'd only known the sons of rural Catholic farmers and they had a completely different social identity to the Catholic friends I made through punk rock who lived on working class housing estates in Omagh. I was in a band with two Catholic fellas; Doomed Youth was one of the names I seem to remember we called ourselves. One of my best friends is still a Catholic whom I met during that time. If it hadn't been for punk rock I know that I would never have met him. All the youth organisations open to me to join, like the Boys' Brigade and the Boy Scouts, are mechanisms for reproducing Protestant identity; I could never have met him in that context.

Looking back, it's hard enough to know if one is being honest or not about the influences on one's life. I think punk was a coalition of political ideologies some of which, like the swastikas, were designed to shock, and some of which were anti-sectarian and anti-racist. There was a sense that young people had found their own identity, one which transcended sectarian boundaries. The ideology of punk writ large was that we were young people and ideologies like unionism and nationalism were alien ideologies. Punk was just as anti-nationalist as it was anti-unionist. There were groups like the Sex Pistols with their outrageous statement of nihilism which appealed to me, but equally there were other British groups like the Clash who had a vision of the world which was more consciously political within a broad socialism. What punk represented to me was not a politicisation but a depoliticisation, a way of coping with the society around me. Through punk I came to see myself as a socialist but on British terms. I had a sense of myself as being British and belonging to a movement which was British.

The Omagh punk Catholic identity for want of a better description was a 'who gives a fuck' attitude to politics and I found it really weird meeting republicans for the first time when I came up to Belfast to study. That was at the time of the hunger strikes and although I spent a lot of time socialising in West Belfast, I was never moved politically by what I saw. I was vaguely interested in a sociological way but felt that it wasn't anything to do with me. My interpretation of the IRA was the stereotypical Protestant one that believes they don't have very much support and are preying on the community. I remember seeing all the wall murals covered with paint bombs and saying to my friends that it was really interesting to see how the local people paint bombed the murals; that just shows how much they must be anti-republican. My friends burst out laughing and of course I was told the Brits do the paint bombing.

I worked for a time in a large warehouse in East Belfast. That experience made me realise how limited was the world of young working class Protestants. The young men who worked there measured their sense of themselves by what Catholics were doing, how much Catholics were gaining. Ultimately I think it was destructive for them to measure their success by Catholic failure, to measure their freedom by the subjugation of Catholics. I remember being asked had I got 'O' levels. I had a degree; I was three steps away from that rather than one, but to have 'O' levels was to belong to a different world and have different opportunities. There was a real need for some ideology to allow them to struggle against the mundanity of their life even if it was only in terms of the low wages that were being paid. The place wasn't unionised at all. In other circumstances fighting for better pay would have been a consciousness raising experience but they were more concerned about what the fenians were at or collecting for the bonfire. I don't want to stereotype their lives too much, to make it a caricature, but there is a truth to that. I think Protestants in general have been failed by the political and cultural ideology that they are forced to live within.

The big step for me was going to England. I did a Masters' at LSE for a year and then spent two years working the building sites. For the first time I was forced to come to terms with being Irish, which was confusing at the start but ultimately liberating. It really was a series of experiences which in themselves are relatively mundane. Being called a Paddy is quite shocking for somebody who may or may not be anti-Irish but never thought the label applied to them. The shock of people not being able to understand my accent and then being racist in terms of the way that they didn't understand: being thrown out of a party because one Irish fella got himself into an argument and was thrown out but then the rest of us had to leave as well. All of this was compounded in different ways in the academic environment which was just as racist as the building sites. The closer I got to that middle class English world the more I realised that it excluded me. Whatever contradictory sense of Britishness I had then, I just knew that Protestants from the North didn't belong there. The stereotypes that they employed of loyalists were just as offensive as those they used about republicans. There is a further dimension to that if you come from a Protestant background. On the one hand I do laugh at Paisley; I think he is reactionary, but I'm uneasy with the way that the English middle classes laugh at him not because he is reactionary or pro-fascist but as an excuse for anti-Irish racism. It's a complex dividing line but I certainly felt that the English who laughed used anti-loyalism as a convenient way of covering their own anti-Irish racism.

At the start I thought it was great that I passed for an Irish person and that people didn't pick up on the fact that I was a Protestant. I became quite happy to explore Irishness in a way that seemed just as open to me as it was to people from a Catholic background. Gradually I became more uncomfortable with it. I knew that being a Protestant did matter to me. Although I hadn't been actively involved in reproducing sectarianism the political conflict in the North was a part of me and part of my own identity. I wanted to explore that. I suppose, though it's an over-simplification, it was like I couldn't understand Irishness if I didn't understand sectarianism. There is a southern version of Irishness which is unproblematically Catholic and nationalist; sometimes that is quite appealing, but it doesn't include me. I wanted to be Irish, I think that I am Irish, but I wanted to explore how Protestants as Protestants make sense of their relationship to the rest of the people on this island. That I do think I have some personal responsibility towards because sectarian loyalist politicians and individuals will continually talk in a cavalier fashion about Protestants in the name of all Protestants. I challenge that. I'm a

Protestant; I haven't given up that bit of my identity whatever it might mean but I have no problem with being Irish.

At the time I worked all this out for myself I thought I was quite remarkable! I had made this personal voyage; I wasn't sectarian; I had got rid of all the baggage that I was supposed to have. Then I started meeting people who had managed to do the same thing. At first I was a bit annoyed to discover that I wasn't quite as remarkable as I thought I was! Then I realised that it wasn't about my ability to transcend my origins at all but that it was actually a facet of Protestant identity. All of us can discover a more progressive political and cultural identity.

Whenever I talk to unionists and loyalists in Belfast I am struck by the sense of defeat that they have. They talk about holding the line for 30 or 40 or 50 years but they all know that the end is coming. The British are going to sell them down the river and a united Ireland is inevitable. If that is so then the next question is why don't they do something about it? Why don't they sit down and construct a different relationship to the rest of the people on this island? Why not protect their interests? It's illogical not to say, 'How do we get a deal?' That is not to pretend that loyalism and unionism are not real forces but it is an acknowledgment of choice. Being a Protestant does not mean that one has to be a loyalist.

Through reading about Irish history I discovered that at different times Protestants have been radical and there is no reason why they can't be so again. With the benefit of hindsight I think that the United Irish movement was remarkable. They took on board the democratic ideals of the French Revolution and maybe to a greater extent the American revolution but unlike the American Revolution, which was able to theorise its relationship to British colonialism but couldn't sort out its relationship to native Americans and African Americans, the United Irish movement went further. Its ideas for citizenship included the people that they had colonised.

For me they were way before their time in recognising that the difference between Protestants, Catholics and Dissenters is real and in understanding that Protestants have to negotiate a relationship with everyone else living on this island. That recognition is missing from most anti-colonial movements in the world, certainly missing from anti-imperialist movements which are led by colonial blocs. White people in South Africa as a body didn't develop ideas like that, white Americans didn't and yet for all their millenarianism and shortcomings and their lack of social analysis, Irish Protestants did. I think they also set in motion a character for Irish republicanism which has always had to appeal ideologically to anti-sectarian sentiment. Without that Protestant involvement in the construction of Irish identity I think Irish nationalism would have been much more clerically based; it would have had a religious fundamentalism whereby the identity between colonialism and the colonial bloc was unquestioned and the identity between religious fundamentalism and anti-imperialism was also unchallenged and unquestioned. For me it's not just the survival of the ideas of the United Irish movement which are important but the fact that they prevented the development of a much more reactionary and sectarian anti-imperialism which even today holds out the possibility of a genuine anti-sectarian political settlement in the North of Ireland.

I recognise that some Protestants have renewed their interest in socialist ideas within the newly formed loyalist parties like the PUP and UDP but I can't see how those parties will be able to deliver socialism within a six county set up. The big difference today is that the Northern Ireland state, premised as it was on the notion that whatever you did you had to keep the Protestant class alliance happy, has gone completely. Britain is clearly committed to building a relationship with the Catholic middle class. It has reinvented itself in its attempt to accommodate them. In the past if you were a Protestant you knew that if you were a man you would have a job and your son too would have a job. That's gone. It can't be reconstructed. I can't see how loyalist socialism can ever get the same bargaining power because that state formation will never be put in place again. Stormont needed working class Protestants on its side to survive; the British government doesn't care. Protestants only account for 1% of the vote.

I think that if Protestants stop thinking in terms of being the majority in Northern Ireland and accept that they will be one of the minorities in a united Ireland then it will free them to be progressive in constructing a political settlement which protects all minorities. Finally Protestants can fight for their rights rather than forever hanging on to a privilege they can only have by denying other people their rights. I think it's better for all of us to live in a society which is multi-cultural, multi-religious and multi-ethnic. Irish Protestants have a key part to play in that, not just in terms of their tradition but also in terms of their sense of vision.